Explorations in Wood

The Furniture & Sculpture of Tim Stead

Giles Sutherland

with a Foreword by Dr David Bellamy

CANONGATE

To Dee and Bryan, Raymonde and Jos:
'The apple doesn't fall far from the tree'

Also for Lys and George. Thanks for sowing the seeds.

First published in 1993 by
Canongate Press Ltd
14 Frederick Street
Edinburgh EH2 2HB.

The publishers wish to thank the Royal Botanic Garden, Edinburgh, for their permission to use their assistant photographer Debbie White. Thanks are also due to the following photographers: Antonia Reeve, Iain Mackenzie, Roger Lee, Eric Thorburn, Alex X. Fraser, Sean Hudson and Ken Kirkwood.

Cover photographs by Antonia Reeve showing two boards of burr elm.
Photograph on frontispiece by Debbie White showing detail of ash boards.
Photograph on page vi by Debbie White showing part of the 'botanic ash' in the Caledonian Hall, the Royal Botanic Garden, Edinburgh.

British Library Cataloguing-in-Publication Data
A catalogue record for this book is available on request from The British Library.

ISBN 0 86241 433 4

Design by Ann Ross Paterson
Phototypeset by Hewer Text Composition Services, Edinburgh
Printed and bound in Great Britain by B.A.S., Over Wallop, Hampshire

since feeling is first
who pays any attention
to the syntax of things
will never wholly kiss you;

wholly to be a fool
while Spring is in the world

my blood approves,
and kisses are a better fate
than wisdom
lady i swear by all flowers. Don't cry
– the best gesture of my brain is less than
your eyelids' flutter which says

we are for each other: then
laugh, leaning back in my arms
for life's not a paragraph

And death i think is no parenthesis

e.e. cummings

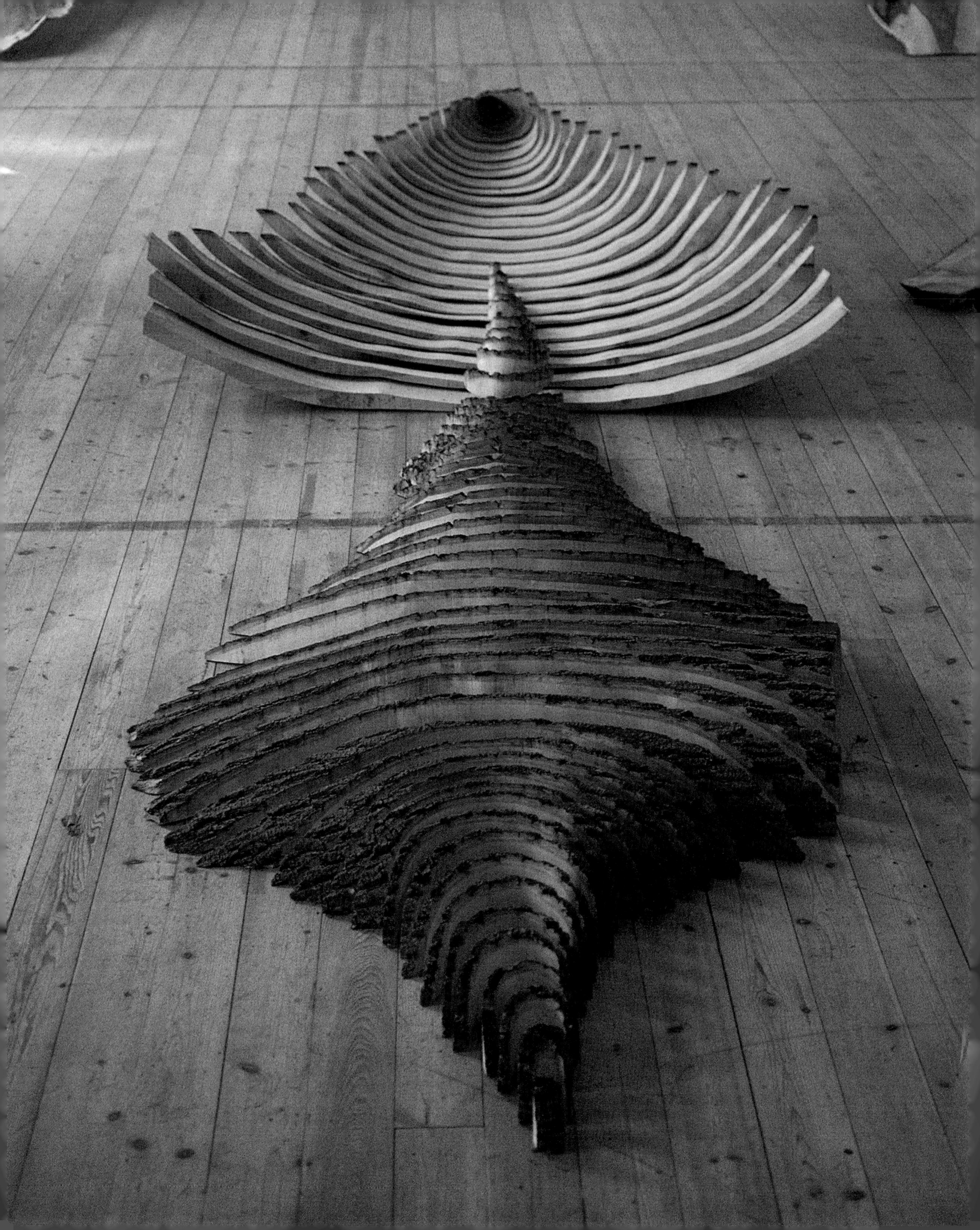

Contents

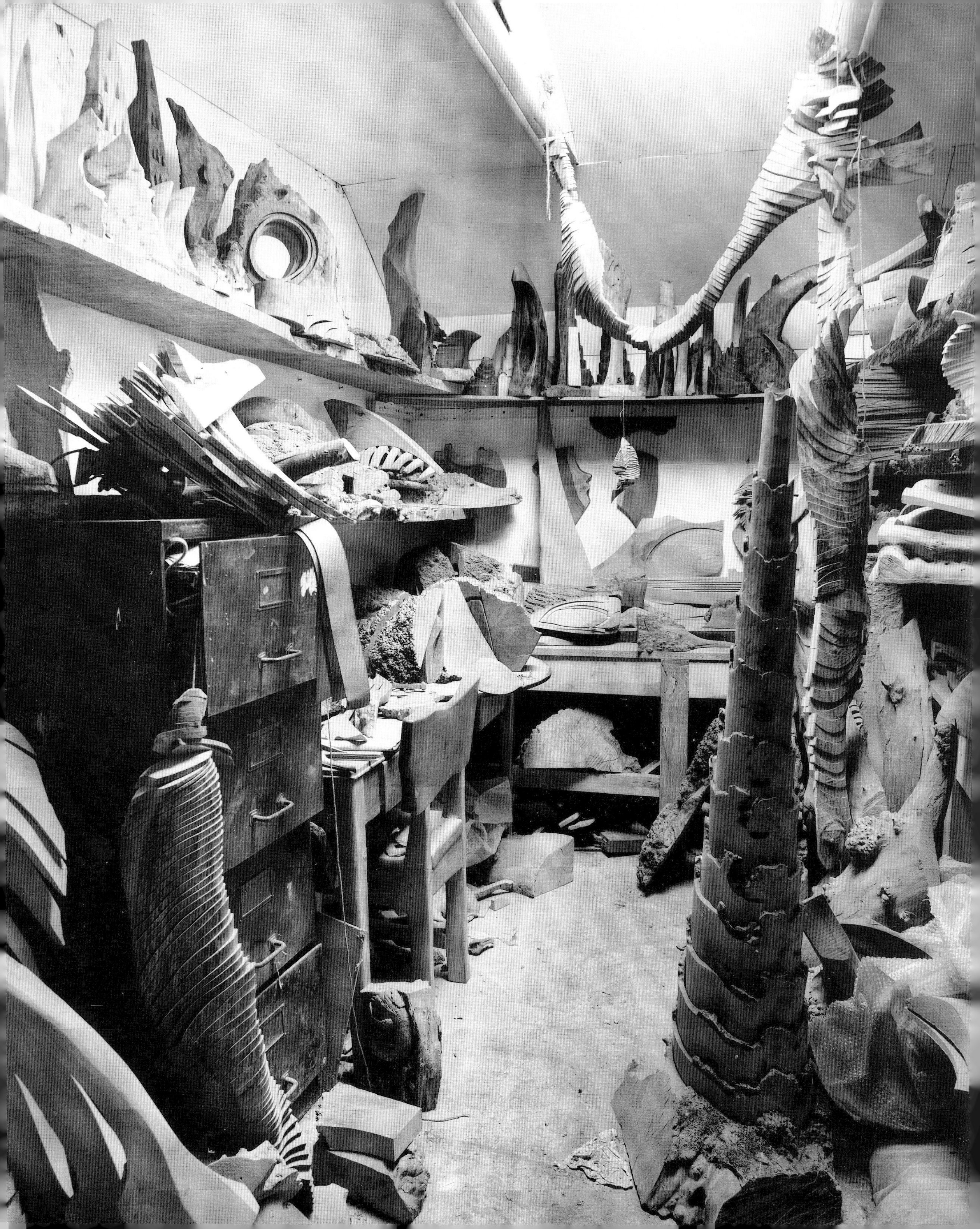

Foreword

I have a number of key books in my library, treasured possessions which have helped make me what I am. The most important is *Sources of Wisdom*, by Ananda Coomaraswamy, a cardinal figure in twentieth-century art history and in the cultural confrontation between East and West. In this and in his many other books he argues, in elegant terms, that it is the continued destruction of human cultures based on the art and craft of living which threatens to destroy the world. *Explorations in Wood* celebrates a living example of these ancient traditions.

Like 'soil' the word 'timber' has been devalued by so-called 'modern' minds. Soil is the complex living thing which not only supports all natural vegetation but also allows all our crops to grow – and yet we speak of 'soiling' our hands. We 'preserve' folk songs, while at the same time our way of life destroys the singer. We are proud of our museums, where we display the damning evidence of a way of living which we have made impossible. Timber, the most versatile of all natural products, when shouted aloud – 'TIMBER!' – warns that another living tree has been destroyed.

The many cultures which lived, with trees as part and parcel of their lives, would say prayers before such a sacrifice was made to resource the many needs of their lives. Others would only harvest part of the tree – what they needed – leaving the rest to continue its vital work making and holding the soil; itself ready to resprout and grow a new crop of wood. It was thus that the ancient craft of pollarding and coppice came into being, a living example of how people made and managed diversity.

Tim Stead is a vibrant part of that tradition. He gives much more back to the forest than he ever takes and every product of his craft is a prayer of thanks and a celebration of the creative power of people and wood. As a tree grows it locks up carbon dioxide from the atmosphere and makes oxygen into the bargain. As it dies and decays away it uses up that oxygen, releasing the carbon dioxide into an already overburdened atmosphere. Tim Stead helps to balance the equation because everything he creates is destined to become a treasured possession and so the carbon it contains will remain locked up for many years to come – antiques for all our futures.

When I die I would like my ashes to be cast into one of the woodlands of the Border Country which gives Tim and many other people so much joy and inspiration. Then I might have a chance of becoming part not only of a living tree but also a product of a future 'new wood age' worker in whom this book has sown seeds of inspiration.

David Bellamy
Bedburn, March 1993

P.S . In the meantime this book will take its pride of place in my library.

Opposite:
'Chaos Practice'!
Photograph: Antonia Reeve

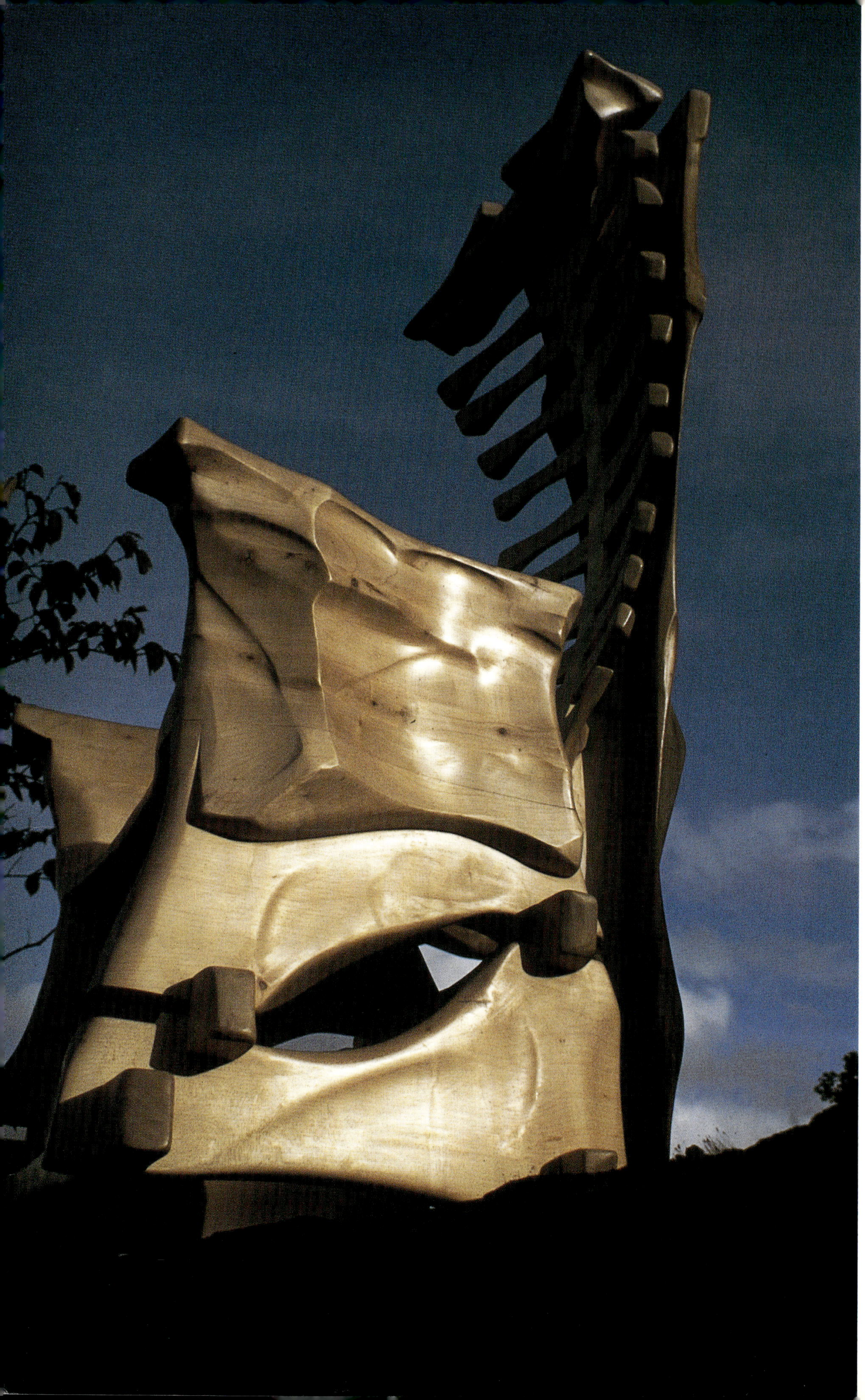

The 'Skeletal' armchair, forerunner of the 'Strata Chair'

Preface

In my work I hope to convey the amazement I feel for wood, and nature. I am very wary of the 'pedestal' that a book implies. A finished object always looks as though it was thought out from the beginning to the end. In my own case this is often far from the truth. Exploration is about risks and 'mistakes'. Often, things which work out well happen by chance – wood by its very nature allows these opportunities to occur. It is often me who adapts to the wood rather than the other way around; on many occasions I have had to modify what I originally wanted to do because not to have done so would not have allowed the wood to achieve its maximum potential.

I am not a finished product either and am equally full of faults – the prospect of perfection fills me with boredom. Twentieth century life seems to be too much concerned with formality and perfection – and frightened by the seemingly infinite possibilities which natural forms can offer. To work in harmony with a natural material is wonderful and each piece of my work is a partnership between myself and the tree. Often the tree is older than me and I bow to the superiority of its age and beauty. None of my work would have been possible if I were on a wavelength of my own, because the individuals who have bought and commissioned my work in the past have allowed me the space and time to develop my ideas freely. I hope that this book will encourage rather than intimidate the individual patrons of the future.

Like the seeds of a tree each person has to have the opportunity to germinate, grow and flourish – and it is often through chance that opportunities occur. For me the Scottish Development Agency was an important link in my development through their financial support. The Scottish Craft Centre, Café Gandolfi, Lothian Estates, The North Sea Oil Industries, Glasgow Museums and Galleries, Viz and The Royal Botanic Garden in Edinburgh are also all owed a debt of gratitude.

Tim Stead
Blainslie, April 1993

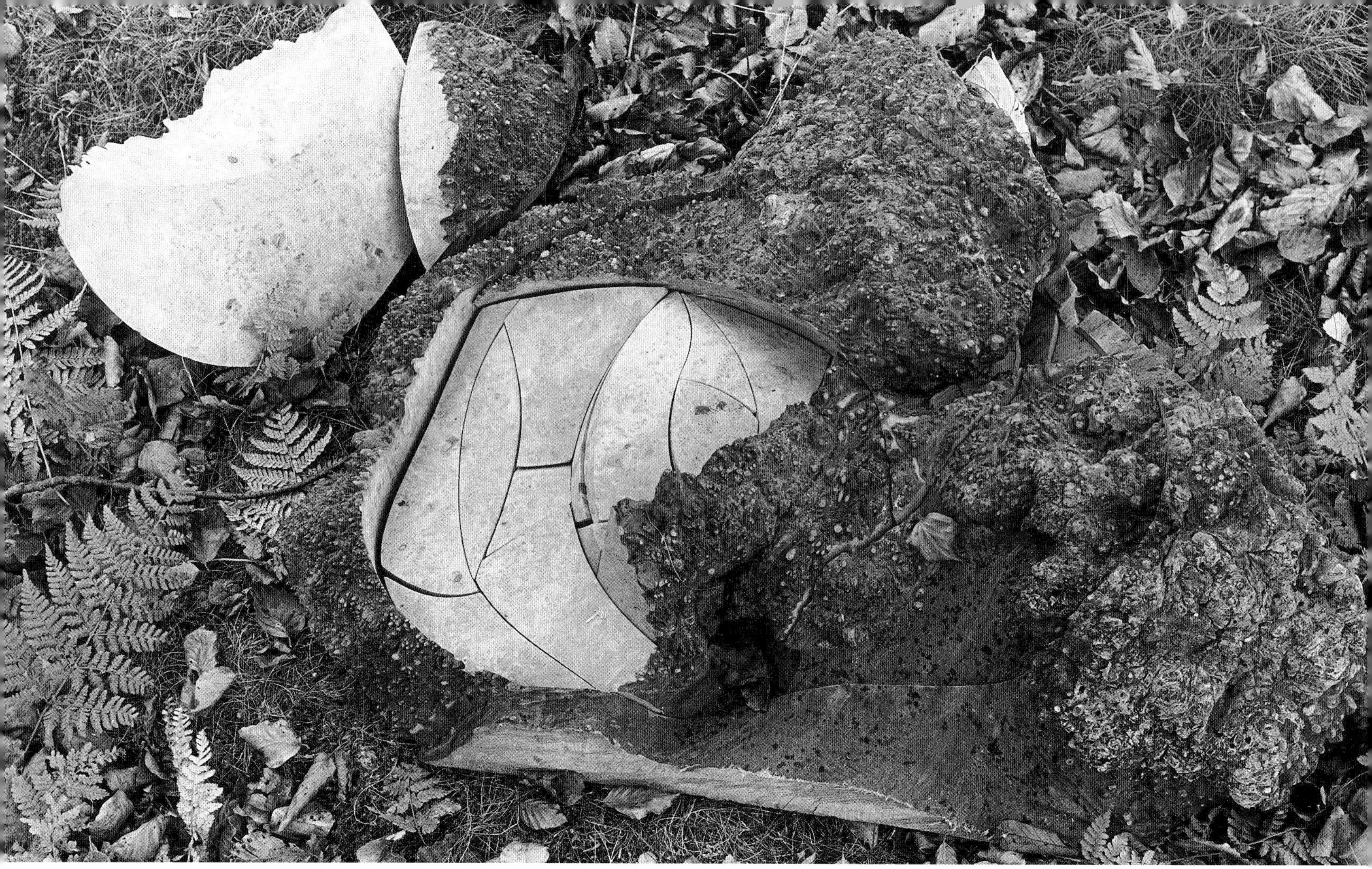

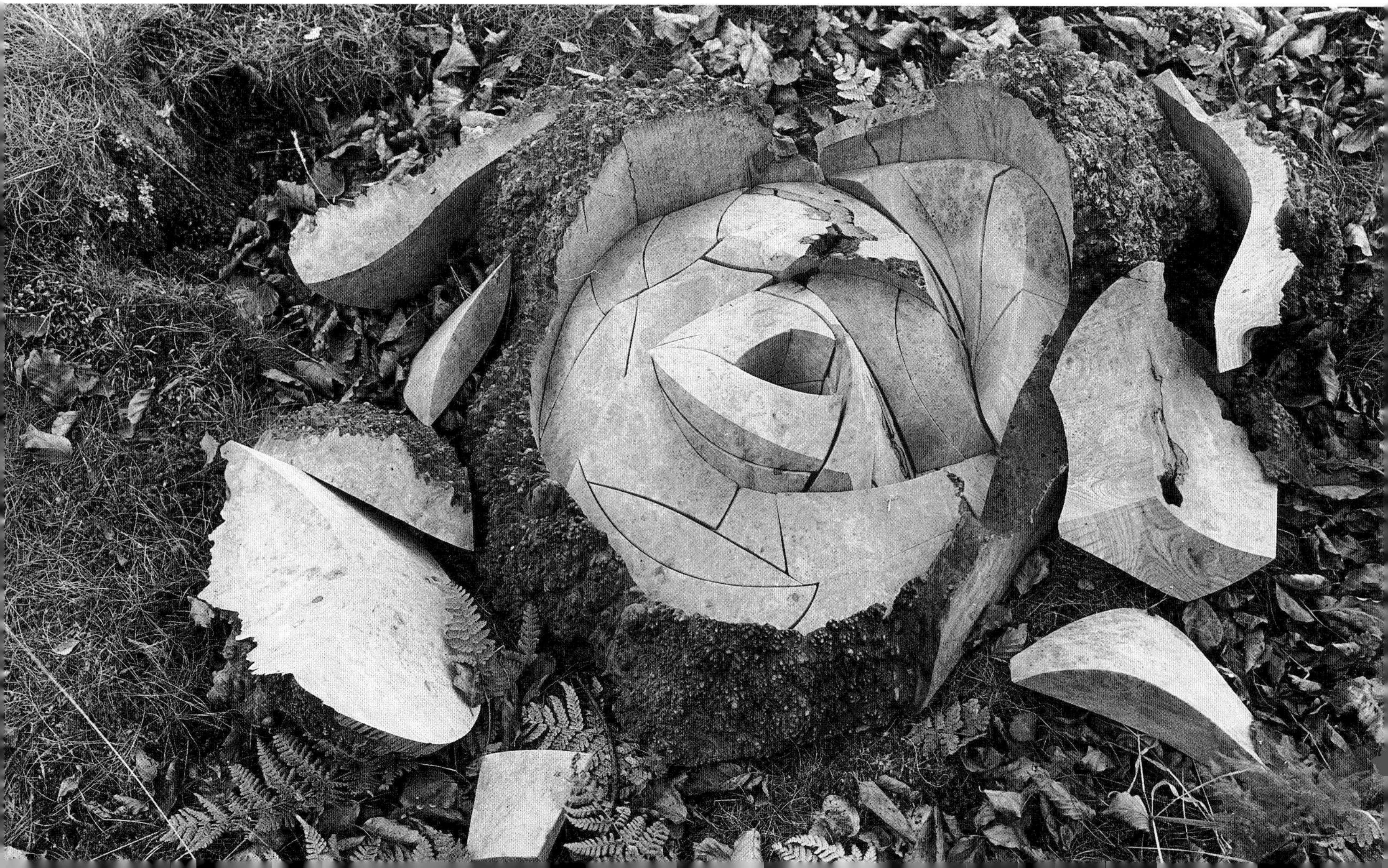

Opposite:
'Rising Mound'. All of Nature interrelates and within the wood there is landscape, history, sky, water, interlocking forms and infinite scope for speculation.
Photographs: Iain Mackenzie

Introduction

There are certain truisms which bear the weight of repetition. Once stated, the meaning can be turned over in the mind like an object and when we do this new facets may catch the light and compel us to think or feel differently. 'Wood comes from trees' is one such statement that appears so self-evident that to utter it would seem to invite ridicule. Tim Stead lives and breathes wood. He is surrounded by it in his home and works with it every day of the week. He plants trees and gives money and help to tree-loving causes. He derives a very good living from wood. And yet he never tires of stating the obvious. 'Wood comes from trees', he will say to a journalist, or a forester or a sculptor. The point is that this isn't at all obvious to increasing numbers of people. The link between the objects in our everyday lives and the raw materials from which they are derived becomes increasingly difficult to unravel. Supermarkets supply us with washed potatoes as if they want us to forget that these plants grow in the earth. Christmas trees are discarded, rootless and withered a few days after the event – yet another commodity. Wooden objects often bear little reminder of the trees from which they originate. An ancient link is lost and to many, wood comes from 'nowhere' or is taken for granted in the orgy of consumption which our culture has become.

Wood has been with human beings from the beginning. It has been an essential component of human life for millions of years – as a building material, a fuel, for weapons and as a raw material from which to fashion art. Intricate systems of belief, mythology and spirituality based on trees have developed. Yggdrasil, the great ash tree of Norse mythology held heaven in its branches, the dark underworld in its roots and temporal life in its trunk. Even today we put wreaths of holly and ivy on our doors, kiss under mistletoe, and place presents under a green tree in the middle of winter. The memory will not allow us to forget, even if we no longer understand the reasons for our strange behaviour. In a sense we have never left the 'Wood Age'. Like all valuable constants, wood has had to be re-invented and re-interpreted for our own times. The tree is a remarkable organism. Through photosynthesis solar energy helps to make wood. The tree locks up atmospheric carbon and produces oxygen. These complex plants are the planet's lungs and we depend on them, literally, for our survival. The tree has become the focus, practically as well as symbolically, of campaigns highlighting the global environmental crisis.

Yet to fell a tree and use its wood is not in itself a destructive act. In many places a balance was and still is struck between human needs and nature. Given due care and attention, a tree can assume a different life for hundreds or thousands of years after it has died. The woodworker, the builder, the craftsman, the carpenter and the sculptor have ensured this.

Tim Stead is part of this long genealogy of wood. He has been working with this miraculous material for the past twenty years on what has become a journey of self-exploration and a process of discovery which he has come to share with increasing numbers of people. Paradoxically the process has also been about learning how to forget. To discover the true nature of wood he has worked backwards to a time before Classicism to find an indigenous vocabulary capable of accurately describing his material. A seminal point in this process was Skara Brae, the stone village in Orkney buried for thousands of years. Its builders knew nothing of the straight lines of the Greek world. Reinterpreting this lost vernacular style in his own work has allowed Stead to feel truly at home. Whereas the straight line can suggest a dominance over nature, the observance of the natural rhythms of wood with its curves and irregularities implies an outlook more appropriate to our own times. If homo sapiens is to survive at all it will not be by conquering nature, but by means of a partnership which sensitively acknowledges the need for equilibrium. The increasing popularity of Stead's work testifies to this need.

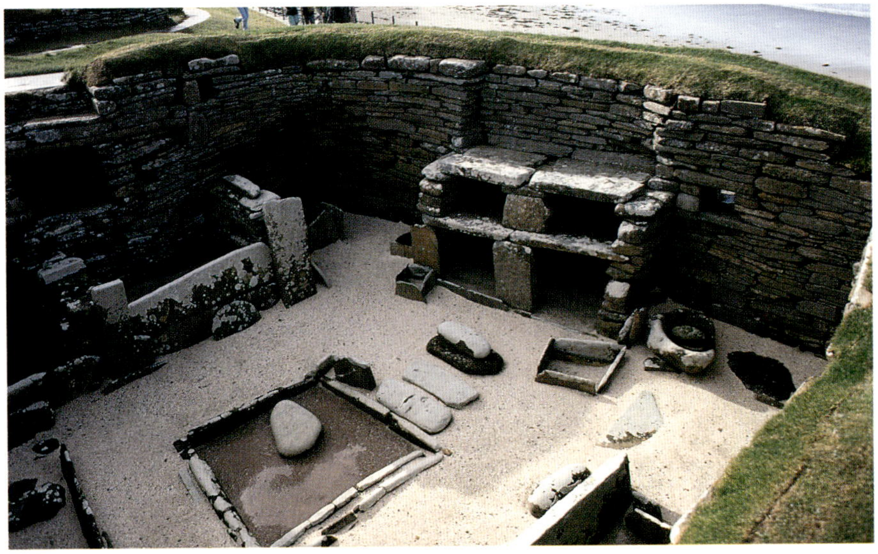

One of the Skara Brae houses on Orkney. The buildings testify to sophisticated construction methods and, by implication, a civilised way of life.

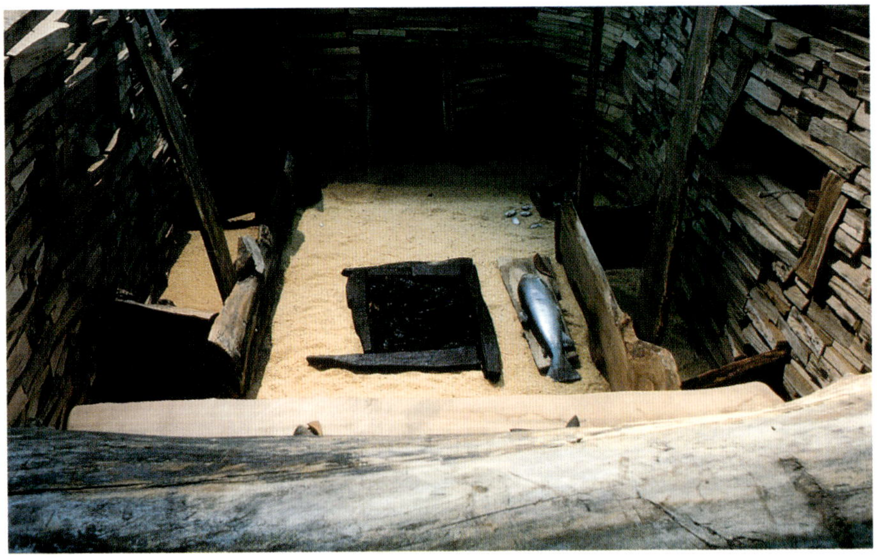

Detail of Skara Brae house showing doorway, hearth and beds.

Part One

Beginnings

Tim Stead was born in 1952 and brought up near Helsby, in rural Cheshire. He later attended art-school at Nottingham and Glasgow. He first became interested in working with wood while a student and has been addicted ever since. To support the habit he has made furniture as well as sculpture, with the former to some extent subsidising the later. However, the two are symbiotically linked with the sculpture providing inspiration for his furniture and vice versa. Tim Stead has exhibited widely both in Britain and abroad and in a career spanning twenty years to date, his work has become widely known, particularly in Scotland, where he has lived for most of his working life.

After living in Glasgow for a period, he moved to Harestanes in the borders and then to Blainslie, near Lauder which has been his home for the past ten years. Stead's house which with typical humour he named 'The Steading', is also home to his wife, Maggy, and their children Sam and Emma. Blainslie is a working village – adjacent to the Steads' home is a small sawmill – this combined with Tim Stead's workshops gives a feeling of productivity and industry.

As one enters the house one is greeted by a large open-plan room, combining kitchen and living area, full of interesting objects, most of them made by Tim Stead or by friends and other artists and makers. At the centre of the room is a large oak table around which life at The Staeding revolves – conversations, warm hospitality and laughter. Initially there is a visual shock at being somewhere so different, but the surroundings seem so simple and natural that this soon wears off. The real shock comes upon re-encountering the 'real world' which, by comparison, seems humourless and where natural materials are kept firmly in their place.

Each piece of Stead's idiosyncratic furniture and constantly evolving sculpture questions the mass-produced world and the homogenisation of culture. His life as an artist and an individual has been dedicated to finding other ways of living and working in an increasingly uniform world whose aesthetic codes he mostly rejects.

TS
I grew up beneath a sandstone outcrop in Cheshire which was wild and wooded. Bracken to roll in, trees to climb, narrow lanes, farms and plenty of space. To the north was a wide view of the marshes whose mysteries of 'great expectation' are now crossed by the M 56. Ever present on the horizon was the vast Stanlow oil refinery with its belching cooling towers and burning gas lighting the night sky. I found the prospect of being a part of the modern world increasingly alarming. The dominant man-made city-based culture filled me with horror, and still does. At the age of twelve I remember

calculating that with eight hours work and eight hours sleep there was very little time left for being alive.

Stead once commented that it was becoming increasingly difficult in Britain to turn down a side-street and find anything noteworthy or interesting. In a sense that remark is the starting point for Stead's work. One possible definition of the artist is somebody who populates the visual world with things which add to other people's visual perception, and makes it a richer and more interesting place. This can certainly be applied to Tim Stead. His work is a homage to the diversity of life, of nature and an irrefutable assertion of the 'impossibility of not being original'.

TS
The role of the artist is still very misunderstood and this is mainly because of the art market which has as much to do with art as the futures market has to do with coffee growing. The artist is taken up, ignored or spat out by the market, but for the most part works away quietly doing only what he or she can do. Generally they are people who are driven; they do what they do because they feel they must, they have a vision and pursue it and through exhibitions want to share it. To have a vision and a drive to do something is unfortunately a minority occupation in this society – and whether it is the arts, sciences, literature or politics – there is a huge weight of conformity which always tries to slow the impulsive visionary.

The ambition to be an artist, which gives me licence to do what I want, and my training, have given me the confidence to look always for new solutions. If my character were different I might have set up a factory to produce my designs in volume and market them, whereas my character gets bored quickly with repetition and wants to move on to the excitement of a new discovery.

One of the most profound motivations behind Stead's work has been his inability to identify a firm sense of what it means to be British. Like many English people living in Scotland he has adopted an identity through Scotland where he has identified facets of the cultural landscape no longer so easily accessible south of the Border. In 1990 Murray Grigor invited Stead to interpret Skara Brae for the 'Scotland Creates' exhibition which Grigor was co-ordinating. Stead revisited Orkney to look at Skara Brae – a Neolithic village (dating from c. 3,000 BC) on the west coast of the Orkney mainland. Until recently, the buildings and their contents were preserved beneath sand which had accumulated over millennia. Because of a lack of wood, the predominant building material was stone, whose use also extended to furniture. The Skara Brae houses contain dressers, beds, fireplaces, clay-lined pits for fresh water (or perhaps fish) as well as indoor sanitation. In Skara Brae, Stead recognised an indigenous vocabulary of architecture and design which seemed to confirm the aesthetic principles of his own work.

TS
This has been a very strong influence on me. It was really a point where I felt incredibly at home – a place where, at last, I had discovered some roots. In Orkney I saw many buildings of a much earlier period which were powerful and incredibly civilised. This had much more to do with my culture than the Roman or Greek culture.

Stead questions a British education system, particularly in respect of its teaching of history, which lays too heavy an emphasis on the importance of the Romans as a 'civilising' influence on ancient British culture. This is reflected too in the importance of Latin in the school curriculum which denied the equivalent 'Classical' period in our own civilisation. The Celtic languages of Britain have been so neglected that they assume only a minority status; and only a few words of Celtic origin (with the exception of place-names) are in current usage.

TS
My education said that before the Romans came and 'civilised' us, we were rushing around in woad and were as uncivilised as the native people that we had colonised – just 'savages'.

Murray Grigor described Stead's own work as 'pre-Hellenic post-Modernism'. The label is not altogether whimsical in that it challenges the pervasiveness of Classicism with its order and straight lines. The reheating of the same Greek soup as an aesthetic base for our architecture and design, Stead feels, should be challenged.

In many ways Stead's work is ahead of its time in that the organically-inspired forms suggest a harmonious relationship with nature. Stead associates Classicism in architecture as 'power-building'. The styles belonged to military states intent on imposing their will on other cultures. The architecture is of an age when humankind's relationship with nature was one of marked inferiority. Architecture was therefore a way of challenging nature's supremacy by making a distinctive impact on the landscape. In many ways a similar attitude prevails today, although we can explain most natural phenomena and control most of the natural environment. Stead feels it is time for a change.

TS
Our society has moved into a different era. Nature can be dominated by man. We can change the climate and we can damage nature. We should therefore adopt a more harmonious relationship with nature. Buildings should begin to convey these values.

It is perhaps worth remembering the building styles employed by the Austro-Hungarian empire, the Nazis and more recently in Ceauçescu's Romania. The Romanian dictator employed a deliberate policy of ethnocide, destroying peasant villages and housing the inhabitants in concrete blocks; correspondingly he flattened a large hill and demolished an entire quarter of

Outside the sun-lounge, winter.

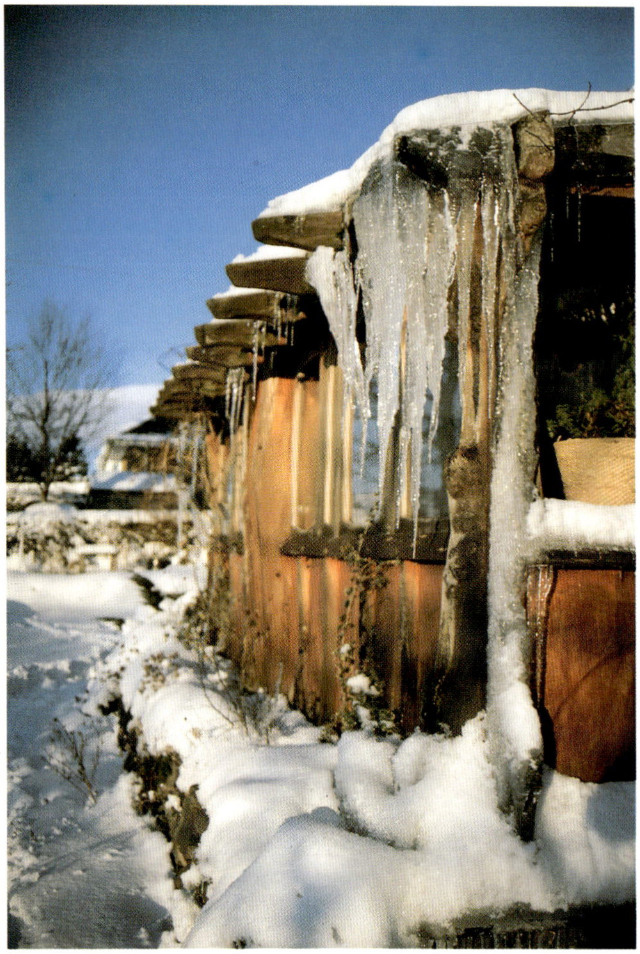

Opposite:
Fish-eye detail of four-poster bed. This derives its inspiration from Orkney – the Neolithic tomb of Maes Howe has a corbelled roof made from immense stone slabs placed on top of each other. The roof of the bed echoes this structure. The timber is held firmly in place by massive steel bolts.
Photograph: Antonia Reeve

Below:
Maggy and Emma on the thyme roof. The pitch of the roof was too shallow for slating. The idea of a turf roof had always appealed to Stead, but he rejected turf or heather in favour of creeping wild thyme. Thyme never grows too tall and is easily taken from cuttings (over 400 plants were needed). The thyme spreads rapidly and has the added bonus of millions of small, purple, sweet-smelling flowers in June and July. Below the thyme, the roof is fully insulated and waterproof. A two-inch air gap is formed by the batons which support a deeply corrugated metal roof, angled to allow the rain to run off. Putting soil on a roof, essentially burying it, can seem a very strange thing to do. The JCB driver took a lot of persuading. Up to the last moment he suspected he was having his leg pulled. The planners had no regulations about thyme roofs and were quite amenable to the idea that this wasn't really a roof at all, but a series of forty-two gutters.

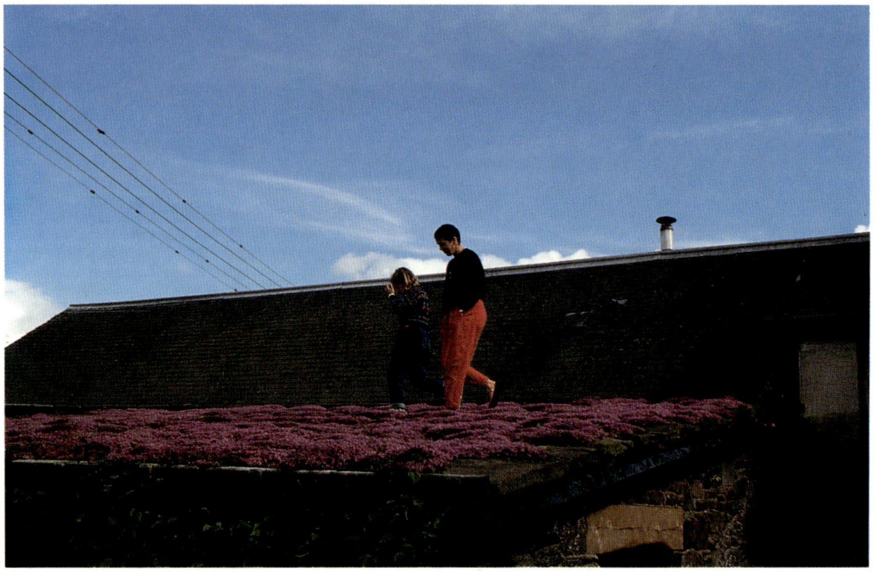

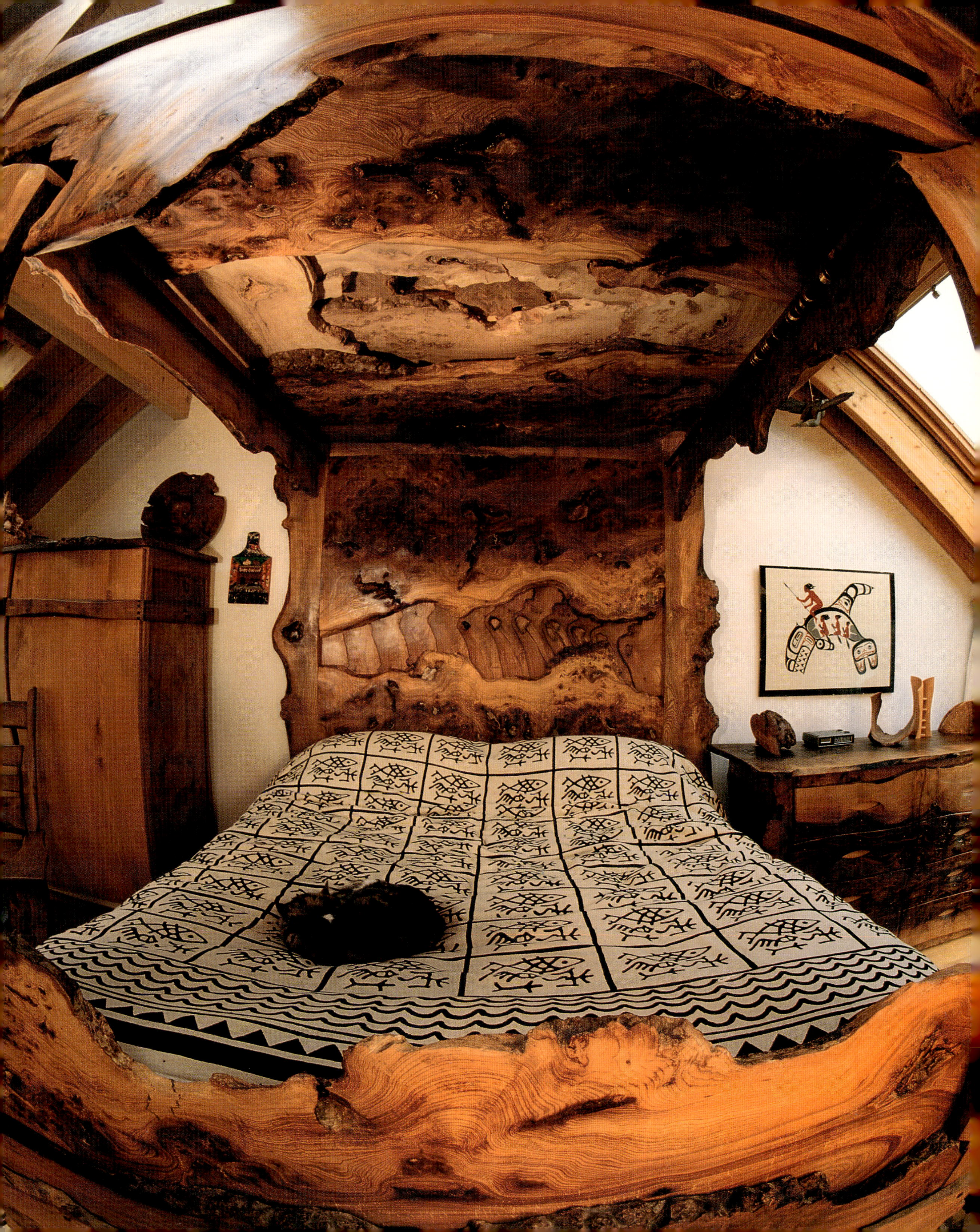

Bucharest to erect a classically-inspired 'palace'. It was a symbol of power, of megalomaniac delusion, of a state held together by military and paramilitary force.

If Stead's work is a reaction against militarism and classicism, and is about a turning towards roots, it is also a product of the times. In 1992 it was more difficult to view Columbus's 'discovery' of America as an event worth celebrating. By pointing towards indigenous Celtic or British styles and suggesting the possibility of a new aesthetic vocabulary Stead implies that the Roman conquest and our subsequent addiction to Classicism was a similarly unhappy event.

Opposite:
Twenty-four thin boards cut from a small limb to form a tunnel – one of many possibilities.
Photographs: Debbie White

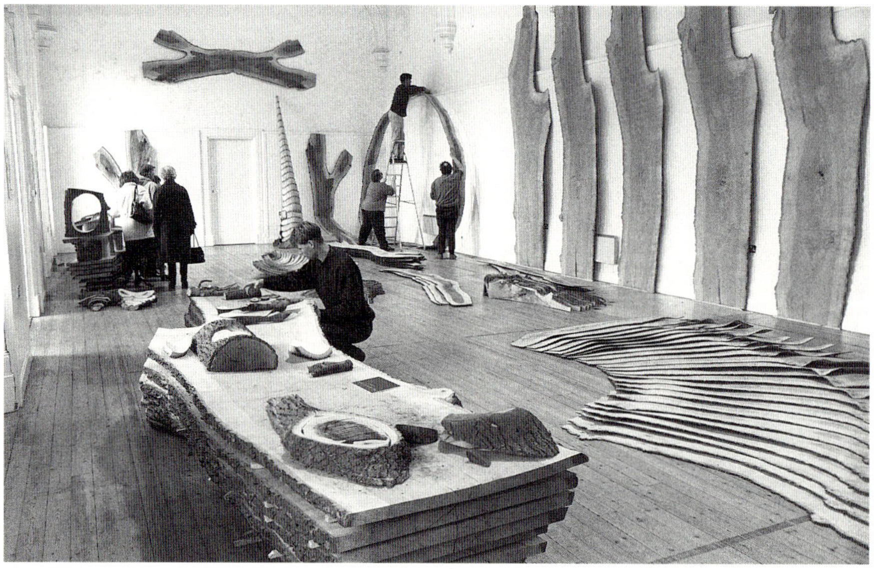

Setting up 'The Botanic Ash' exhibition, Royal Botanic Garden, Edinburgh 1993.
Photograph: Debbie White

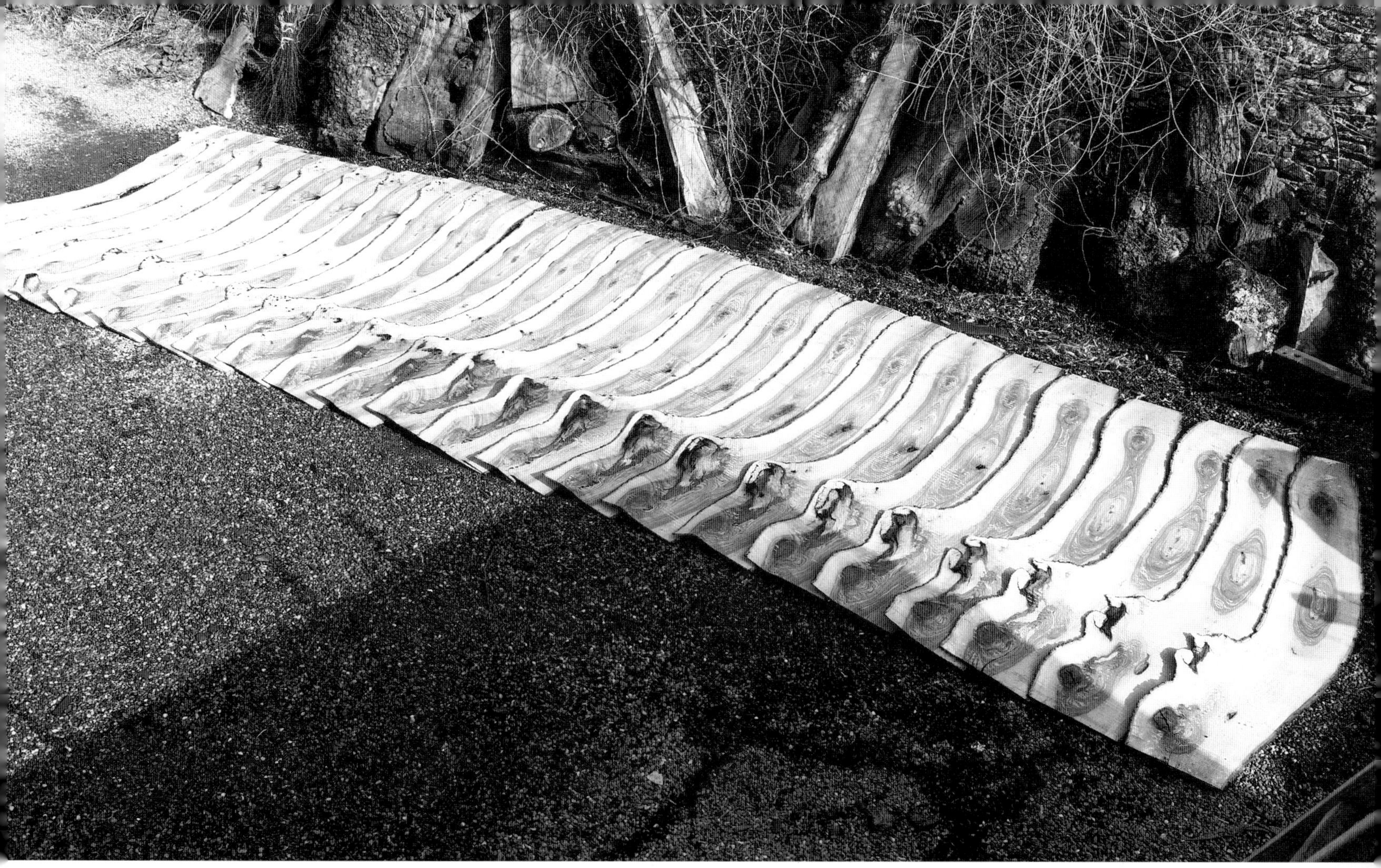

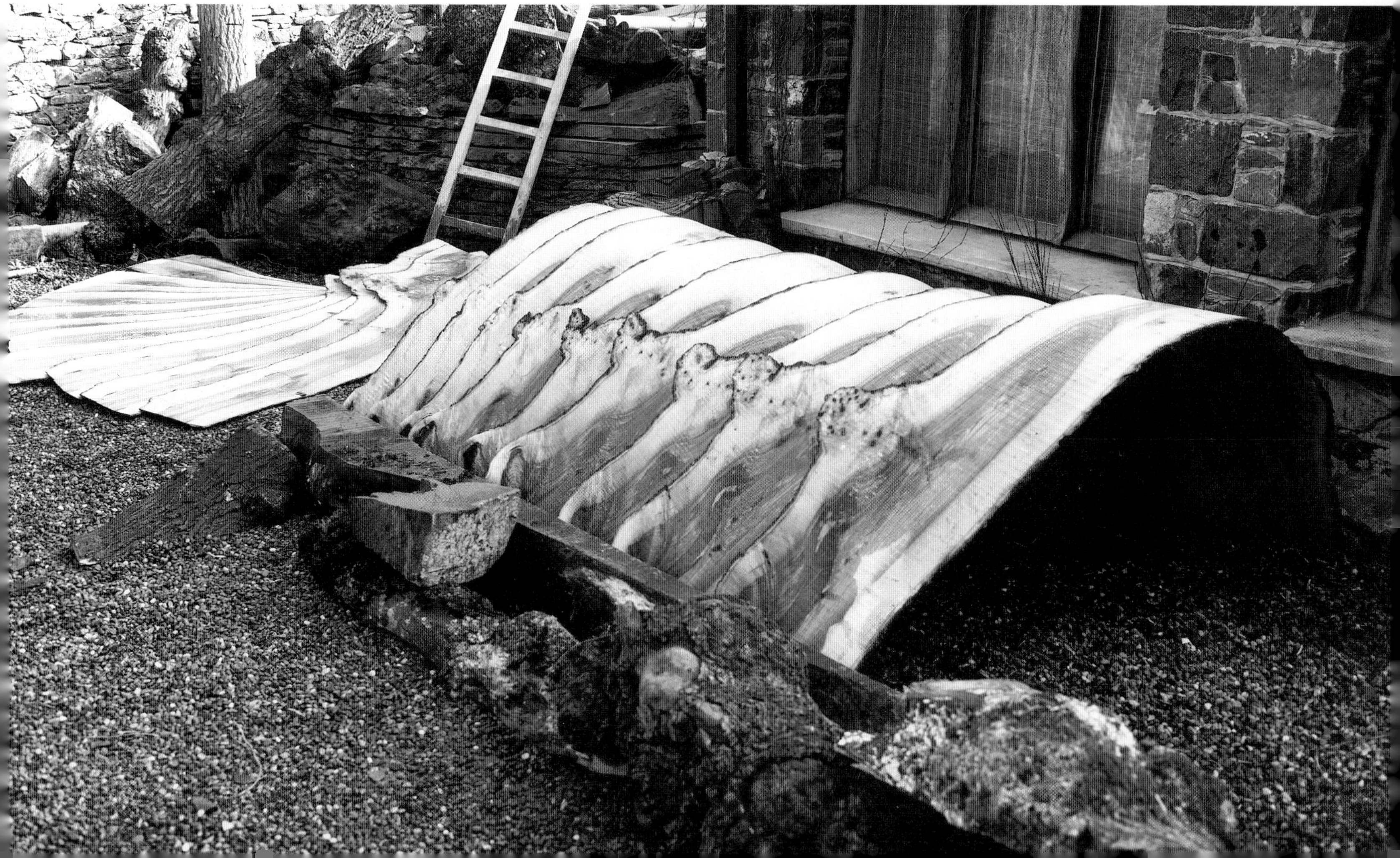

One of the huge 'trilobite' sculptures shown at the 'Spirits of the Forest' exhibition which was held in Glasgow in 1991. This shows the sculpture in the yard outside Stead's workshop.

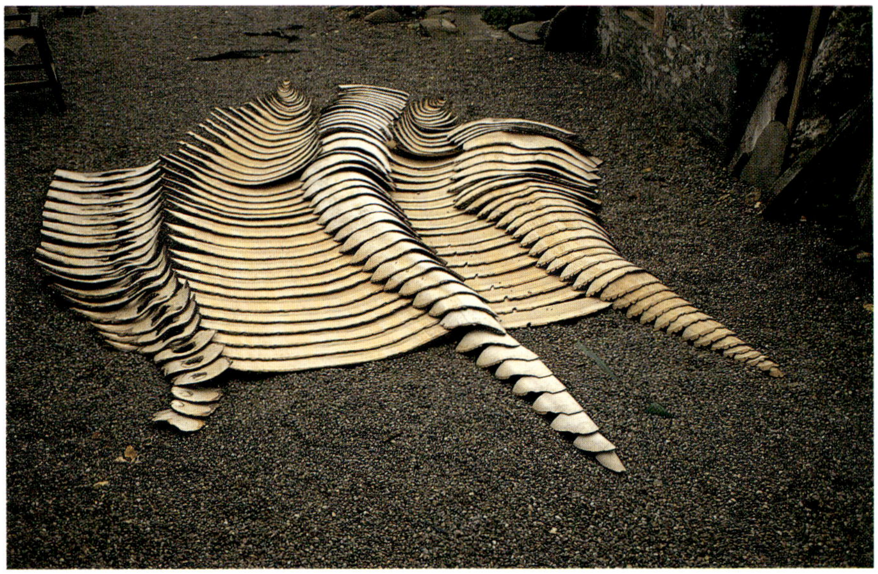

Opposite:
Detail of bar, in burr elm, with corner unit. Commissioned by a client in Greece who has bought many pieces of Stead's work through 'Indesign'. The client wanted this particular bar to be 'really burry and unusual – a fantasy'.

'Claws', from the 'Layers' exhibition.

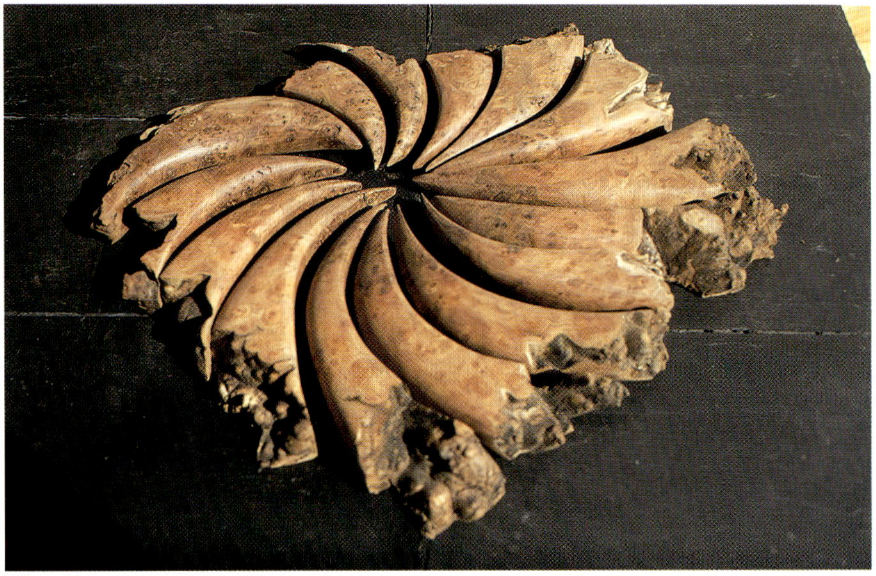

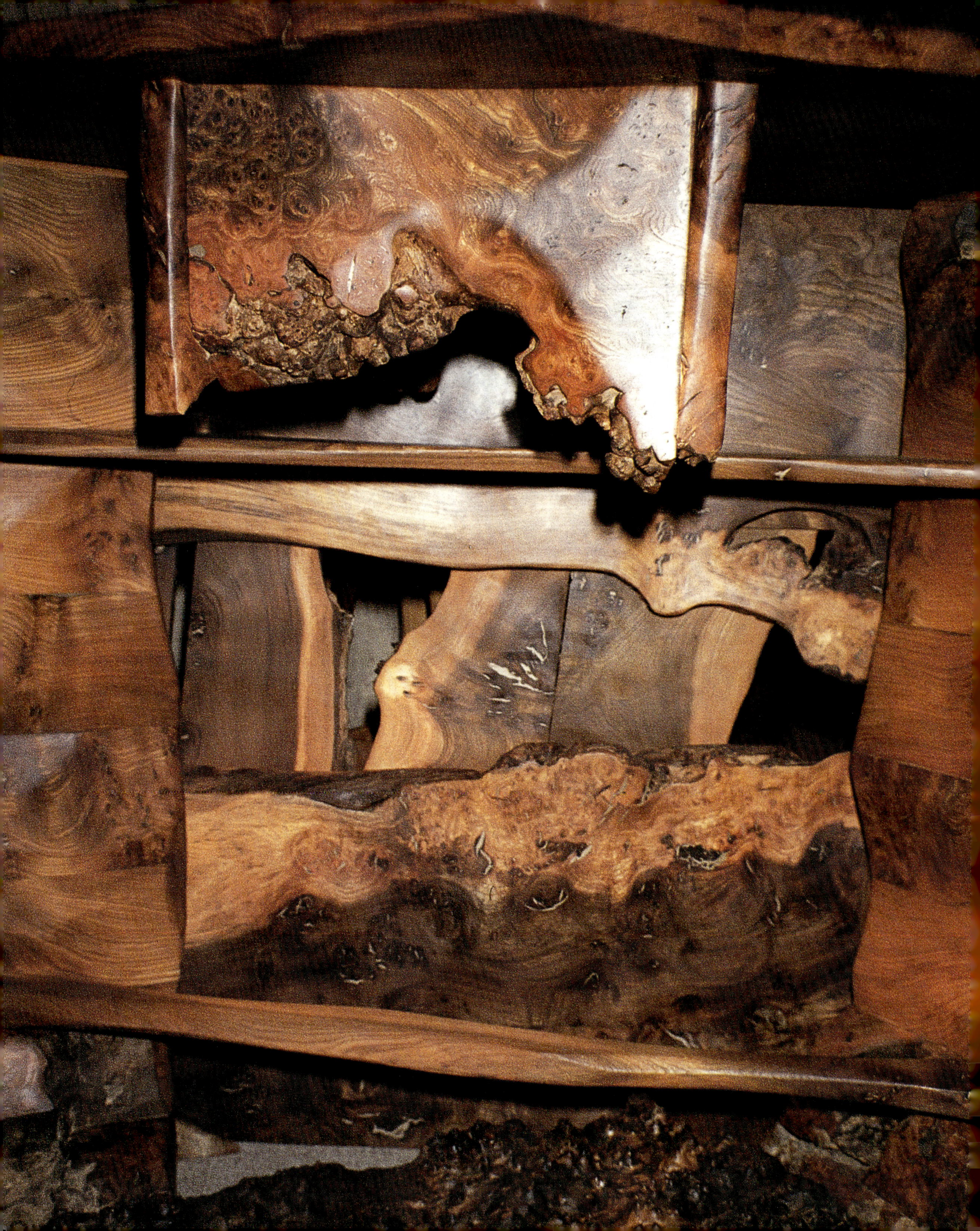

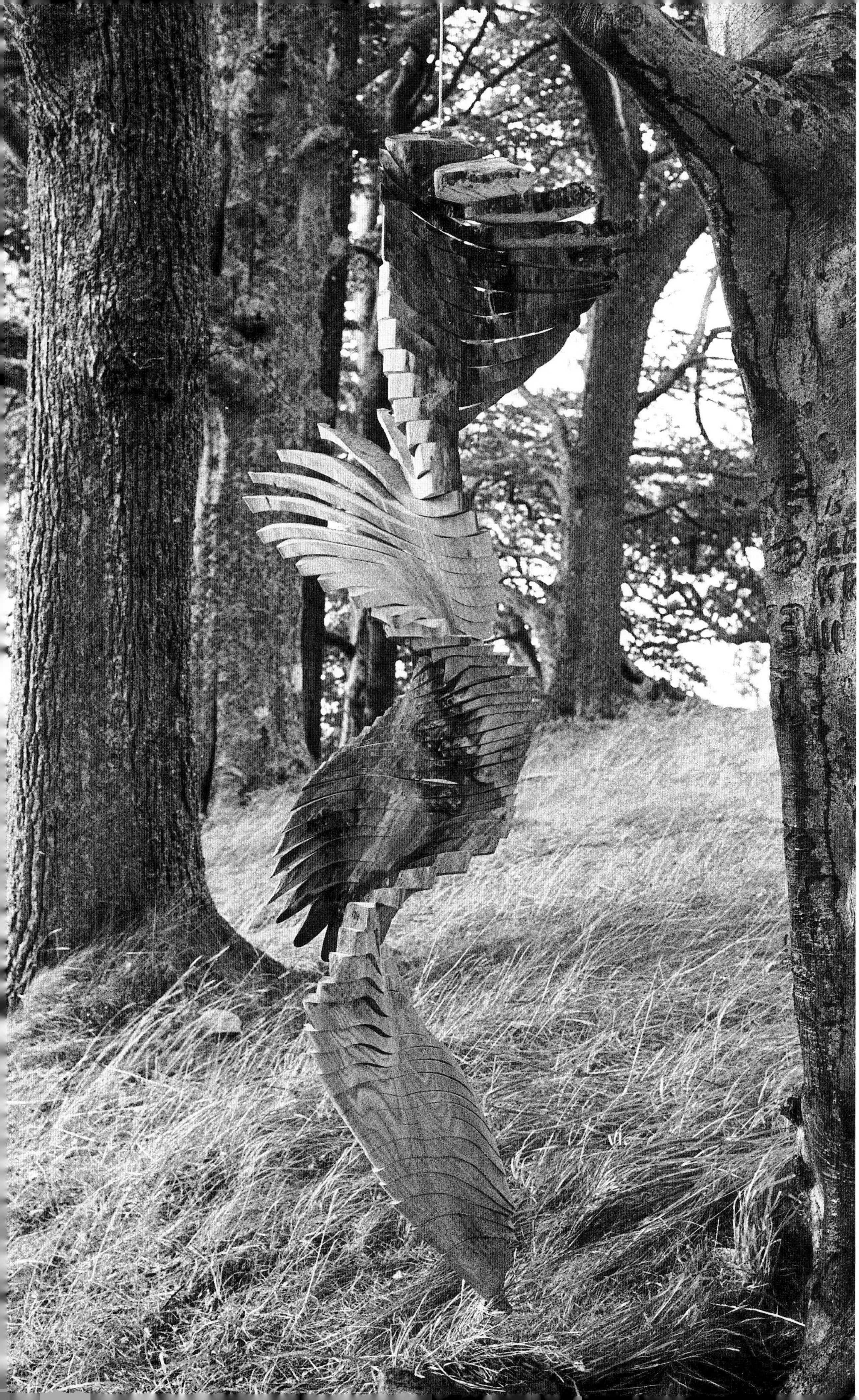

A 'mysterious' sculpture made from a slab of elm cut into fine sections. A wire runs through the centre allowing for articulation.

Photograph: Iain Mackenzie

Influences?

Stead is hesitant or unable to name almost any direct positive influence on his work by other artists or makers. Although not negative in outlook or personality, Stead cites only those things which he has reacted against as being influential in his work – Conceptualism, Minimalism, the 'Brutalist' architecture of the sixties, the mass-production of identical objects. All the high-flown 'isms' with which the world of art, craft and architecture has surrounded itself over the past thirty years or more.

One of the positive influences Stead acknowledges is the Austrian artist Hundertwasser. Stead's debt to Hundertwasser is not stylistic; rather he admires the Austrian artist's robust stance, his forceful language and an uncompromising spirit. Stead is fond of quoting Hundertwasser's axiom 'Beware the straight line and the drunken line – but above all, beware the T-squared line. The straight line leads to a loss of humanity.'

In a speech at the State University, San Francisco in 1982, Hundertwasser stated:

> 'Art must create values and not destroy values. One should feel with art protected as if you were really at home. Art must be beautiful, true and positive. Art must return to simplicity in our more and more complicated world, and find solutions to reduce the problems in which we are more and more entangled, and not to create new problems.'

Although not consciously part of a movement or '-ism' (it is, after all, art critics and art historians who create these categories, not artists) it is difficult not to place Stead's work alongside that of other artists with whom he shares certain ideas. For Hundertwasser it is a reverence for natural forms and an abhorrence of the straight line which motivates his work. Andy Goldsworthy builds upon natural forms, emphasising the variety of colours, shapes and textures to create his own inimitable artworks. herman de vries, a meticulous collector and categoriser, delights, for example, in the variety of colours found in different soils or the differences in tone and texture between twigs from different species of tree. David Nash's large wooden sculptures, often organically derived, also share some parallels with Stead's work. George Nakashima, a Japanese American, is perhaps the closest to Stead in his use of wood for furniture making. Nakashima passionately emphasised the true nature of wood and many of his pieces showed a delight in the 'waney' edge (the original surface edge of the tree) and the rich patterns of 'burred' timber. But Stead made his own work for many years without any knowledge of Nakashima.

These artists are best characterised by a need to place nature to the fore; the personality or the feelings of the artist remain in the background. In responding to criticism that his work leaves too much to nature and is therefore not really 'art', Stead, perhaps surprisingly, agrees but with an interesting proviso.

TS
It takes a certain amount of integrity to leave things alone. I would agree entirely that in much of my work the wood is making a much bigger statement than I am. But perhaps that is also the statement that I want to make . . . Normally the wood I use wouldn't get into a furniture maker's workshop and if it did it would tend to get squared-up or have a man-made design imposed on it. I like the idea that it's man-made, that it's jointed and that it has a function but also that it still has a very strong reference to the natural form. The natural form is the powerful element. Often, I can't find better shapes or images that are as strong as those of nature. Maybe it's a question of throwing in the towel and admitting that nature has the star part and that is where the focus should be – not on 'what a well-made and well-designed piece. How clever I am!' But rather what an extraordinary piece of wood and how enjoyable it is to see wood in context. I think the idea of a message in art is very much out of fashion. The justification in what I do is beyond a simple aesthetic and making something which people will buy; there needs to be more than that. That extra is the natural element and the awe which I think we should all feel for nature in all its forms.

Three-part coffee table in elm whose pieces can be used separately or in combination – an alternative to the traditional 'nest' of tables.
Photograph: Antonia Reeve

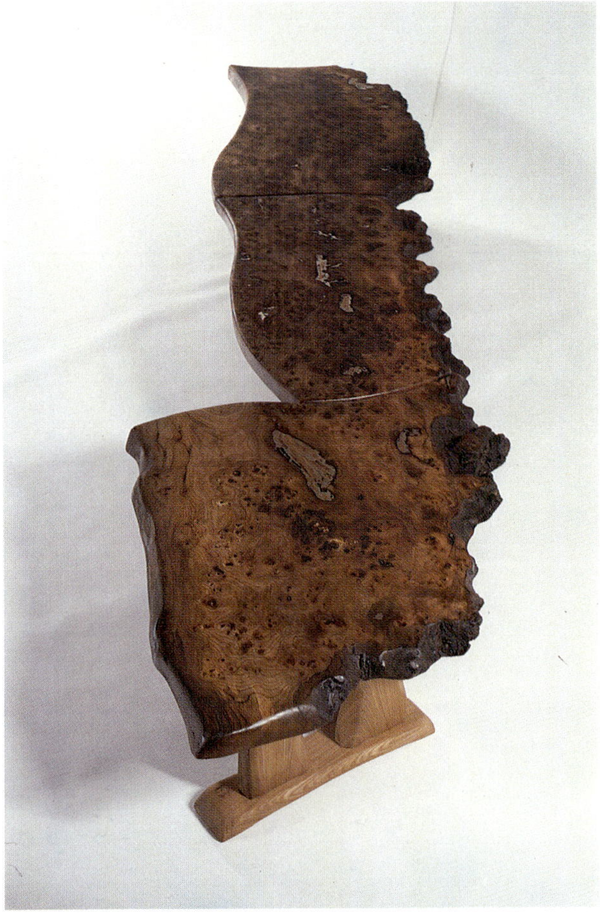

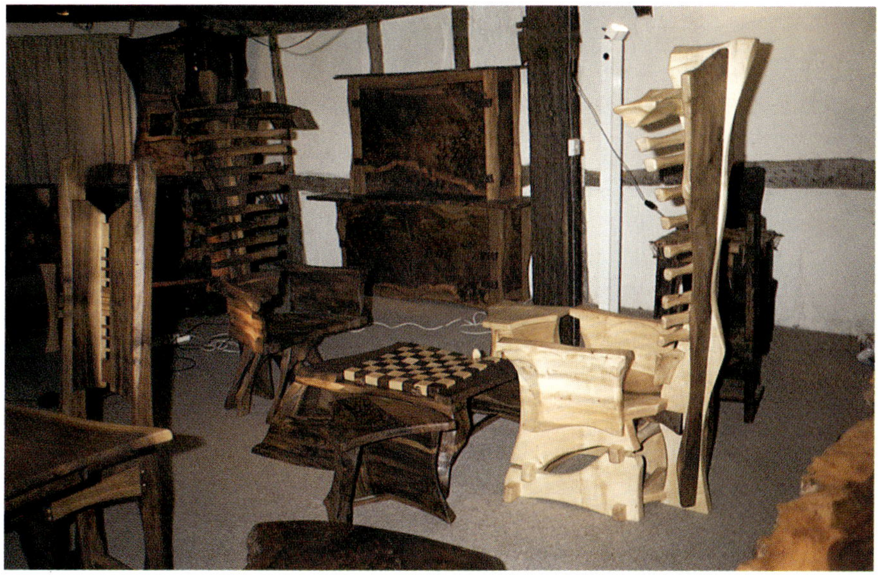

'Indesign', Chester

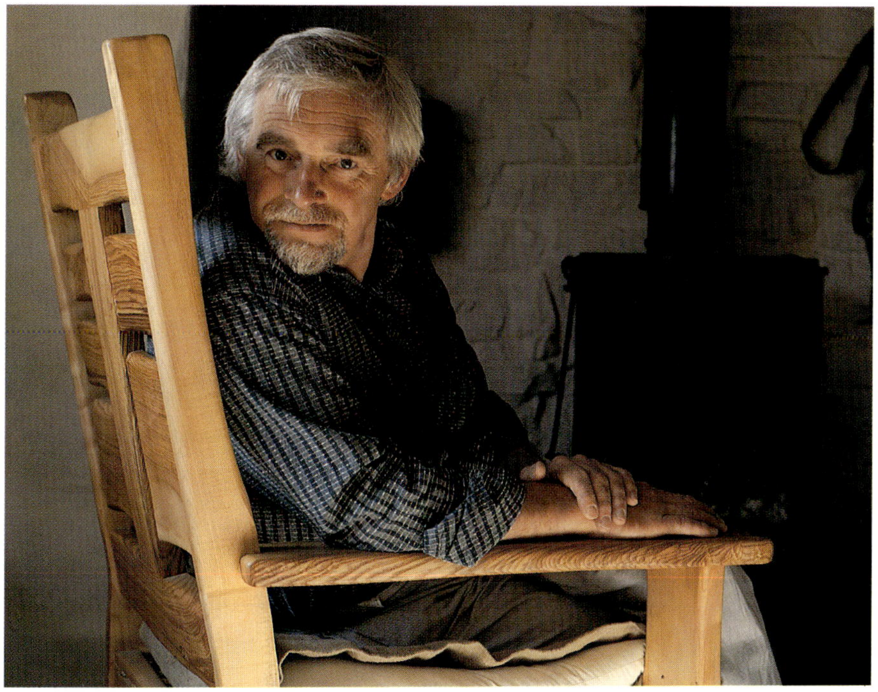

Alan Brown.
Photograph: Ken Kirkwood

The Fundamentalist Manifesto

An important influence on Stead's development, particularly in the area of furniture design, was Alan Brown. Brown ran a shop in Chester, 'Indesign', which specialised in modern furniture.

TS
The shop dealt with European design with quite hard lines. I showed Alan some photographs and he said 'you're making what I've been trying to design for ages!'. It was very exciting. 'Indesign' allowed me to put my furniture into a modern and serious furniture, rather than the craft, context.

Stead's relationship with Brown extended well beyond that of a manufacturer with his retailer; it was a nurturing friendship which Stead feels was instrumental in his development.

TS
It was a voyage of exploration with Alan – we were always having discussions of extreme philosophies and debating aesthetic issues. He wasn't concerned with the idea of developing a chair, say, for a particular market and then finding a way of producing it in bulk. He said: 'This is successful; what about the next?' So I had to design something else which people would then want . I was continually changing and evolving ideas. The work became a lot more exciting through working with him. Alan was a catalyst – he drew people together and encouraged experiment.

Brown, who had attended Liverpool Art School at the same time as John Lennon, was a rebel who frequently delighted in challenging the accepted order. His circle of friends included the Merseyside poets, Adrian Henri and Roger McGough. Along with Stead and two others he issued, quixotically, 'The Fundamentalist Manifesto'.

The Fundamentalist Manifesto

Design, architecture and craft are expressed in the intellectual language of these disciplines. The messages are often only clearly understood or used by members of the same profession. The standards of beauty (the aesthetics) are required to be capable of formal definition and critical judgement.

The fundamentalist resource is the emotional language (art) related to the direct experience of natural form and texture – rocks, old bones, driftwood, – which have the qualities produced by erosion, use and accident.

The objective of a fundamentalist group is to propagate this concept and to liberate creative people from the nunnery of the design/architectural/craft establishment.

Alan Brown
Caroline Bailey
Tim Stead
Paul Mountain

Stead is philosophical about the manifesto's purpose, as well as realistic about what it could achieve.

TS
A manifesto develops ideas which cut across a lot of common ground – almost a 'Gestalt' thing. It's the same as the creative process – like a knot for a particular function. You play around with the string and you find what works; there are some knots which come undone. The manifesto had implications which were larger and much wider. However, the main ideas remain and I'm convinced there is a very wide area of visual language that can be copied and used in buildings, furniture and graphics.

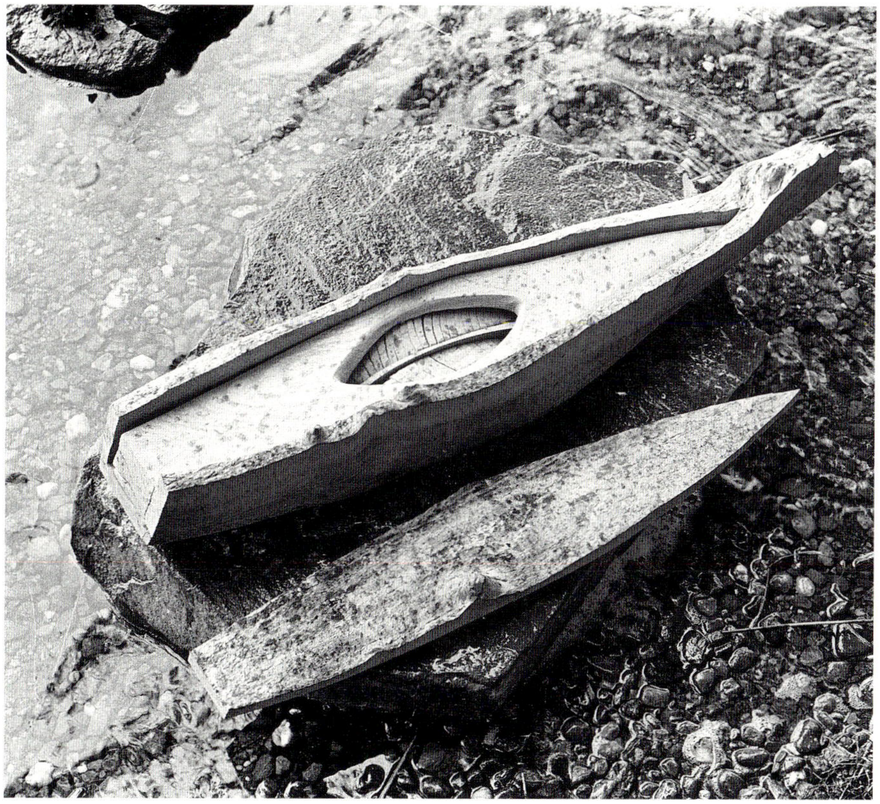

'Spawning Voyage'
Photograph: Iain Mackenzie

Driftwood platform

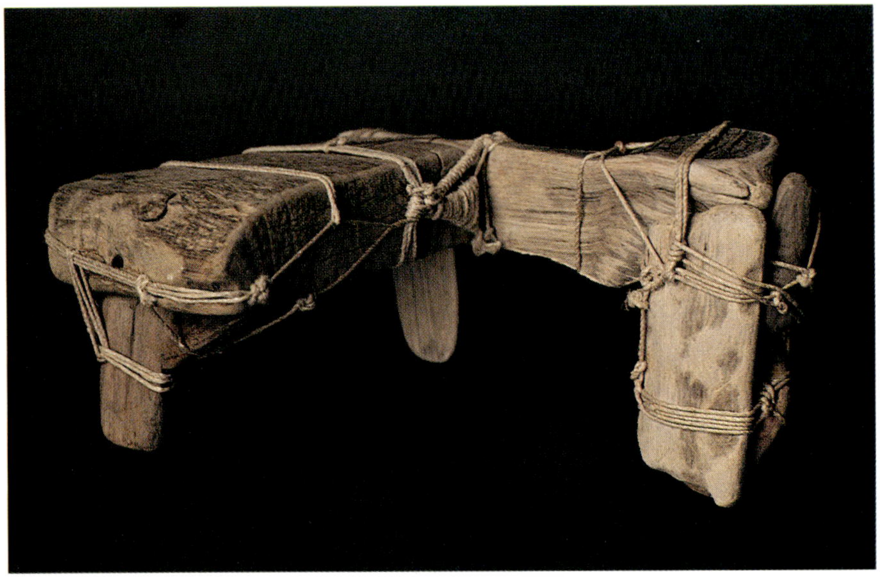

Opposite:
A collection of Stead's notebooks and burr elm desk.
Photographs: Antonia Reeve

'Ancestor and Seed' from the 'Layers' exhibition.
Photograph: Antonia Reeve

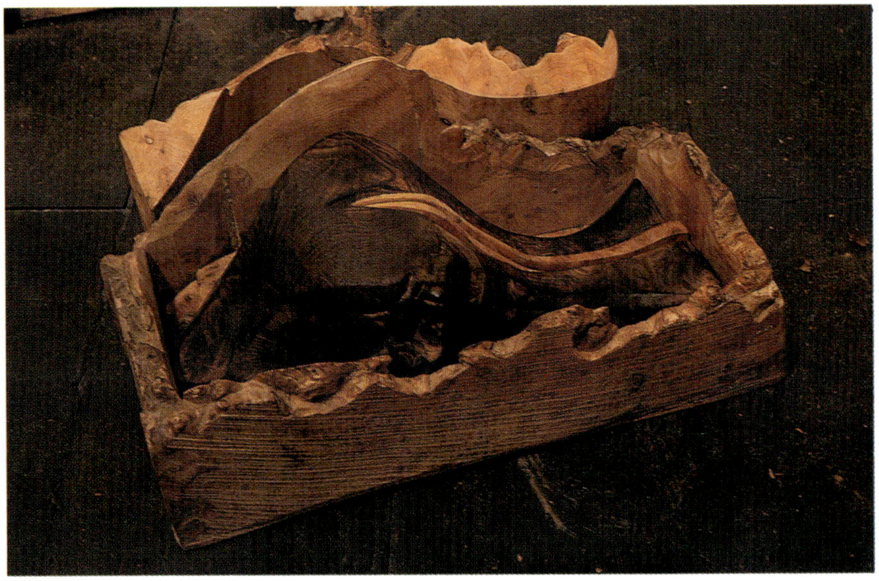

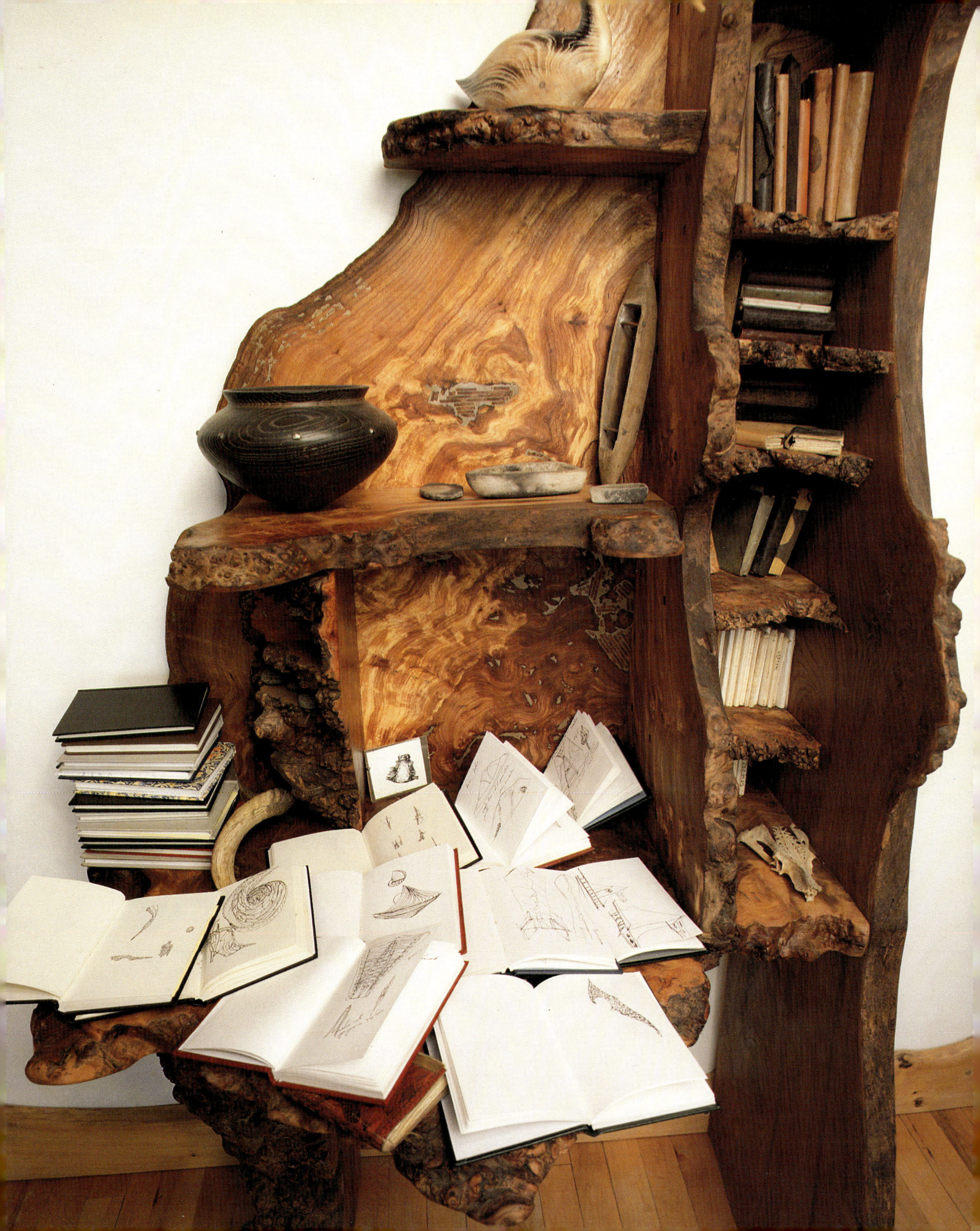

Driftwood & String

TS
My big breakthrough came when I stopped taking myself seriously and started playing. I started with small pieces of driftwood, moving to larger pieces, eventually collecting and carving railway sleepers. I wanted to make things which could be left outside and appear like discarded parts of something functional rather than as 'pieces of art'. The sculpture which followed was always about a balance between the man-made and the natural. There is a very strong dynamic. A totally clear landscape is beautiful in itself, but somehow the straight line of a dyke going over a hill can have more poignancy by harmoniously combining the man-made with the natural. Through the driftwood I became addicted to wood . . .

Stead has used wood from the beginning and a continuity can be traced from his earliest pieces to his most recent work. In some of his earliest work Stead used driftwood which he bound with string. He exhibited examples of this work in his degree show at Trent Polytechnic. As well as driftwood, he also salvaged timber which had been dumped in the nearby canal.

TS
There was a big bonfire heap with tons of old bits of wood: two ends of a thirty foot boat; parts of lock gates; big oak ribs from a barge. It went very well. I felt that could balance my own interests with what was required of me by the art school. I've never really looked back since then.

Stead feels that the relationship between landscape and the forms and shapes of eroded or naturally-shaped wood cannot be ignored. Many of his earliest pieces echo the folds of landscape; and very recent pieces like 'Ancestor & Seed' reinforce the feeling that a similar logic informs both tree and geomorphology. 'Ancestor & Seed' refers to the late Bruce Chatwin's book, *The Songlines*:

> 'The aboriginals tread the earth lightly and by not taking out more than can be replaced they respect their ancestors who sang the world alive and still live in every fold of the landscape.'

Just as landscape in a sense contains the lives of all those who lived upon it, so a tree will reflect its shaping forces. When a tree is cut down it does not die. If it is burned it releases the energy of which it is constituted. If it rots it returns to the soil, allowing more trees to grow. If it is retained as furniture or sculpture it is given new life as ornament or functional object.

Burnt tower with creaking pendulum.

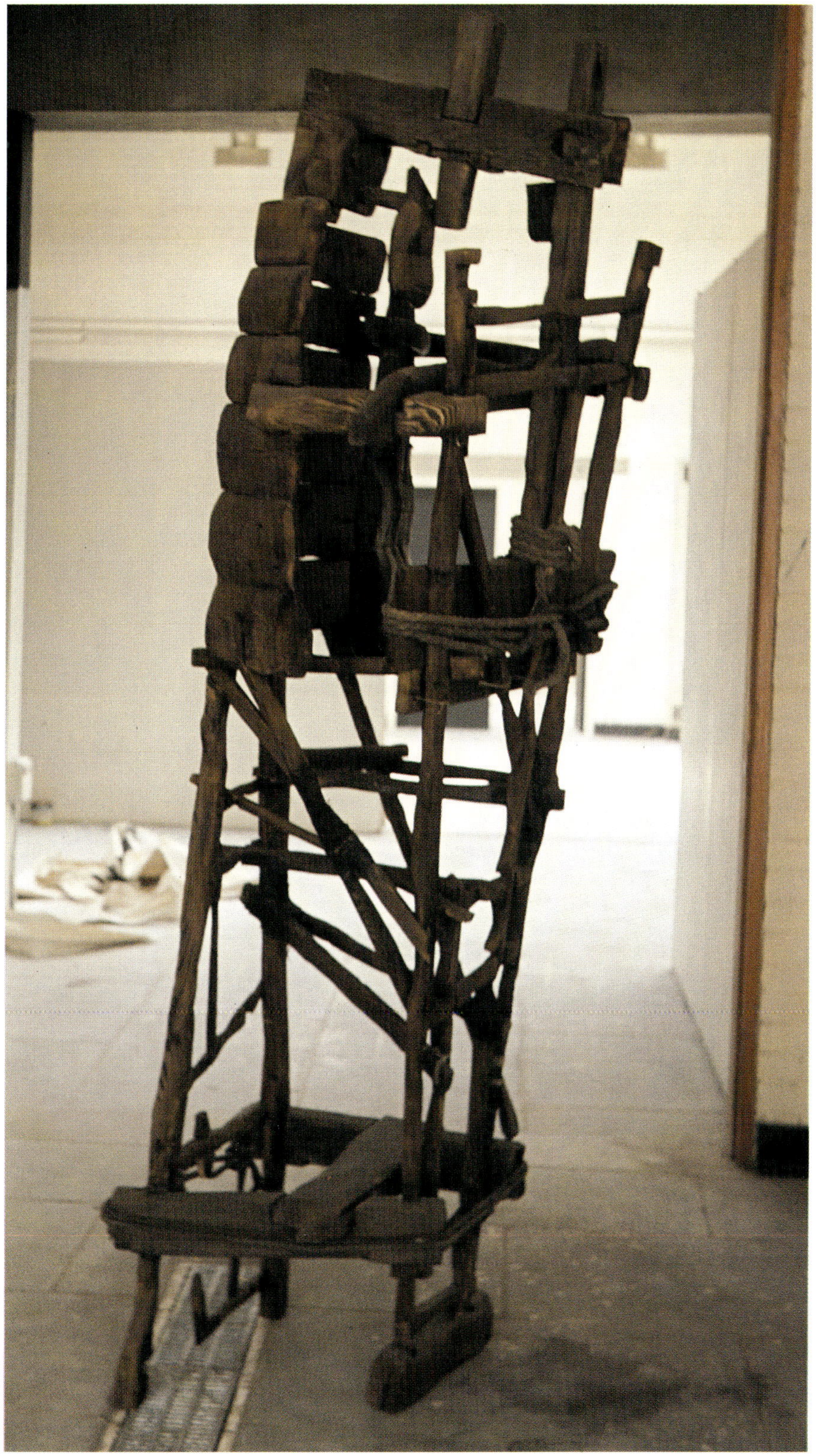

Stead's first chess-set showing detail of pieces.

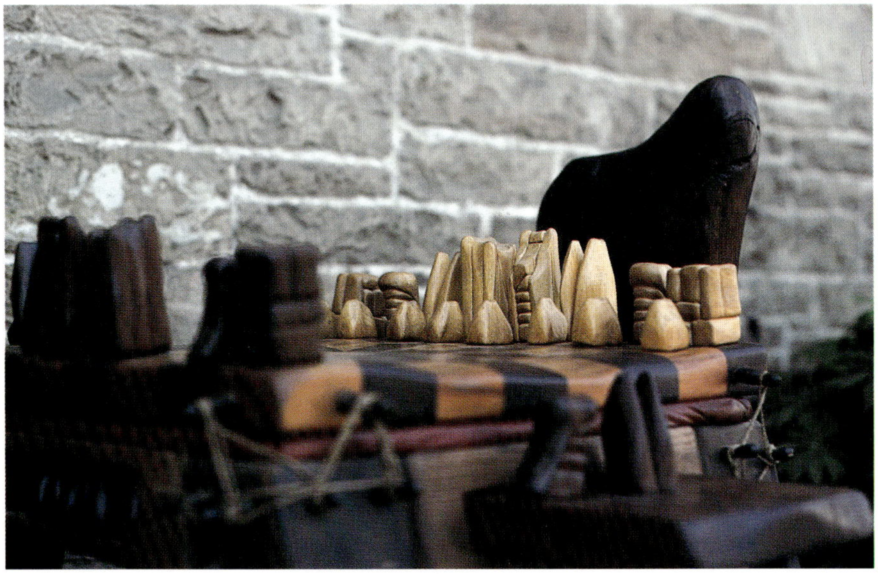

Detail of burr elm, repaired with cold-cast bronze.
Photograph: Alex X. Fraser

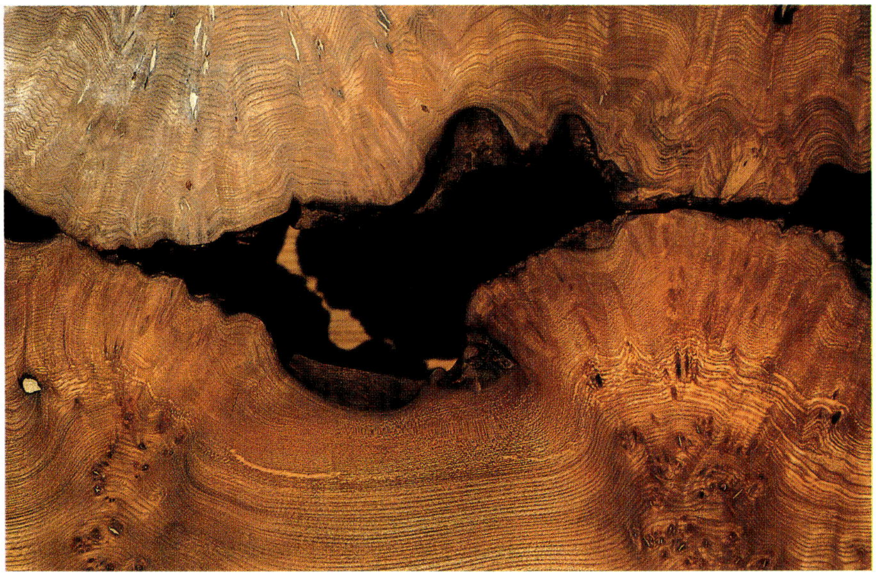

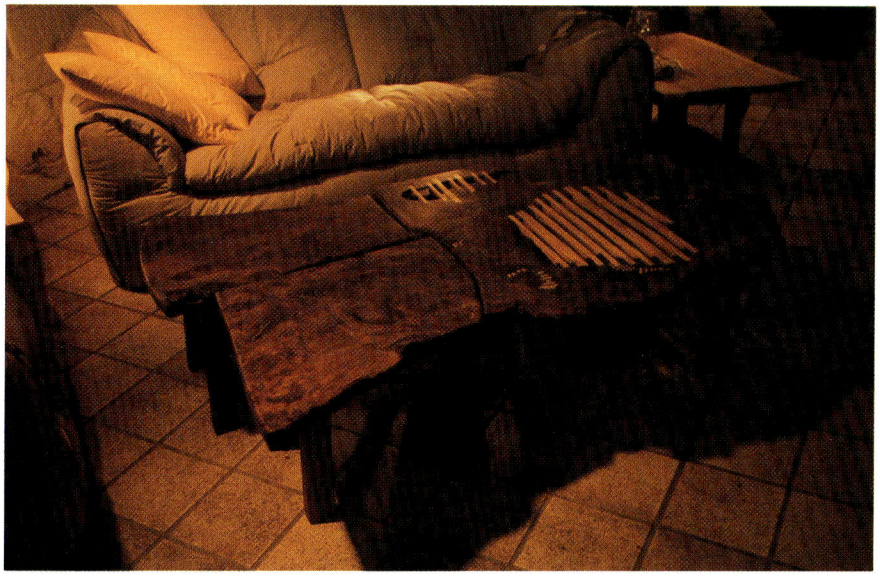

Three-part burr elm coffee-table, repaired with sycamore.

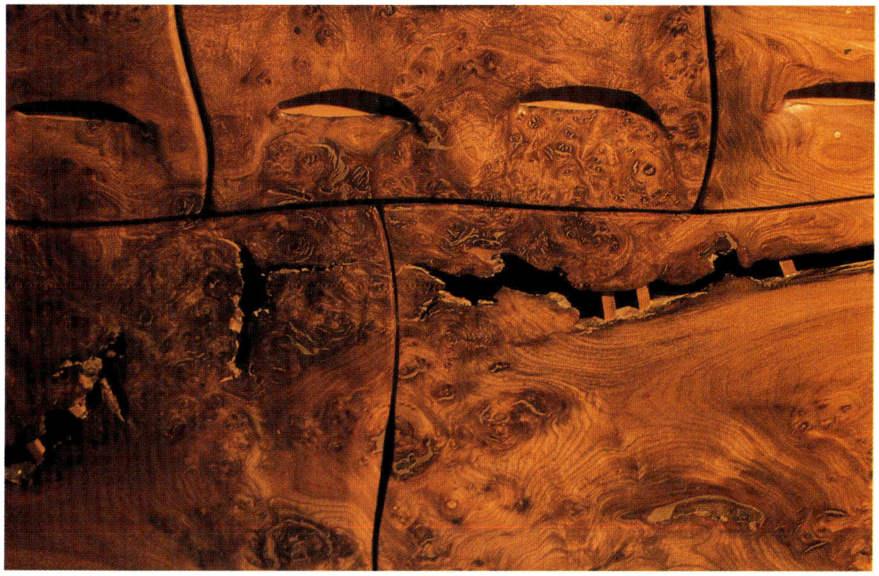

Detail of drawer and cupboard fronts on burr elm dresser.
Photograph: Antonia Reeve

Creativity

TS
Creativity is not exclusive to the arts – everyone has creative potential. We subject children to a process of 'adultification' which seems to dull their creative edge, or remove it altogether. . .Within each day I hope to be absorbed by what I do, and better still, excited by it. The best of all is to start on something new. To do a good day's work and to make something well is very satisfying. To make something which is 'original' is spell-binding. At one moment you are very blank – you're not sure how you are going to proceed. But there is that excitement of finding a new way of approaching something and coming up with something which is fresh and hasn't been seen before. In retrospect it's always very obvious. You should have been able to see how to do it years ago. It is just some sort of quirk of looking at it differently that sets you going on a different way.

As well as working directly on to the wood Stead continually uses small notebooks which he fills with sketches and ideas – a discipline which he has maintained over the past twenty years. The drawings often start randomly with a line and develop in the same way as a doodle, each one beginning and ending differently from the last. Themes occur, forms repeat themselves but total repetition is impossible as the artist simultaneously explores seemingly infinite possibilities and his own limitations. On the one hand he is unaware of the extent to which he constrains himself while on the other he continually tries to surprise himself by adopting new approaches.

TS
I am not totally disorganised but certainly not tidy either physically, mentally or spiritually. I find chaos more exciting and friendly than order and extreme organisation. There is no virtue or sin in either. It is perhaps more interesting to find order in chaos than chaos in order. I doubt that if my character were more ordered I would make what I do.

The creative process finds many parallels in current scientific theories of 'chaos'. Although the possibilities for creativity are potentially infinite, in practice they are always delineated by certain constraints. In Stead's case, these parameters extend to areas of the visual world which he finds aesthetically pleasing. The majority of his work is inspired by the natural world where a straight line is rare and ugliness only a relative term.

TS
There is a simple power and beauty in natural forms – the body of an insect, the wings of a bird, bones, skulls, (particularly of birds and water mammals), of wood-grain, rock, minerals and crystals. I find a similar beauty in man-made objects which adopt natural forms to solve the problems of natural forces – the bow of a boat, a kite or 'plane, a plough and especially the axe, which brings in rhythm as well. For visual stimulation I am drawn towards natural history, ethnology, geology and pre-Greek archaeology rather than to European art. This is not an intellectual decision but simply a gut

response. Everything comes down to a question of character and it is much easier to pursue a course which I enjoy rather than to work within a discipline. Nature is always making me aware of my ignorance,which is good, and it provides a framework for valuing work. My work succeeds only if it surprises me, and I have unknowingly tapped into a natural vocabulary which refers to a number of forms.

Repair

Stead often retells a story about Japanese Raku masters whose pots are fragile and prone to breakage. The master repairs his pieces with a glue made from gold which adds a different value to the work.

TS
The skip and the bin are the destiny of most of our material possessions. Often we do not become sufficiently attached to these to consider repairing them. There is a beauty in repair which is visible, and an ugliness in a botched job.

Stead began making furniture with demolition timber full of nail-holes which he didn't want to show. The 'botch' solution would have been to fill the holes with putty or wood-filler. Instead, he cut small blocks of contrasting wood and made an inlay to cover the defect. This random inlaying broke up large table surfaces with small decorative details. The clusters of inlays can be seen as repair, decoration or like runic markings on stone. With large home-grown trees repair became a functional necessity. A large tree with a difficult and long past will have the most interesting figure. It will also have small holes from small branches dying and being re-absorbed, and more extensive markings from larger branches breaking or being sawn off. It will contain deep pockets of bark which the tree has grown over, as well as cracks and fissures. A kind of geology of wood. Stead fills smaller cracks with cold-cast bronze, creating veins of light and energy. Repair is a measure of value and is therefore enhancement, not merely patching. Once again Stead draws an analogy between wood and landscape. Although the cold-cast bronze is in contrast to the wood, the dynamic provides interest rather than conflict. Man's impact, although marked, should also be harmonious, not obliterating or destructive.

TS
Not to use such wonderful pieces of wood would be a terrible waste. The man-made element is on a small scale compared with the natural lines of the tree and the relationship is therefore balanced.

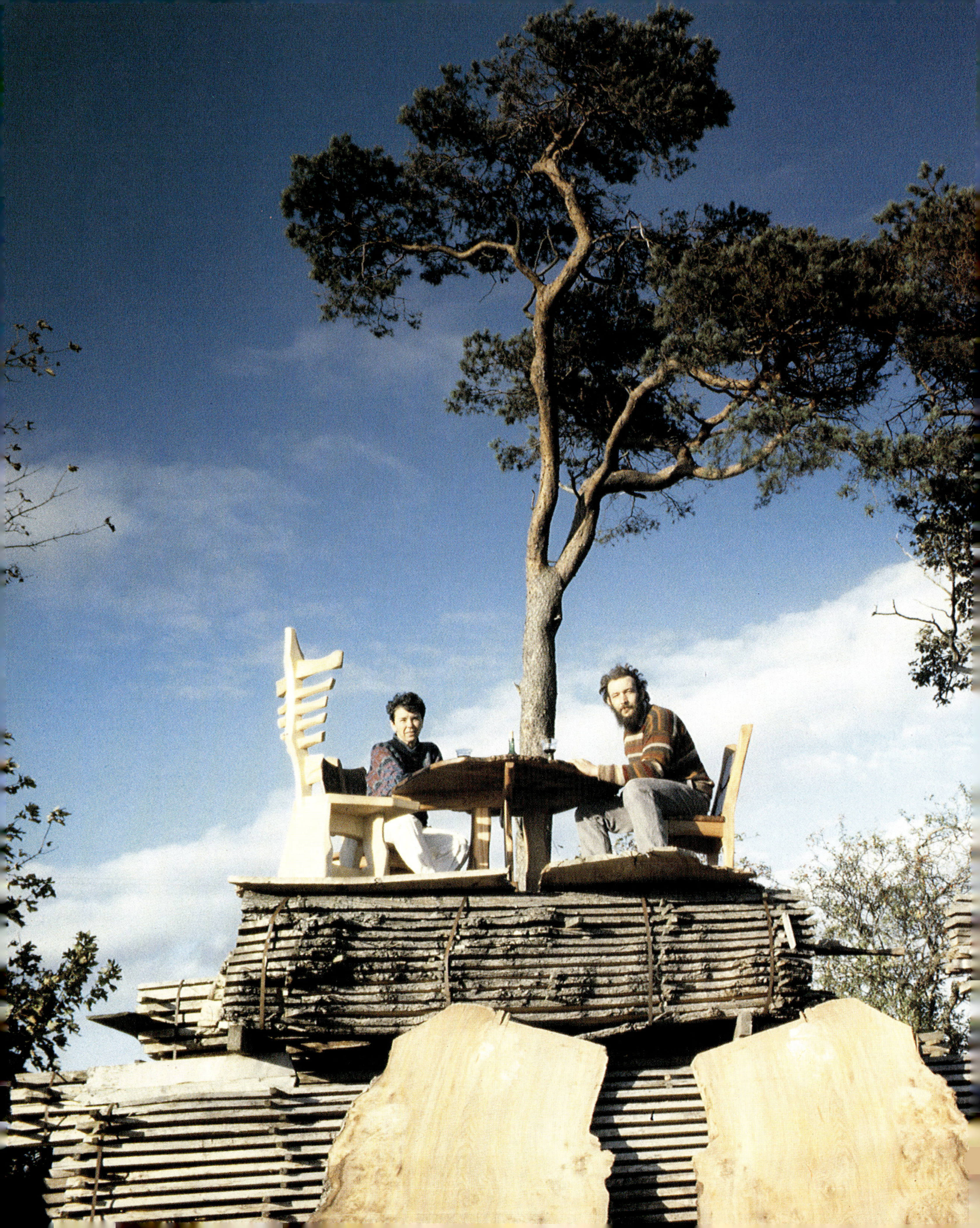

Opposite:
Tim and his wife Maggy sitting on top of a stack of timber near their home in Blainslie.
Photograph: Roger Lee

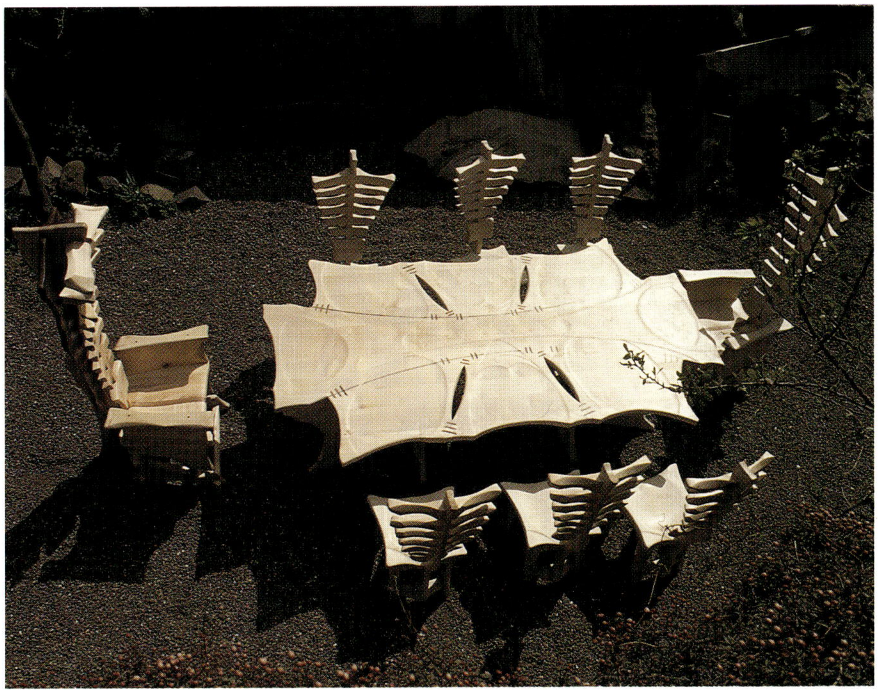

Sycamore table with skeletal chairs.

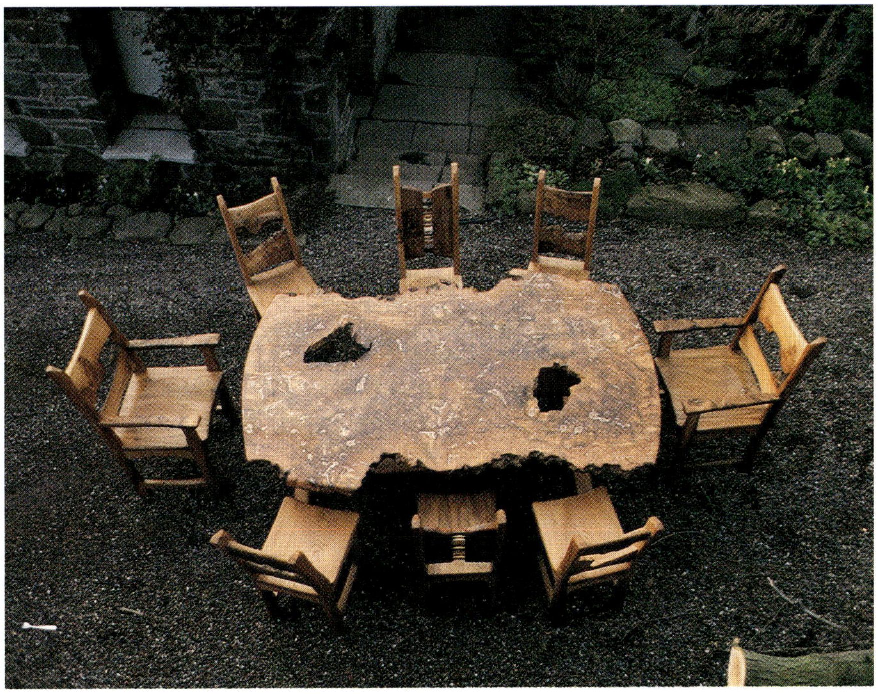

Burr elm table with holes. This was commissioned by clients who wanted an interesting outside edge and many faults and much character. It was decided to leave the holes visible but with removable covers.

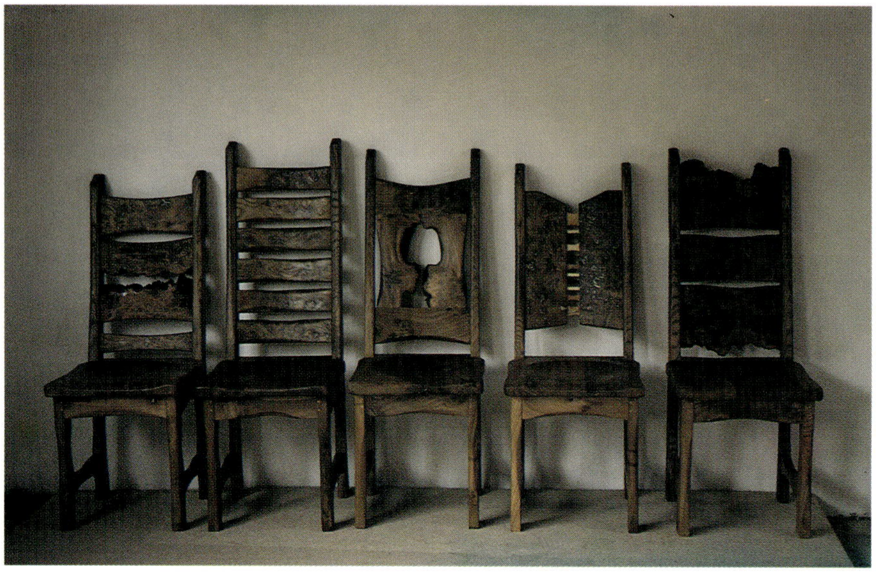

Collection of burr chairs

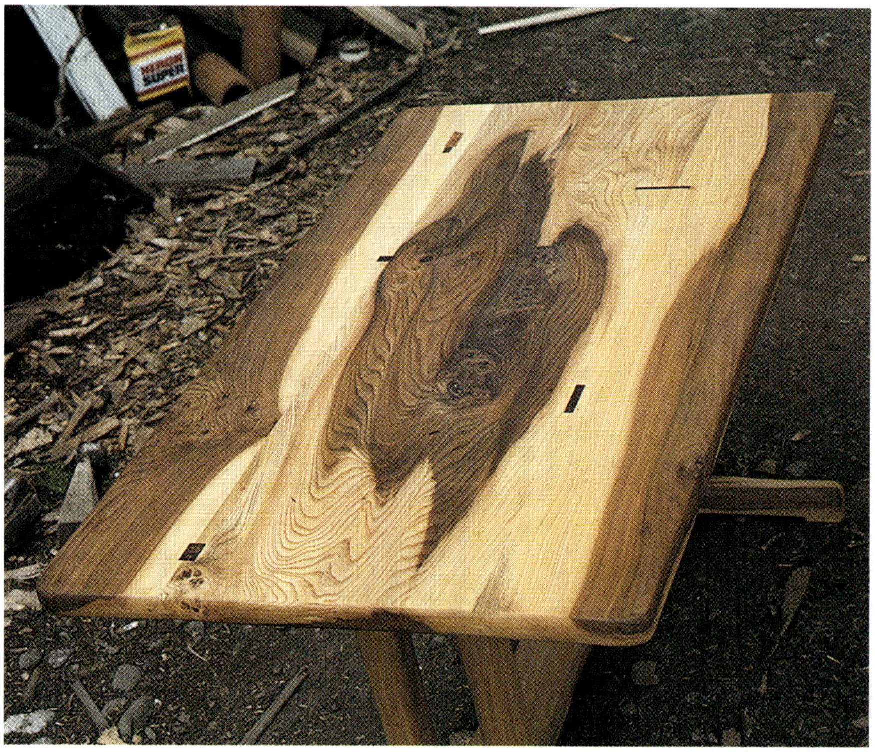

An elm table which emphasises the differences between the darker heartwood and the lighter sapwood. The joints appear to be from dark to light. Stead was asked to make a kitchen table with an inlay in the centre. Using this technique, the planks themselves did the work and achieved the desired effect.

'Landscape' coffee table in burnt pine

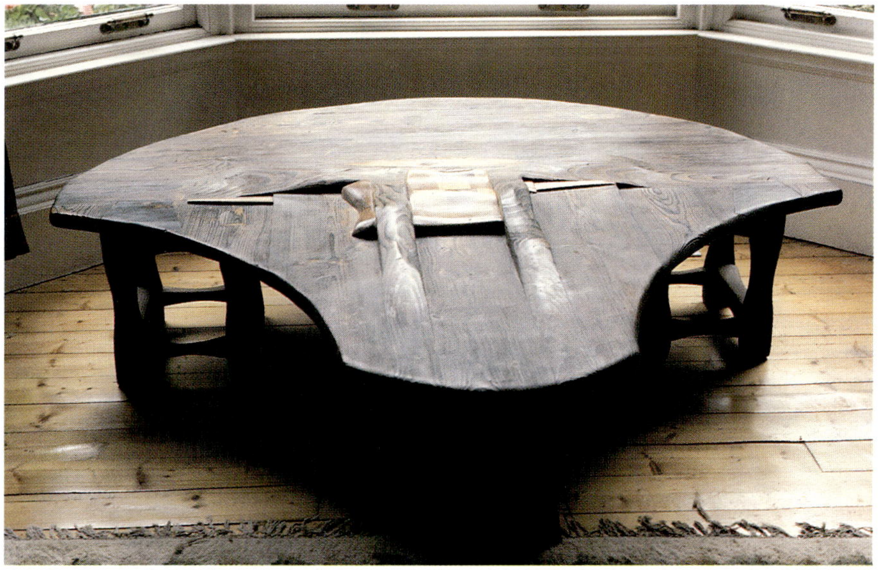

Overleaf left:
Ash dresser with axe-head shapes on panels

Overleaf right:
Burr elm dresser using the natural or 'waney' edge. This creates an interesting space and makes the top part less bulky.

Two linking coffee tables cut from one board which fit in different ways

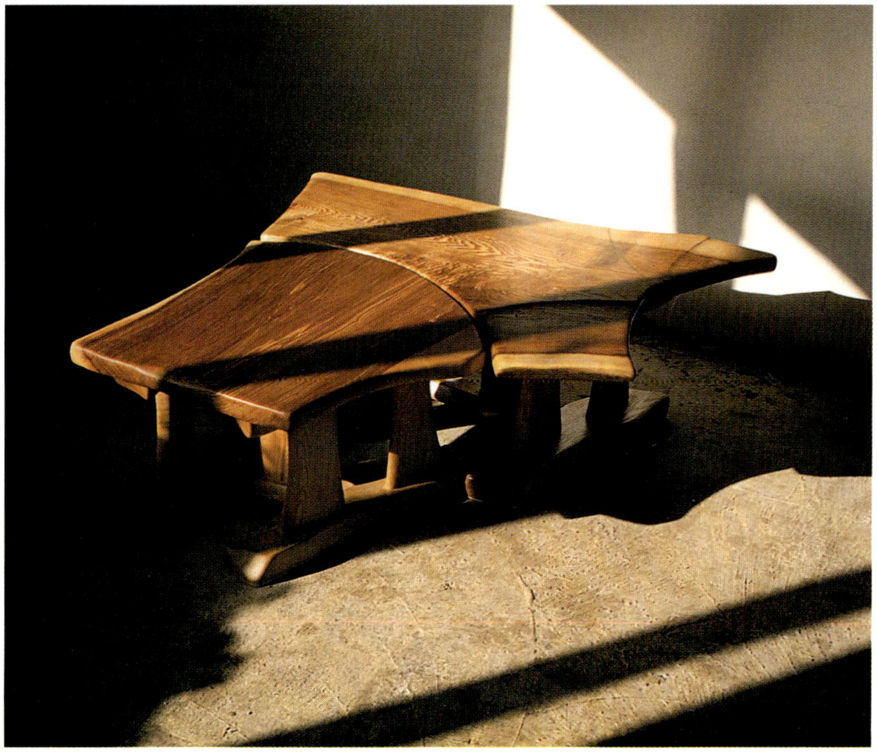

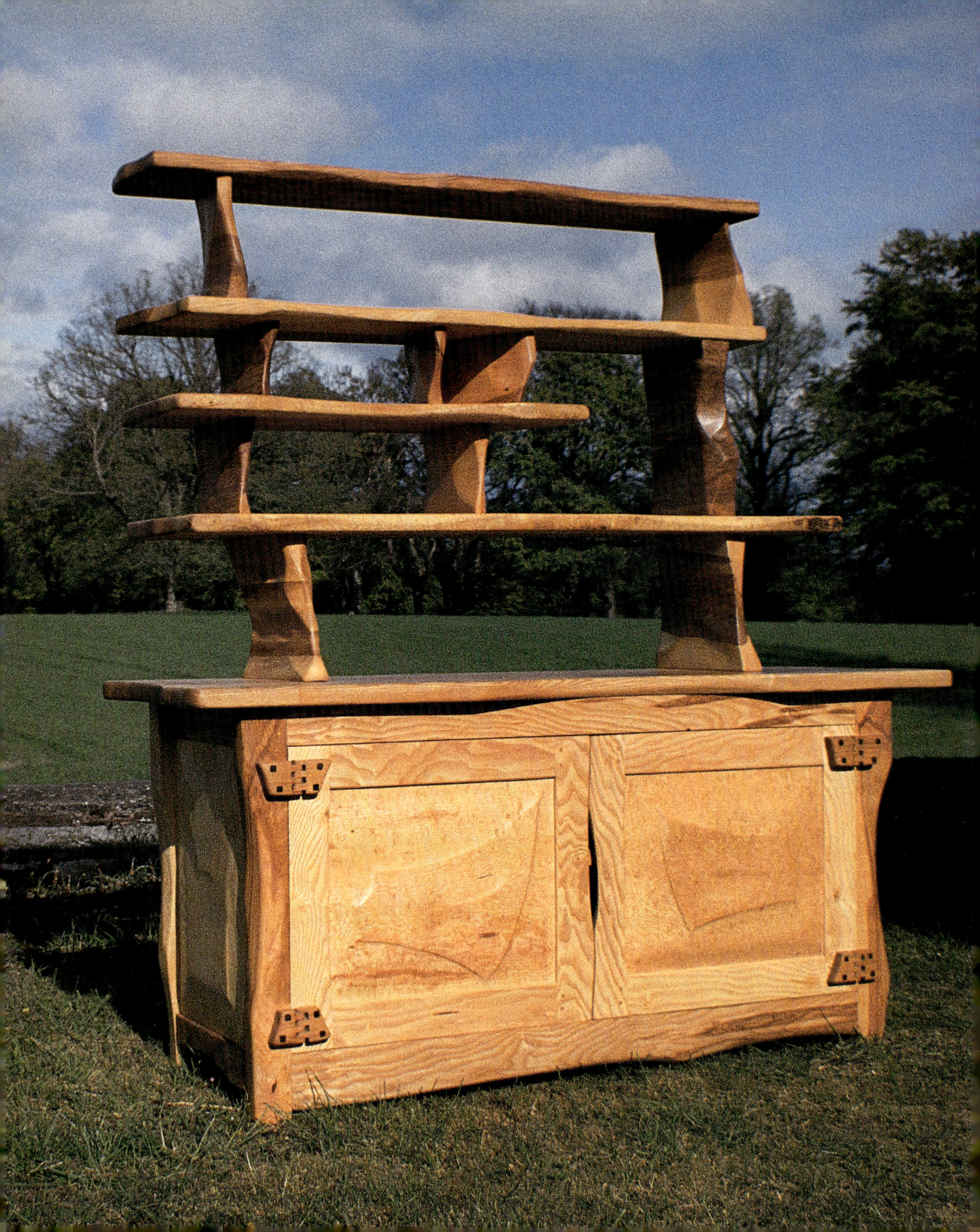

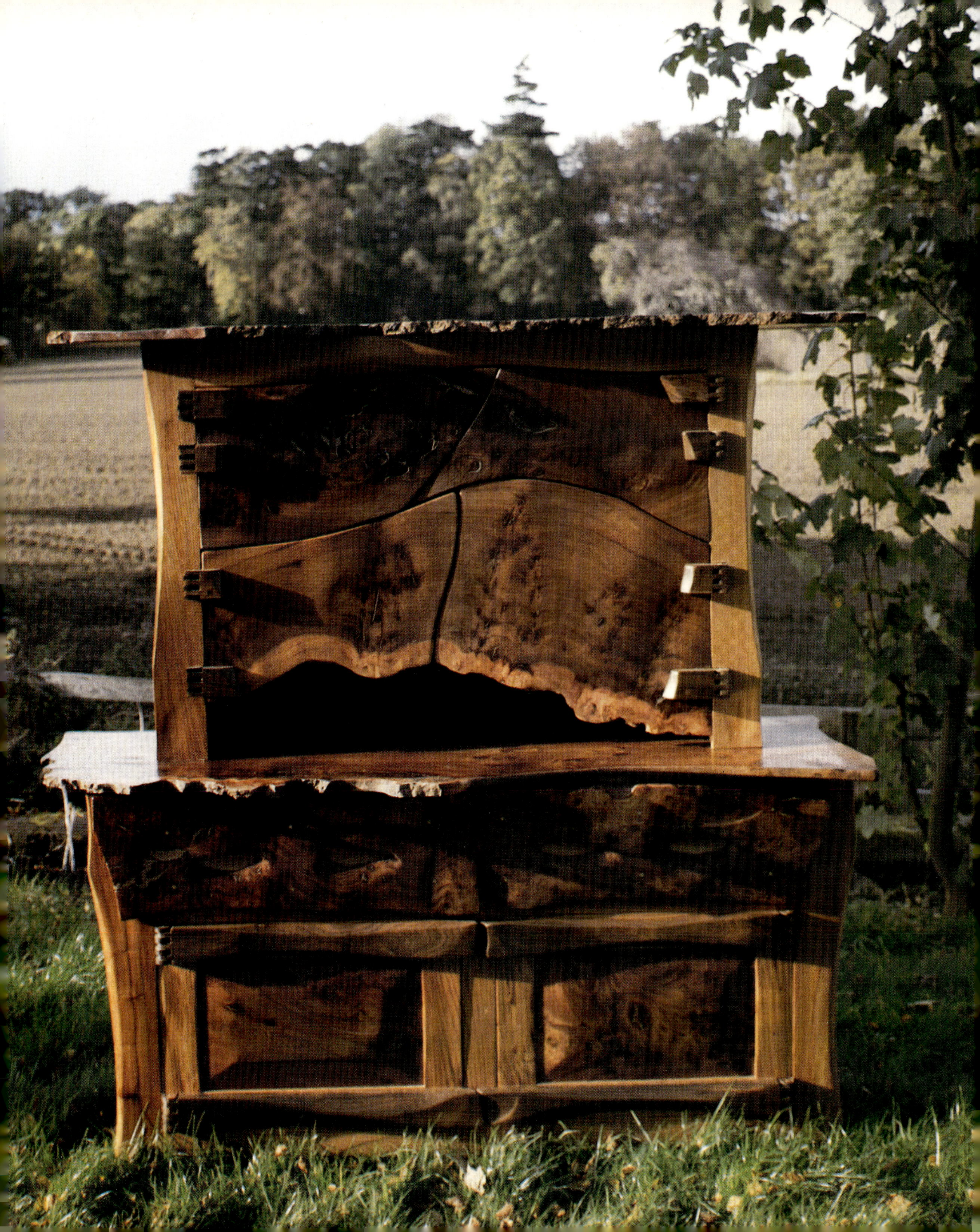

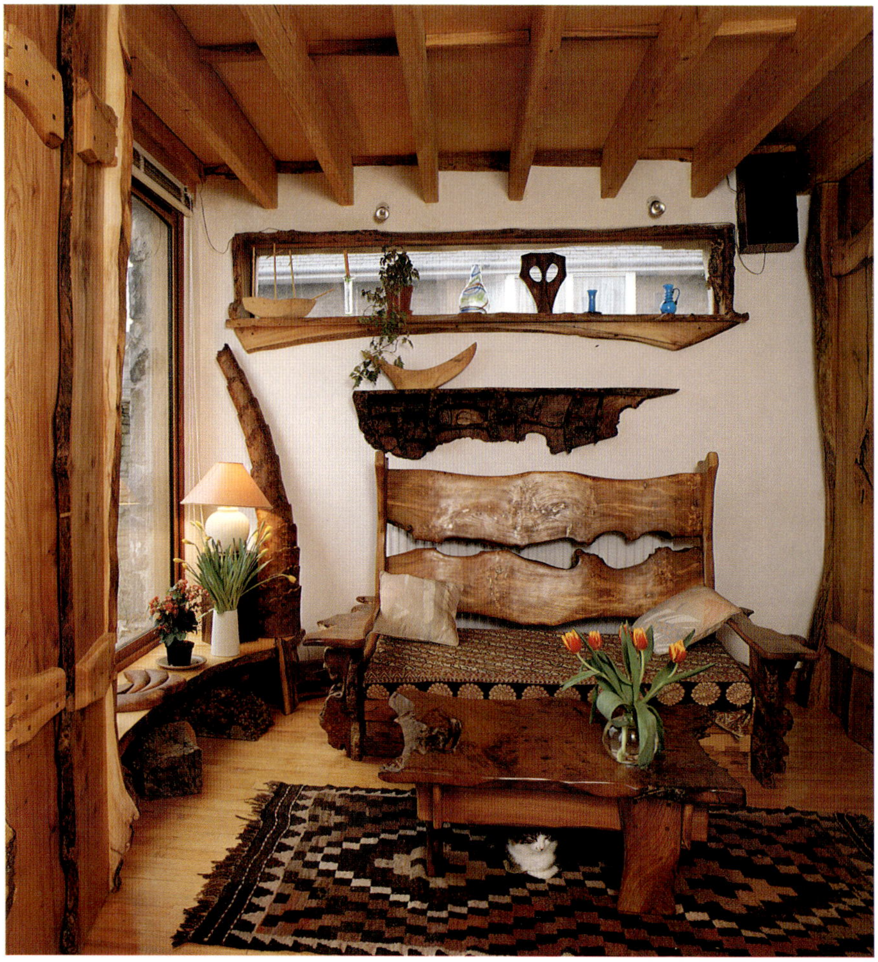

Opposite:
A burr elm settee downstairs in the new extension, which opens out as a bed.
Photograph: Antonia Reeve

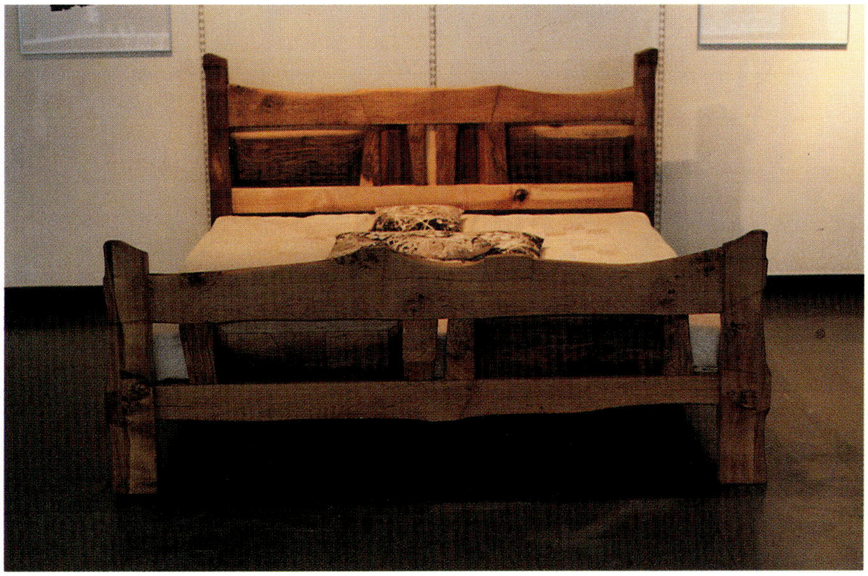

Oak and mixed hardwood bed, photographed at an exhibition in Sweden.

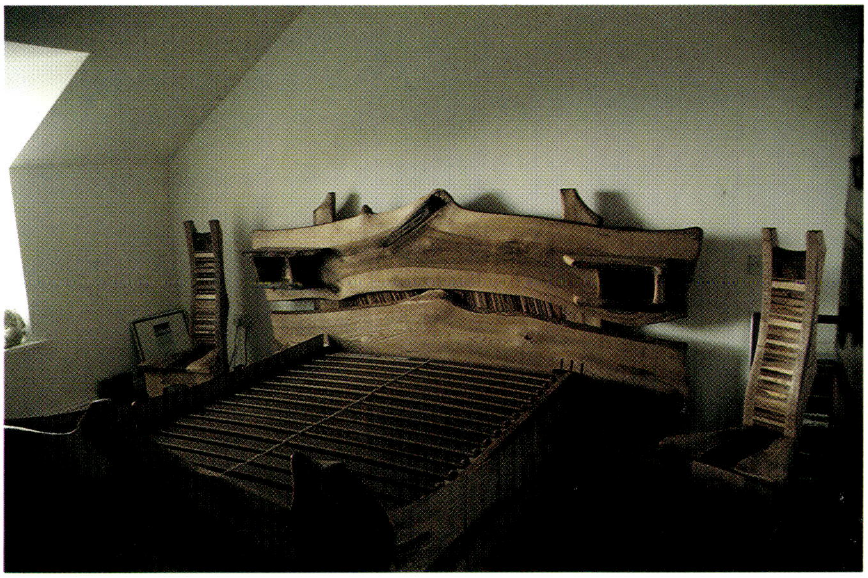

Ash bed with drawers underneath

Desk in burr elm
Photograph: Alex X. Fraser

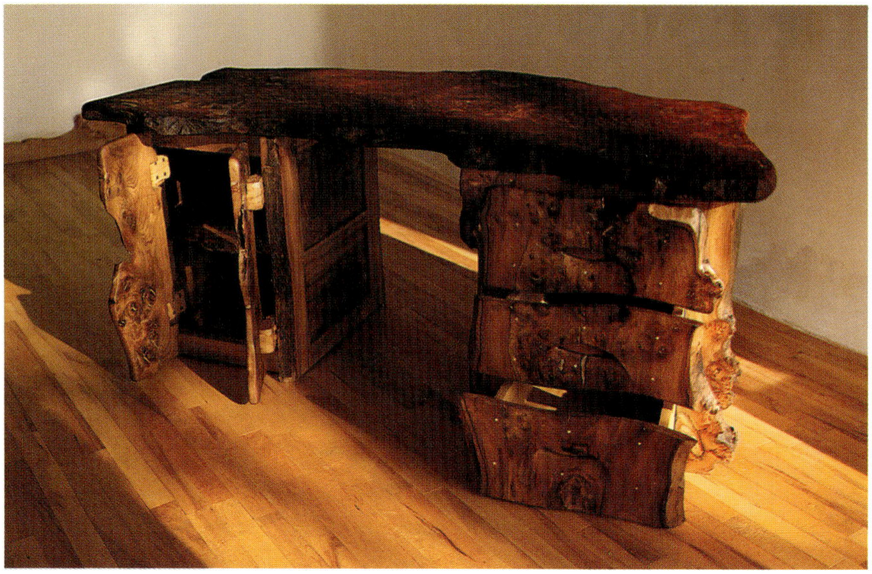

Opposite:
Corner cupboards in elm

Corner shelves
Photograph: Alex X. Fraser

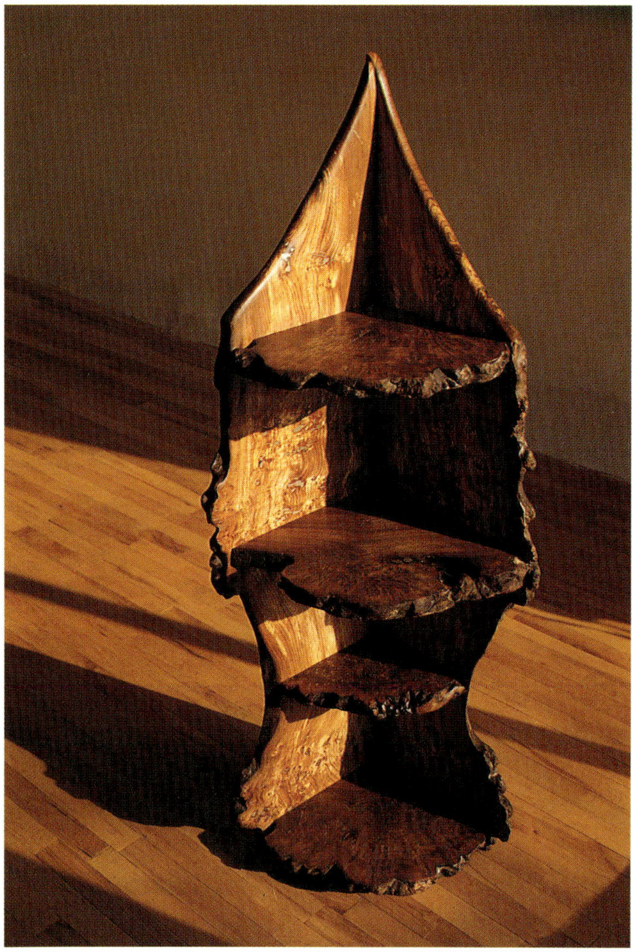

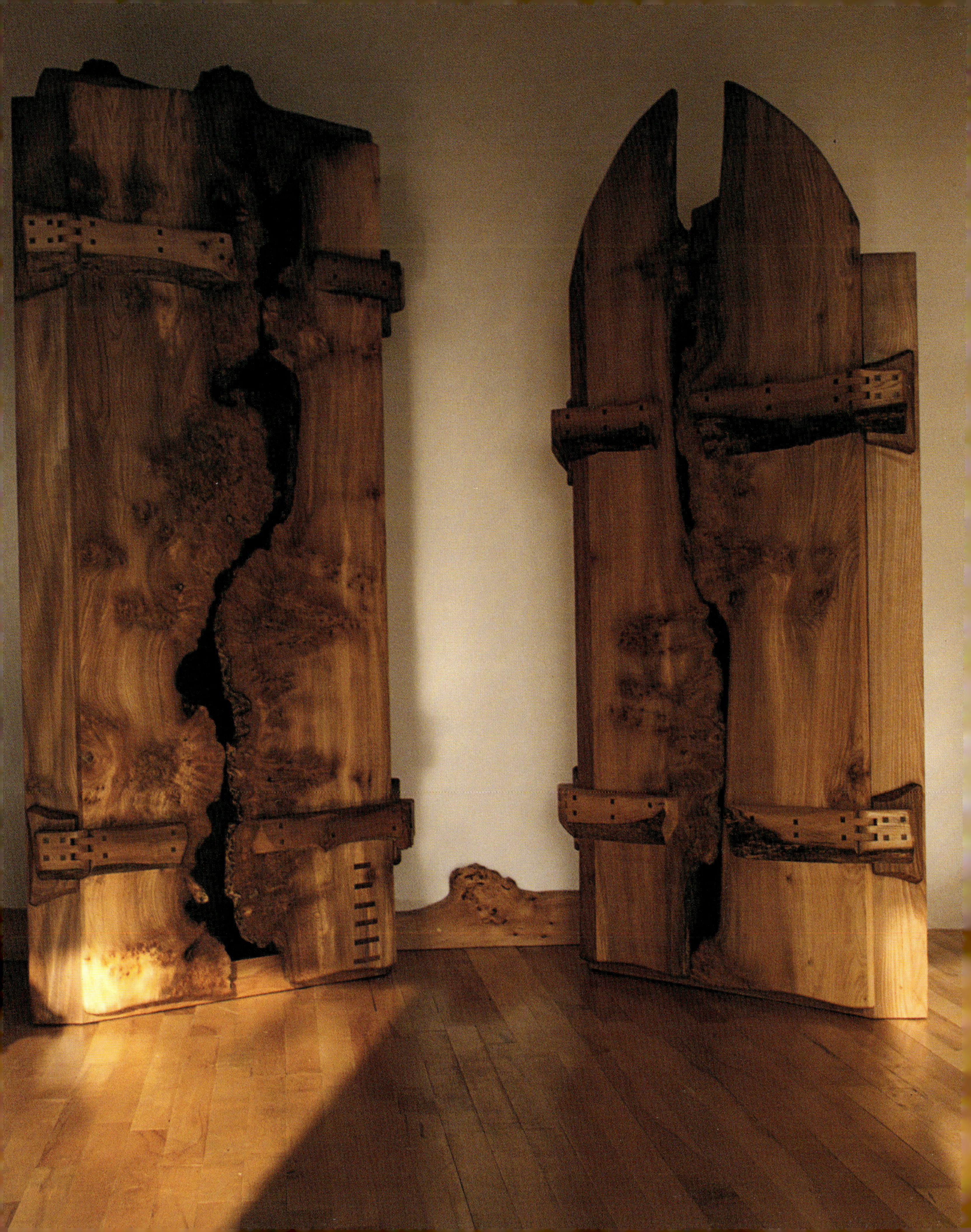

Round-ish table with 'Porter', 'Corset', 'Tall-gnasher' and 'Short-gnasher' chairs.
Photograph: Antonia Reeve

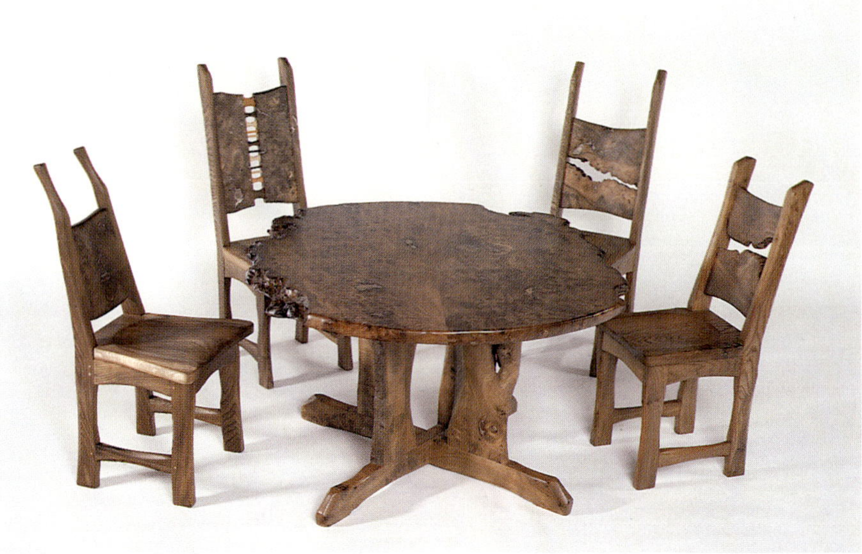

Vertebrate armchair with strung seat

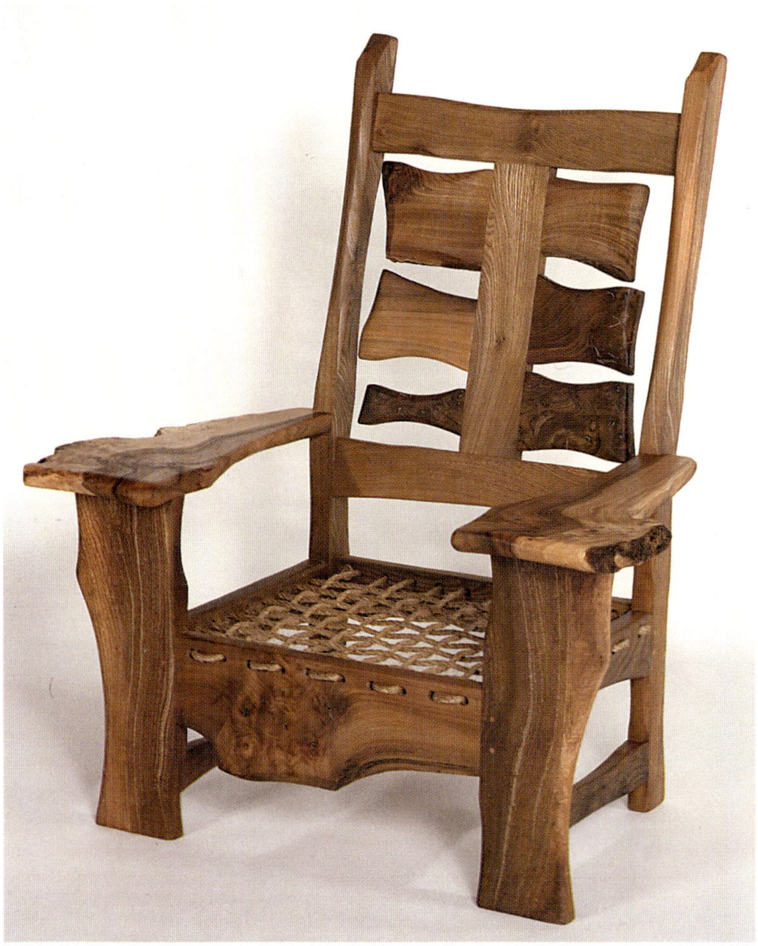

Getting at the Wood

It is generally accepted that the progress of 'civilisation' seems to be leading to a diminished contact with natural materials. Similarly, the relationship between a finished product and its source becomes increasingly obscured. For some people the connection between 'wood' and 'tree' is distant and outside their direct experience. Not everyone will question why the types of trees they pass daily in the park are not the same timber they can buy in the local DIY superstore.

TS
My strength is based on the wonderful qualities of the wood itself which can come from any tree. There are factories which will bleach a veneer, impregnate it with silver nitrate and use this as a 'paper' on which to print a photograph of an interesting wood grain. I take a slice of tree and use its own properties. People want to touch this; they feel a much greater affinity with it than a photograph.

Britain is no longer a tree culture. About ninety percent of the timber used in this country is imported. A significant proportion of the ten percent grown in Britain consists of 'exotic' softwoods, like Sitka spruce. This is used only to make products like paper, particle-board and fencing. Only a tiny fraction of the total wood used in Britain comes from species indigenous to this country.

The reasons for our dependence on imported timber have a basis in history. The British Empire provided access to almost unlimited amounts of this precious raw material; the sources were often exploited unscrupulously. This is still reflected in the low prices and easy availability of imported timbers. The demise of empire and growing environmental awareness have shifted the emphasis towards sustainable sources, although widespread abuse still occurs, particularly in the temperate forests of Canada and Siberia.

All of Stead's work is made from British native species – the majority of this is elm – ulmus procera. The reasons for this are aesthetic, circumstantial and environmental. Stead used to use any timber which came to hand – this included tropical hardwoods like teak and mahogany, although most of the wood, mainly pine, came from demolition sites. Aware of the increasingly problematic environmental arguments surrounding tropical hardwoods, Stead switched to home-grown timbers. Because of Dutch elm disease this particular wood was in ready supply, or at least more easily available than other British woods.

TS
The breakthrough really came when I moved from my first workshop, in Ibrox, to Harestanes near Jedburgh. I lived on a big estate where trees were felled and buyers would come to look at them. I had no idea of prices. On one occasion I saw a burr elm log with an amazing grain and I eventually plucked up courage to ask how much it would be. I think it was about £60.

Overleaf:
Chests of drawers in burr elm (detail).
Photograph: Antonia Reeve

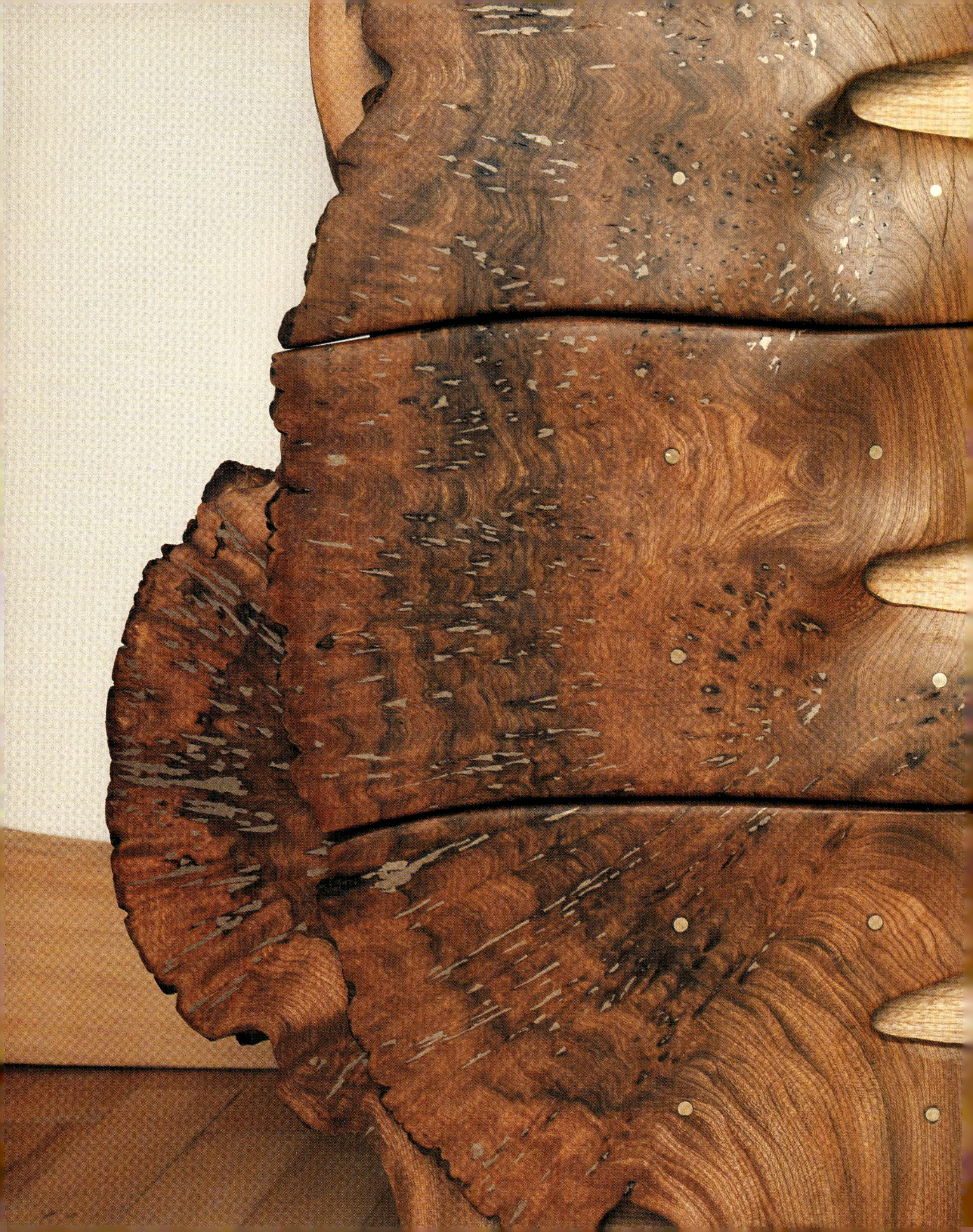

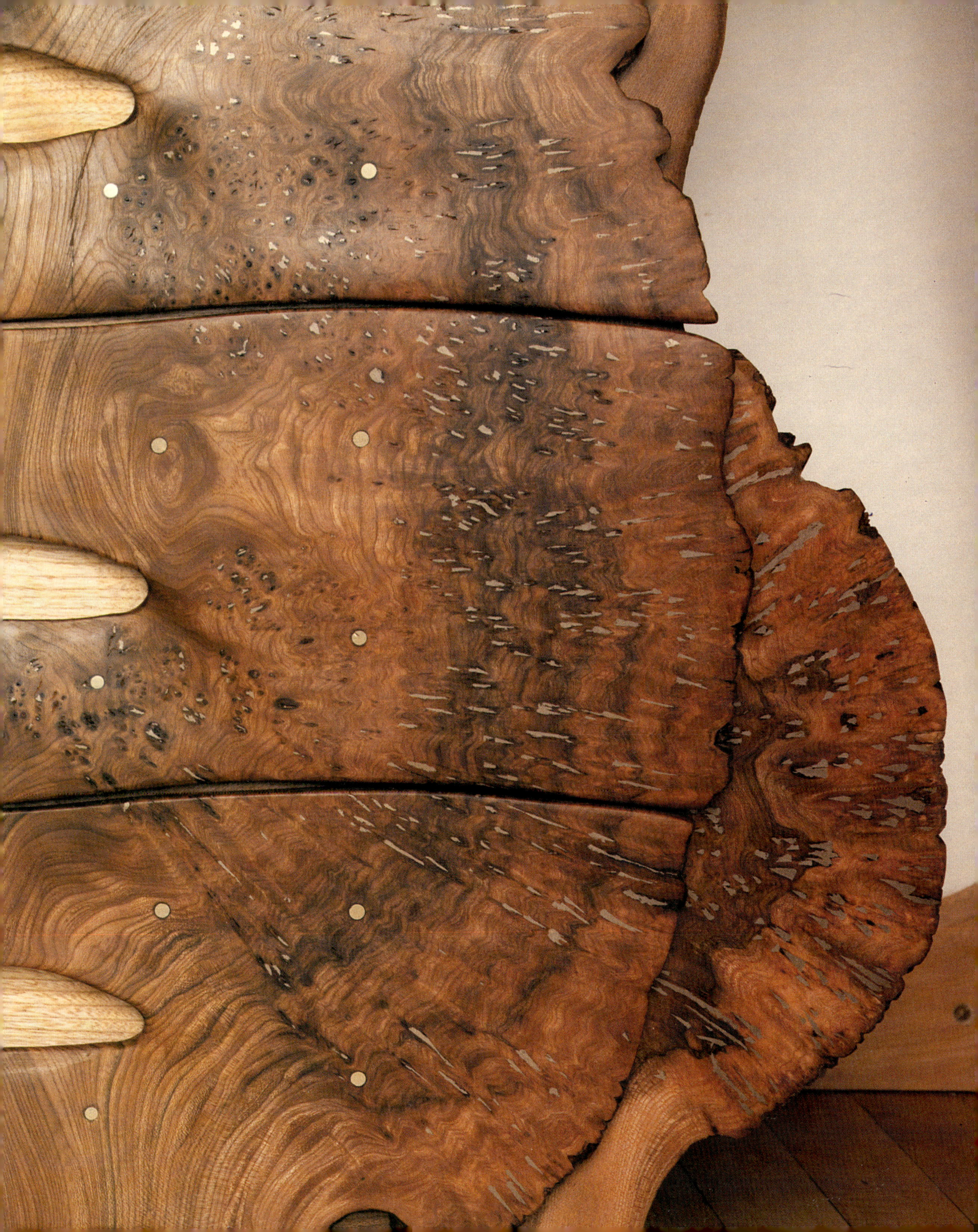

So I got a lorry load and took it to a saw mill. There was a kiln on the estate which I learned how to operate. I never used imported timbers again.
Stead finds the natural patterns in the wood (often referred to as the 'grain', but technically the 'figure') infinitely more interesting in elm than in, for example, mahogany. Mahogany was popular as a timber source because of the straightness and regularity of its growth and therefore the ease with which it could be 'converted'. It is curious that, in the past, we have imparted more value to the exotic than to the indigenous and the 'familiar'. Often the most interesting territory and the greatest surprises are to be found on our own doorsteps.

Most interesting of all in any wood is the figure caused by burring – growths on the exterior of the tree. Because the burr often occurs in a restricted area, it tends to engulf itself in bark and continues to grow. This can sometimes continue for the duration of a tree's life, giving it a rich, continuous figuring. Although the burrs on the exterior of the tree appear bulbous and wart-like, they are neither deformities nor the result of disease. Small branches sprout from the burrs and the process is a natural response, therefore, to the tree's need to capture additional sunlight.

Trees surround us almost everywhere, but the difficulties of getting at the wood are enormous. The felling of a tree can be costly and difficult, involving careful limbing and removal of the butt by heavy machinery. Once this stage is completed, the butt is taken to a sawmill to be cut into boards. Stead prefers to use a horizontal band-mill which enables both 'waney' edges to be retained. Vertical band-mills require one flat edge to be made on the butt before it can be sawn. Typically the boards are cut to a two-inch thickness, although this can vary. The butt is laid between 'railway lines'. A big circular bandsaw drives across the top of the tree and comes back; the blade is dropped and is driven over the butt again.

TS
With an ash tree you get an olive colour in the centre and whiter wood on the outside: each board reads like a page from a book. As you are cutting through particularly with ash, if you've got a bend, the first board comes out white. Then you begin get a small whirl of dark towards the centre of one board until, gradually, as you get nearer the centre, the dark wood is prominent

Once sawn, the boards have to be seasoned. The moisture content of a newly-felled hardwood can be anything up to sixty-five percent; to be suitable for furniture the moisture content has to be in the region of ten to twelve percent. If furniture is made from inadequately seasoned wood, once indoors it will crack and warp as it continues to dry. Boards for air-drying are stacked *en boule* – in the original sequence they were cut from the butt. Sticks are placed between each plank to allow air to circulate which in turn facilitates the drying process. The length of time varies, but the usual rule of thumb is one year for each inch of thickness, and one additional year 'for the pot'.

Opposite:
The stable is used to store wide heavy boards. The building also contains a big sander which consists of continuous belt of sandpaper situated above a moving table. Boards are placed on the table which is then moved under the sanding belt. To the right is a huge oak board from the same tree as the Stead's kitchen table. Above is a loft for one-inch boards.
Photograph: Antonia Reeve

Opposite:
The barn contains a big band-saw, a circular saw, a planer-thicknesser and a small bandsaw. A sawdust burner powers radiators and under-floor heating. There are lofts above for storing timber.
Photograph: Debbie White

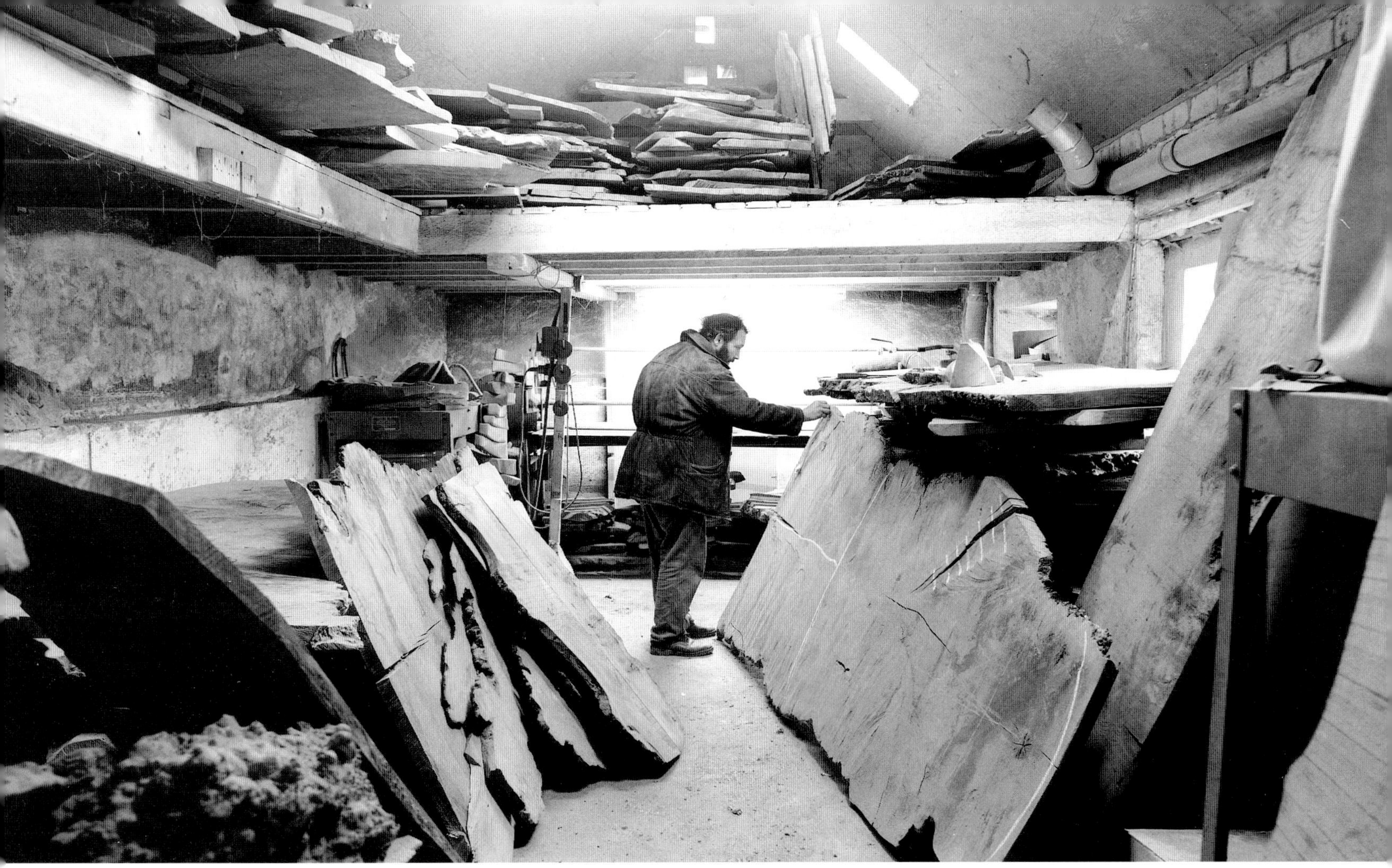

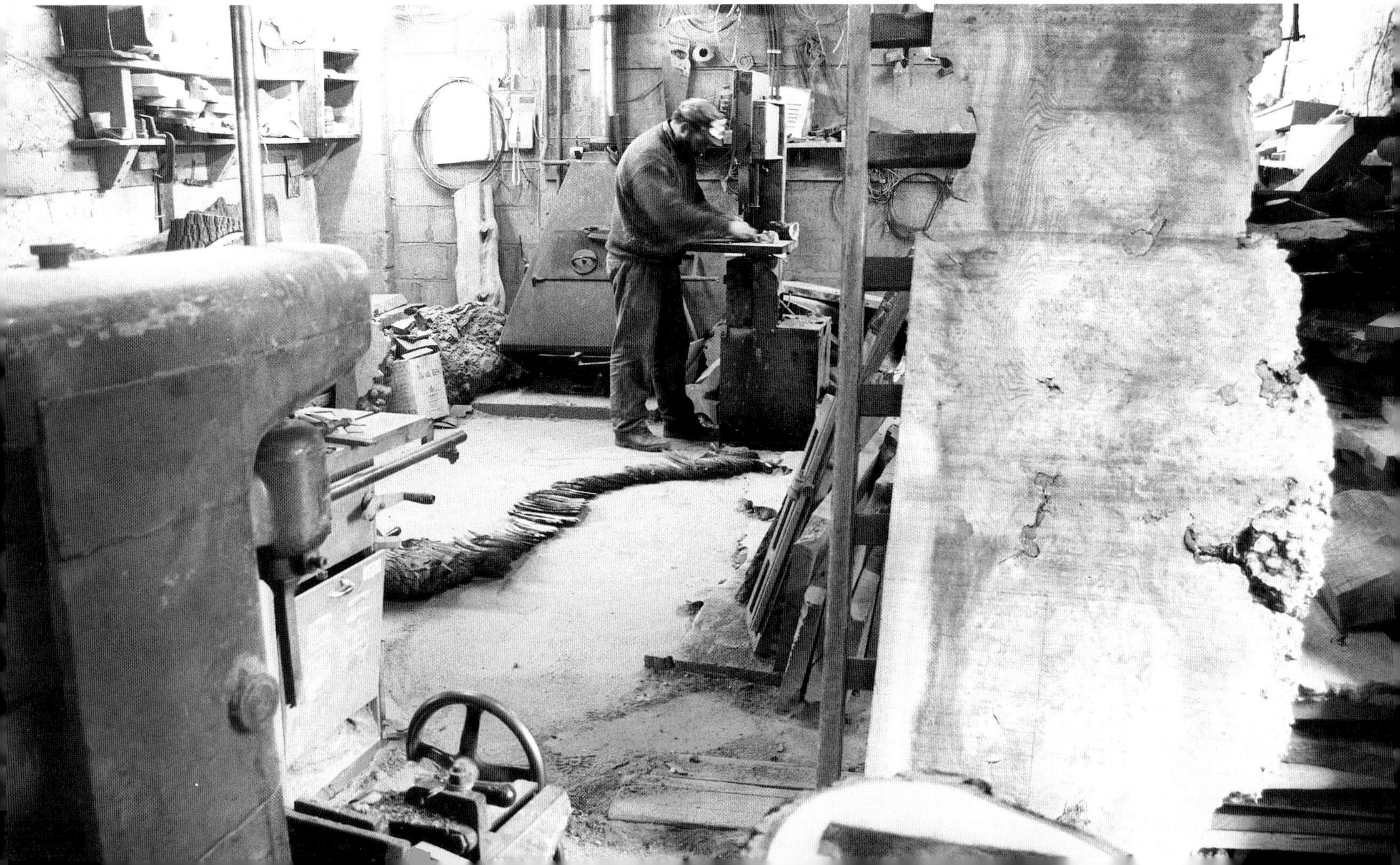

The main workshop houses 'Sarah', a big planer-thicknesser, a small band-saw, a morticer and a circular-saw. John, one of Stead's assistants, is working on a large dining-table, hollowing out the small holes ready to be filled with cold-cast bronze. In this part of the workshop, the wood is jointed, shaped, sanded and assembled.
Photograph: Antonia Reeve

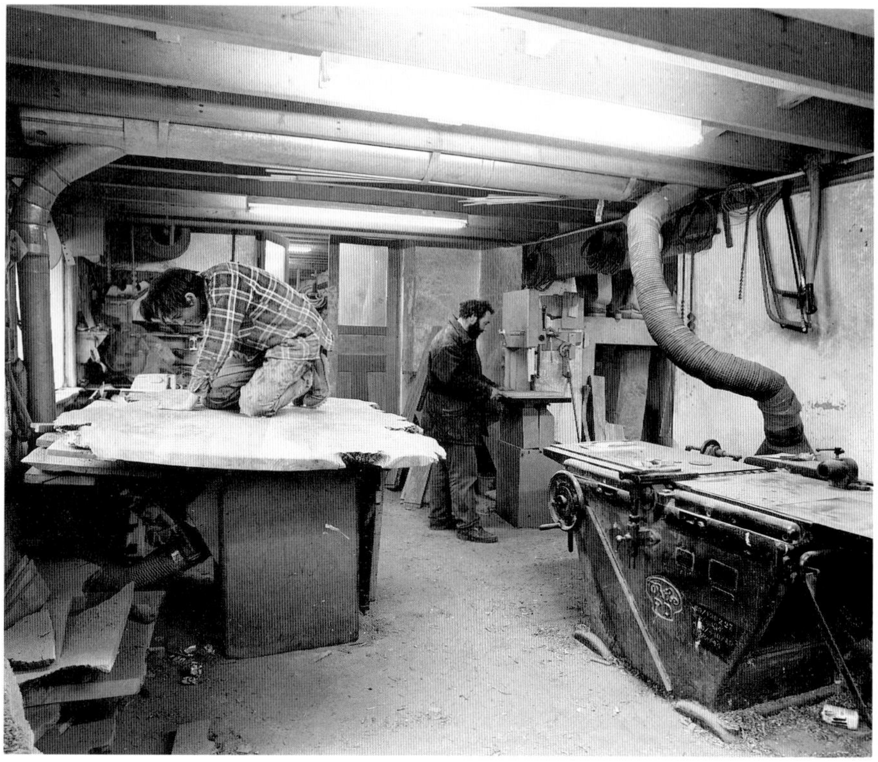

Opposite:
The door of the barn contains a cluster of iron implements – old gin traps, scales, chains, tools – which move and clank when the door is opened. It seemed important to store these items when they were dug up from the garden and give them a new lease of life. They act as a reminder of The Steading's former life as a working farm.
Photograph: Antonia Reeve

John sanding a small table-top as part of the finishing process. In the foreground, a morticer used for making square holes – part of the jointing process.
Photograph: Debbie White

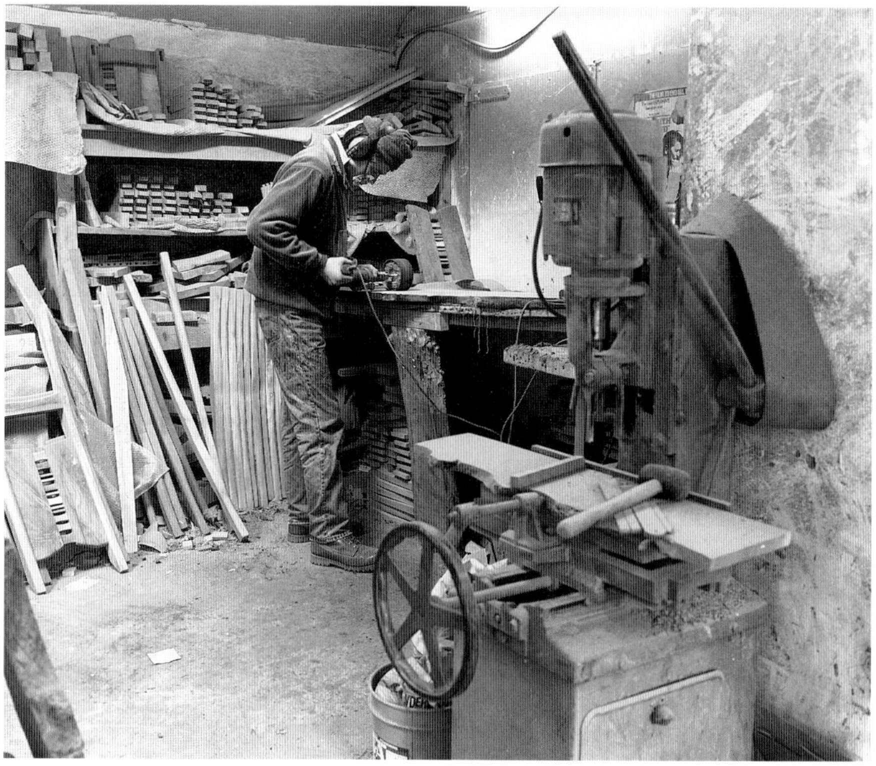

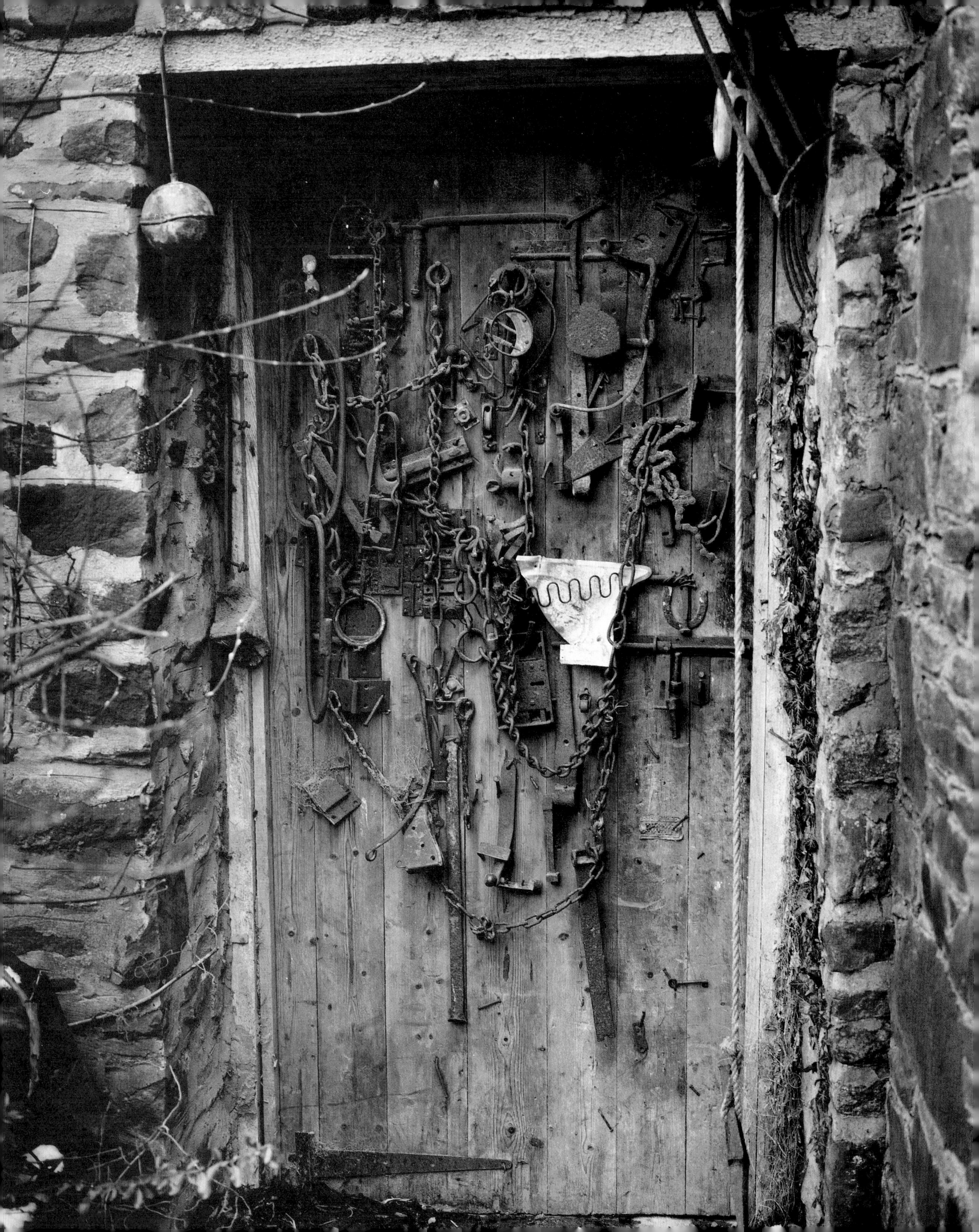

A set of three photographs showing the use of the bandsaw. A block, consisting of a sealed wound in the tree, is transformed into a series of thin slices with an enormous surface area.The bandsaw, which comes in a variety of sizes, is a versatile tool of which Stead makes frequent use – it essentially comprises of a blade running in a continuous loop around two flywheels. Because of the thinness and flexibility of the blade, the cut can be made to curve and change direction. Stead uses this to great effect in his 'Layers' pieces, and the work for the ' Spirits of the Forest' and 'The Botanic Ash' exhibitions.

Photographs: Debbie White

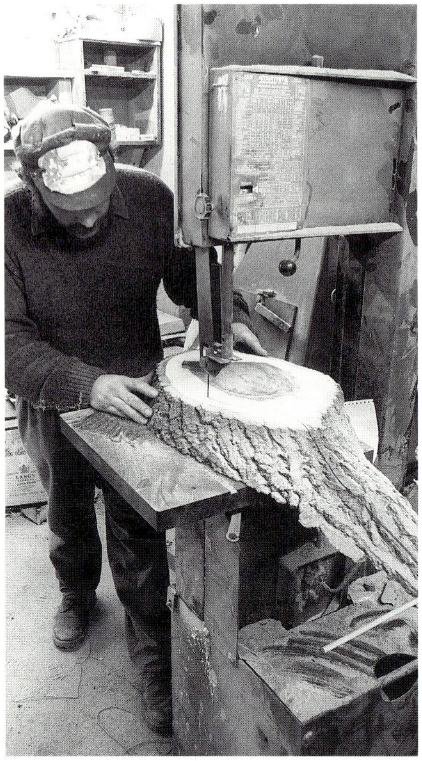

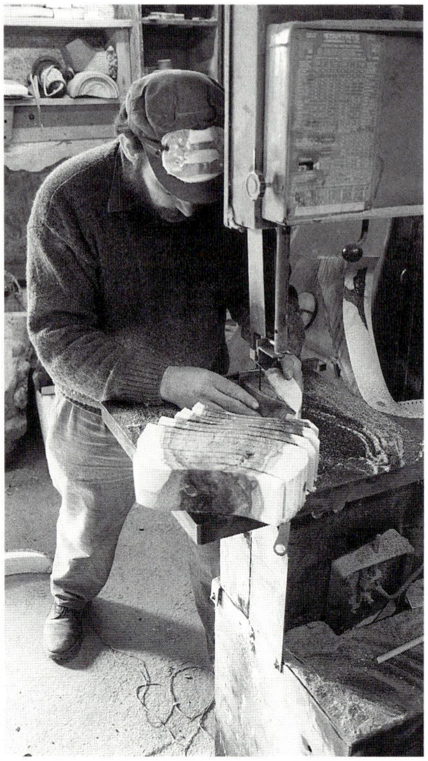

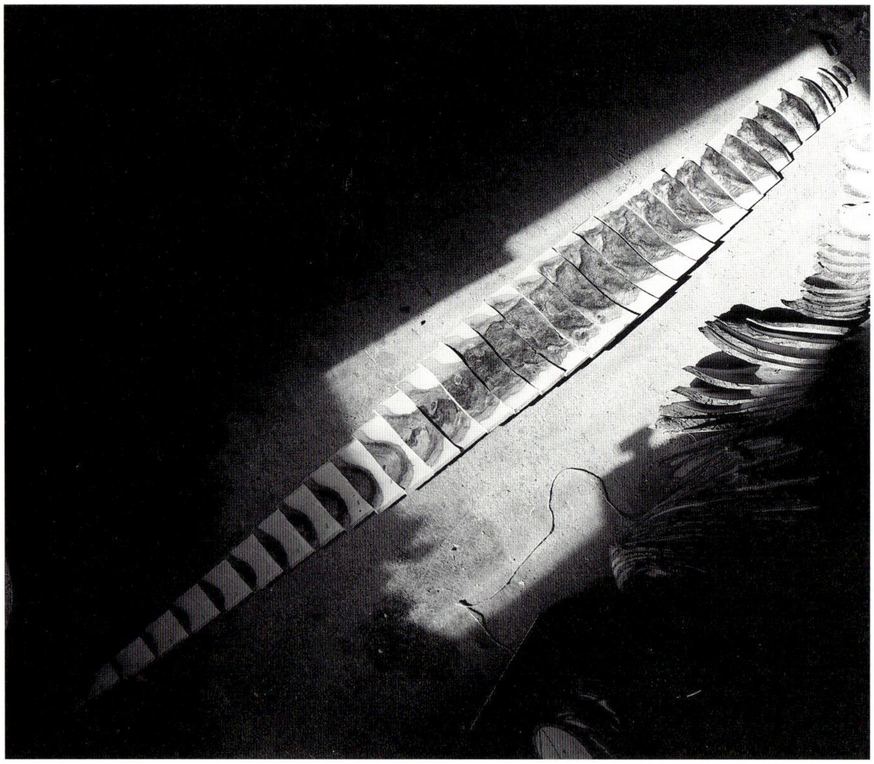

TS
I have always found saw-millers to be very friendly, helpful and interested in what becomes of the wood. Without a doubt, the most amazing saw-mill is Jock Redburn's at St. Boswells. This isn't simply because it's untidy, or that there are hens scurrying round his collection of old cars and historic farm machinery. Jock is a wonderfully friendly, open and enthusiastic man, who fells trees, sells firewood and is the local chimney sweep. Behind his soot-blackened face, his blue eyes are always smiling. He takes photographs of all the work I make, puts aside all the interesting pieces for me, and is determined to make my yard as cluttered as his. It's a real privilege to work with someone like that. He once told a client that he couldn't clear her fallen wood because his crane was out of action. It was 'out of action' because a robin had built a nest in the radiator and Jock wanted to wait until the young had flown the nest.

The humidity conditions in Scotland will never allow wood to dry sufficiently out of doors. Even in the middle of summer, it is difficult to obtain a reading of less than twenty-five percent moisture content in a piece of wood that may be thirty or forty years old. The wood therefore requires to be kiln-dried, which essentially involves heating the air around the timber. Plastic is draped over the wood and a fan circulates hot air around the stack. The hot air is then passed over a cooling element, condensing the water, which runs out through a pipe. Many gallons can be extracted from a freshly-sawn butt.

TS
A workspace has been a vital part of my life for a long time. Before I left home, my room was full of paint and plaster. The flats I lived in were always more full of work-clutter than domestic-clutter. The collective space of an art school is always open; however, I need a space of my own and I have always had a corner where I could work. When I lived on my own I regarded this as a more important living space than an indoor toilet!

As well as retaining the natural edges and forms of the wood, many of the curves and rounded shapes so characteristic of Stead's work are achieved principally by other means. The bandsaw with its thin manoeuvrable blade allows Stead to create shapes which echo the original forms of the tree. An angle grinder, normally reserved for metal or stone, provides a finer finish; buffing with a sander completes the shaping process. Other shaping tools include the spoke-shave and the draw-knife. The wood is finished with a mixture of linseed oil and turpentine.

TS
The owner adds a lot to the finish through use and wear; and a piece will invariably improve with age. When treating a wooden item with oil they used to say: 'One coat an hour for a day. One coat a day for a week. One coat a week for a month. And one coat a month for a year.' Photographs don't get across how nice the furniture smells!

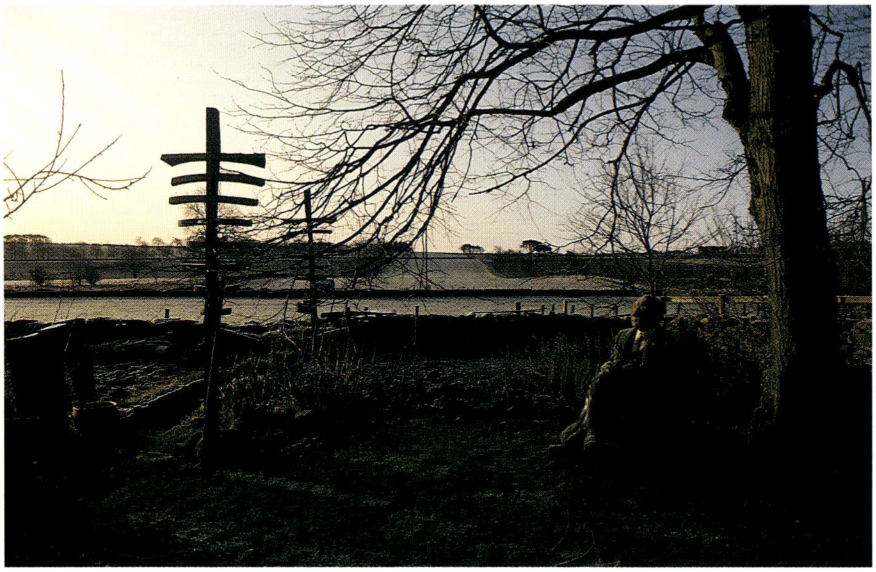

Eybert in the garden at The Steading sitting under a lime tree. A washing-line pole provides a good excuse for making something more visually interesting than the norm.

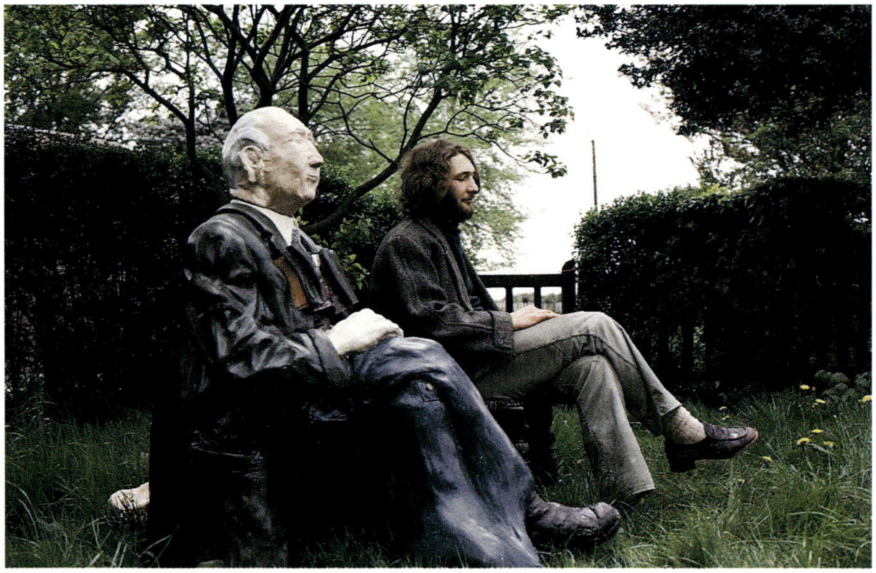

Tim Stead with Eybert

Part Two

Eybert Yafterlaf

Stead was a student at a time when Conceptual Art was in its heyday. Within the art schools he was horrified to find not a place of toil, industry and artistic mess but a sterile environment of 'concepts'.

TS
At Trent Polytechnic there was a fantastic sculpture workshop with huge forty-foot ceilings, big gantries – masses of space. It was filled with type-writers and people using Letraset. The whole atmosphere was really very difficult to work in. At times there is a very strong and restricting pressure from the 'fine art' establishment. I wanted to go into the art school, get dirty, make things, and experiment . . .

In reaction to the prevailing thinking Stead made a fibre-glass figure which he called 'Eybert Yafterlaf'. As the name implies, this was not to be seen as a serious piece of work – in Yorkshire they say: 'Aye, but yer 'ave t' laugh' ! But for Stead it was an important turning point – the point where he stopped taking himself, and art, seriously. Previously he had wanted to make powerful figurative sculpture, with dynamic forms which had 'meaning'. Perhaps deep down he still does. In the Conceptual period, art seemed to be concerned only with other art, while the artist also assumed the role of art historian.

TS
How I hated that intellectually-based art. What I wanted to do was to get dirty, experiment with materials and sweat. Foremost, I am still a maker, rather than a thinker. Instead of this wonderful free world where everyone could do his own thing, it was a self-conscious, self-censuring monastery. This huge free space, which should have been a park full of colour and life, seemed to me like a derelict car park where people stayed only on the edges.

So he gave up and made Eybert, a nice old man minding his own business. He had a drawer in his chest in which his own life could go on in private. Inside the drawer, there were changeable scenes – a garden, rows of cinema seats looking inwards, collections of objects and memorabilia. Stead also made a recording, to go with Eybert, of an old man telling stories.

Around that time Stead had been to a meeting of people 'Remembering old Helsby' in Cheshire.

TS
One old lady told a story about chasing some cattle over the marshes and through fields – the latter all had names. The story was unremarkable but the telling of it was amazing. Some parts had minor alterations to keep the story fresh; other parts were so well worn they were like polished root. . .I remember this story as if it were an object – and I cherish it. It was not a

perfect piece of poetry, yet it had more life and flow to it than anything I had heard. There was humour, suspense, atmosphere and a natural pace and construction; and above all it had no pretension.

It is interesting that Stead remembers this story so vividly and it is arguable that, in retrospect, it had a much more positive influence on his work than a great deal of his art school training.

Café Gandolfi

At Glasgow School of Art while studying for a post-graduate diploma, Stead met Iain Mackenzie who was then working in the photography department. Mackenzie was engaged in a documentary project involving Italian cafés, which held a great fascination for him. After leasing the derelict Old Cheese-market offices in the then run-down Merchant City area, Mackenzie asked Stead to build and install all the components necessary for a complete refurbishment – chairs, tables, an eight-seater bench and a bar. In many ways it was a hopelessly idealistic and romantic notion.

TS
I was exhibiting some work at the MacLellan Galleries. Iain arrived on a bicycle and casually mentioned the idea of setting up a café. Iain was rather prone to fantasy and got carried away with the whole idea! It was more of a continuation of a photography project than a commercial venture! He knew nothing about it – the whole thing was a risk which should never have been taken! The architect, Ian Millican, visited my workshop with Iain and the idea really took off, with the three of us working in partnership. But it opened and has been running very successfully for twelve years.

The project was an enormous challenge and was the first full-scale commission which Stead had undertaken. Working on such a large scale and over a long period of time allowed ideas to develop freely. The result was both a cohesive whole which comprised unique and individual pieces.

TS
I enjoyed the opportunity of creating an environment which did not consist of regimented tables and chairs where each item is the same. The café seats sixty people and was built over a period of two years. It was rewarding to be able to provide a lot of furniture for a place which was going to be used by large numbers of people.

Deriving its name from the famous Gandolfi Brothers cameras, the café opened in 1979 and is now a Glasgow institution. A good deal of its success is undoubtedly due to Stead's furniture.

TS
People identify with and enjoy the warmth of the wood and the fact that each table is different. Different inlays, different colours, different types of

chairs. I find the interiors of most cafés boring and this was a bit of fun. I enjoyed the possibilities of such a large scale work – which included a big bench which divided the place up – and a large bar.

The Steading, Blainslie

Tim Stead's home and its situation in both a practical and emotional sense lie at the heart of his work. In a playful way he has likened himself to a caddis – a type of fly whose larvae encase themselves in tiny fragments of wood and stone for protection. Stead's home and the objects which fill it are, in a way, his protection against a hostile world. Whereas it is not unusual for artists to surround themselves with their own work, Stead's home extends well beyond this norm. The Steading is more than a home and a workplace: it is also an enormous artwork, constantly evolving like the generations of an organism responding to natural selection. In a very real sense it represents the fulfilment of a vision.

TS
I have this dream where the artist, architect, engineer and client have a brainstorming party, leaving their egos outside and really have fun planning a wonderful building. They bring in a musician to make it sound right and a choreographer to make it enjoyable to move through. They invite poets and scientists, gardeners and athletes and the ideas become more and more amazing until an uninvited squad of accountants and building inspectors rush in and suppress the riot with calculators, regulations and cashflow projections.

The Steading comes close to representing this dream, except that the unwelcome guests have not arrived. Stead's home is therefore more than a place to live; it is also an aesthetic statement. And although the Steading is filled with individual objects, it is difficult to consider any one in isolation. Each item of furniture, each sculptural object and every fitting, most of which are considered unimportant or 'invisible' in the average house, resonates harmoniously with all the others. A light-pull echoes various hanging sculptures, birdlike and in perpetual motion; a set of shelving metamorphoses into a staircase. There is always the reminder in almost every shape and edge of the source material – wood – which constantly affirms the relationship with nature. By implication the suggested relationship is one of mutual dependence between the artist and his material, between humanity and nature.

TS
To me working at home is essential and I'm extremely lucky to be able to do so. For most people, unfortunately, this isn't the case. They go off to an office or factory. One should enjoy the details of where one lives. I like to both live and work in surroundings which are visually interesting. In many ways it doesn't take a lot more time to do something which is interesting than to do something which is boring. To make something which is banged together with nails may be a lot quicker, but there's no energy and there's no

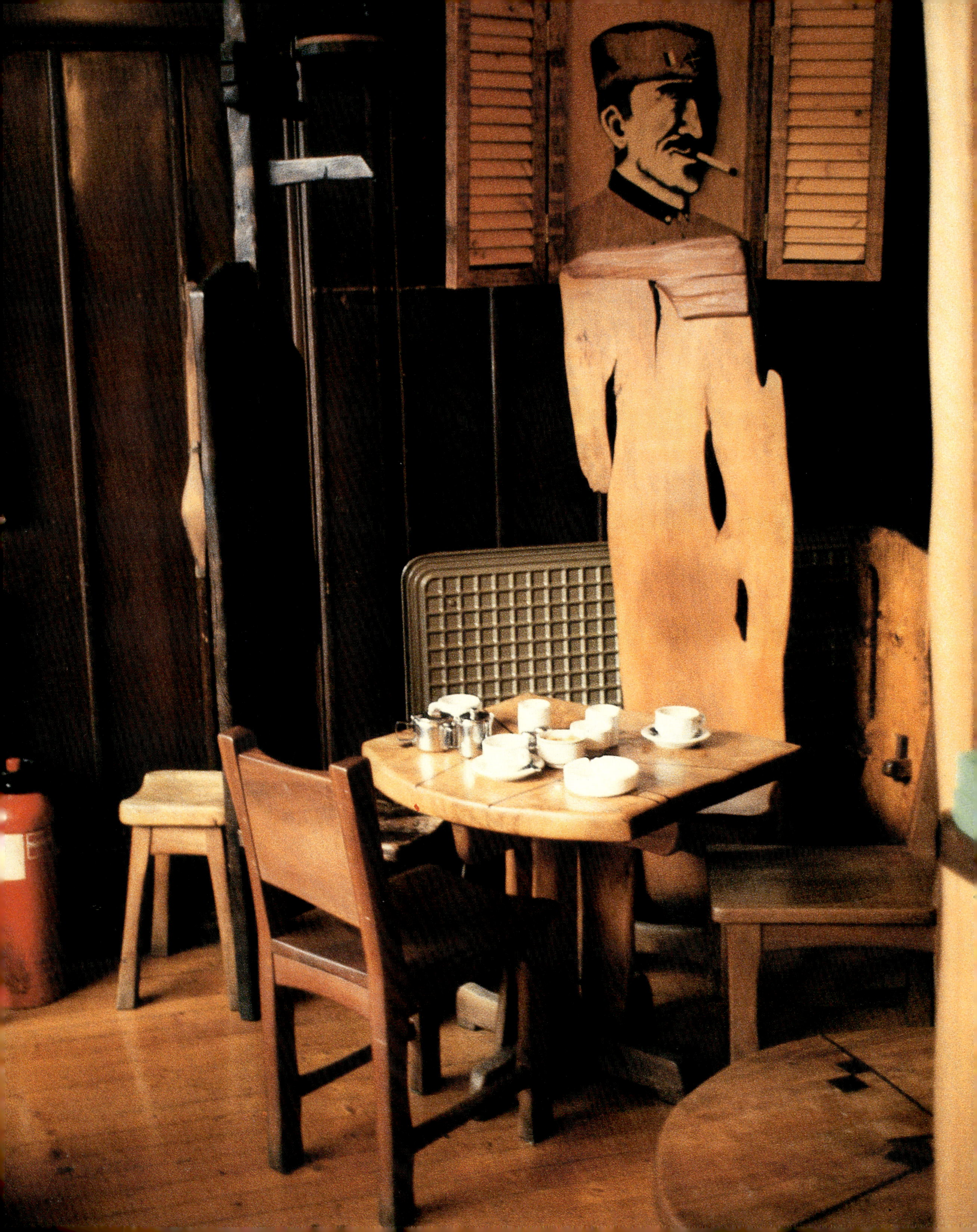

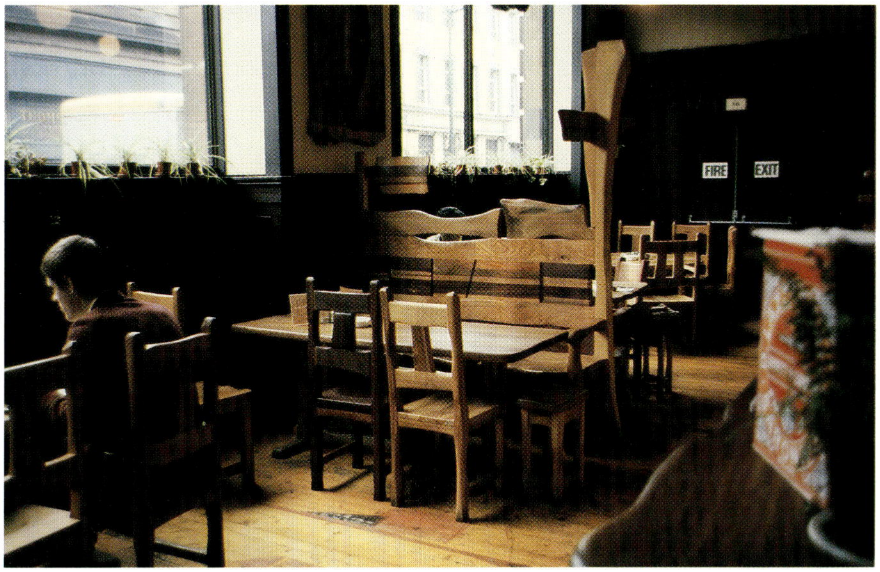

Café Gandolfi. Photographs on both pages by Iain Mackenzie who named his café after the Gandolfi brothers, the well-known camera makers.

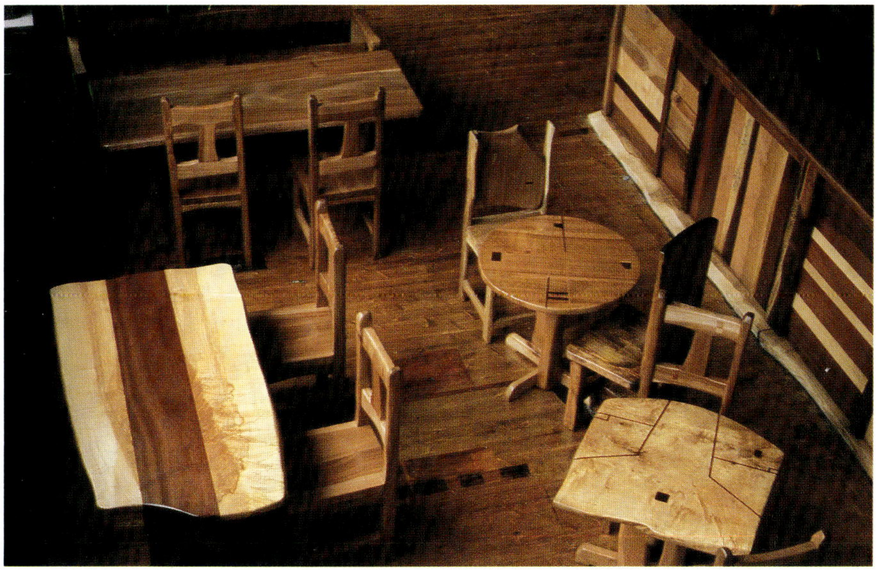

Opposite:
Four-poster bed, The Steading
Photograph: Antonia Reeve.

excitement about seeing what it looks like in the end. There's no pride to it. Finding an interesting or less obvious way of doing something is exciting. You can work very quickly that way, because there is an anticipation in seeing a job finished.

I think that it is important to surround yourself with objects made by individuals – each piece has a story . . . Liz Rowley generally produces drawings before starting on the glass. This was an exception. The commission discussion consisted of me bringing round the templates of the spaces to be filled – and a bottle of wine. We selected through the sheets of beautifully coloured glass and piece by piece Liz cut them and we talked about what should go next. All the glass was cut before we discussed the design. The windows had evolved as a conversation.

A number of years ago Stead received a Scottish Development Agency (now Scottish Enterprise) fellowship to explore the relationship between art, craft and architecture. The work led him to explore some of the seemingly 'invisible' objects which we nevertheless come into contact with on a daily basis.

TS
If more artists were involved at the beginning of projects rather than adding pieces on at the end there could be a greater variety of buildings and structures. Not just 'power buildings' – in fact power buildings least of all – but telephone boxes, bus shelters and small houses. As it is, we have international styles of architecture and multinationals controlling more and more.

The project started with what Stead describes as a 'naive optimism'. He proposed various alternative designs for objects such as bollards, man-hole covers and fences, which could be taken up by architects and planners. He pointed out to the local planning authority that road-side lay-byes were ideal sites for sculpture, stone-work litter-bins, interesting benches and picnic tables. Although the response was enthusiastic the project did not develop. Stead concluded that, with so many facets of the visual world designed down to a boring minimum, we have surrounded ourselves with objects which correctly mirror, and represent, our present culture.

TS
I remember a wallclock at a friend's house which was made with great care – but very badly. It tried to be symmetrical but failed completely. I felt a terrific warmth towards the maker who I felt was a much more approachable man than a perfectionist whose character seems far removed from humanity. The mass-produced world churns out images of perfection by the thousand.

These slabs of wood with the outside edge are so wonderful in themselves that people should really have two or three in their homes as pets – but that is somehow unacceptable. Perhaps what I am doing is to give them a function – like a disguise to allow them inside. The more I can retain the 'treeness' of the pieces, the more pleased I am.

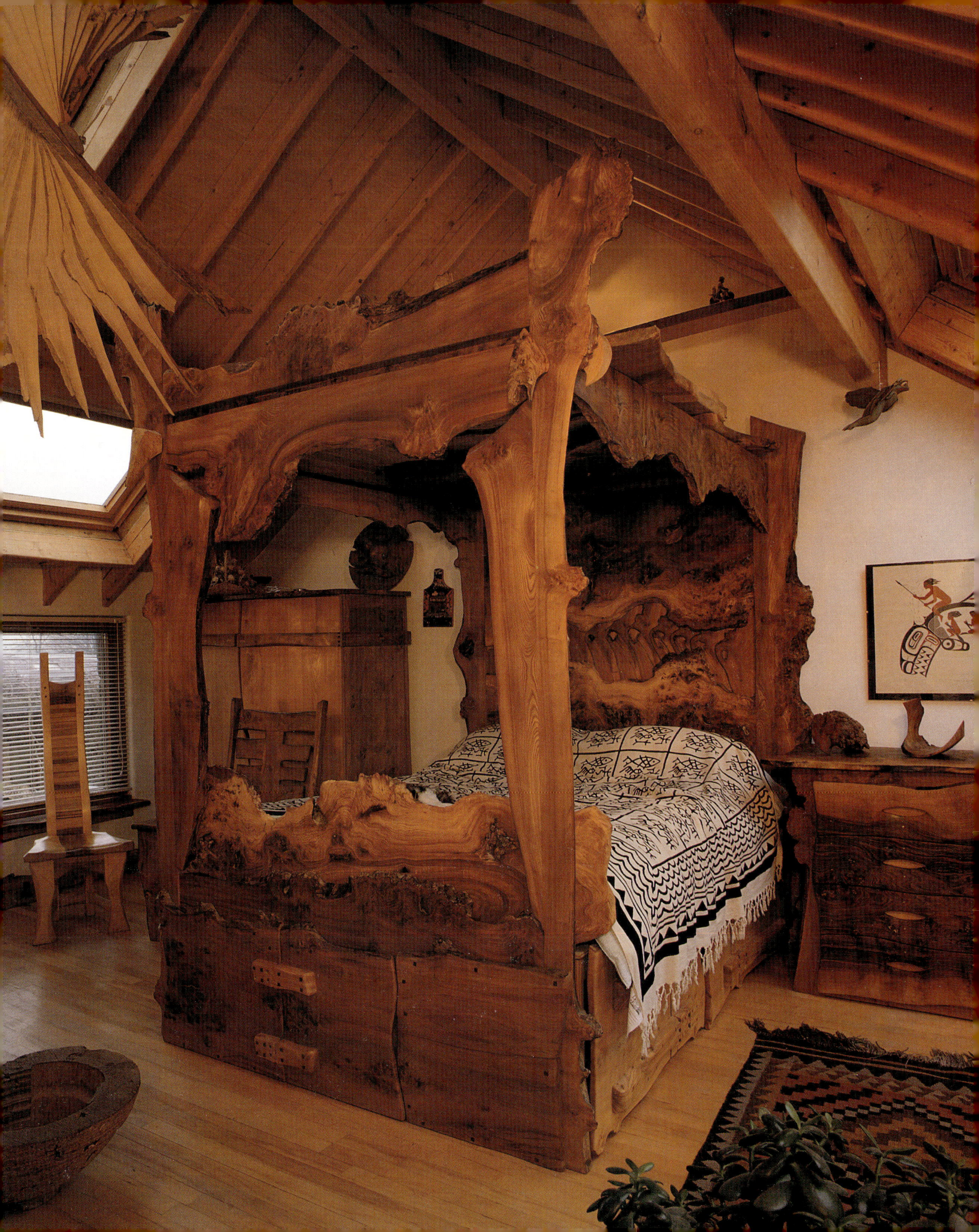

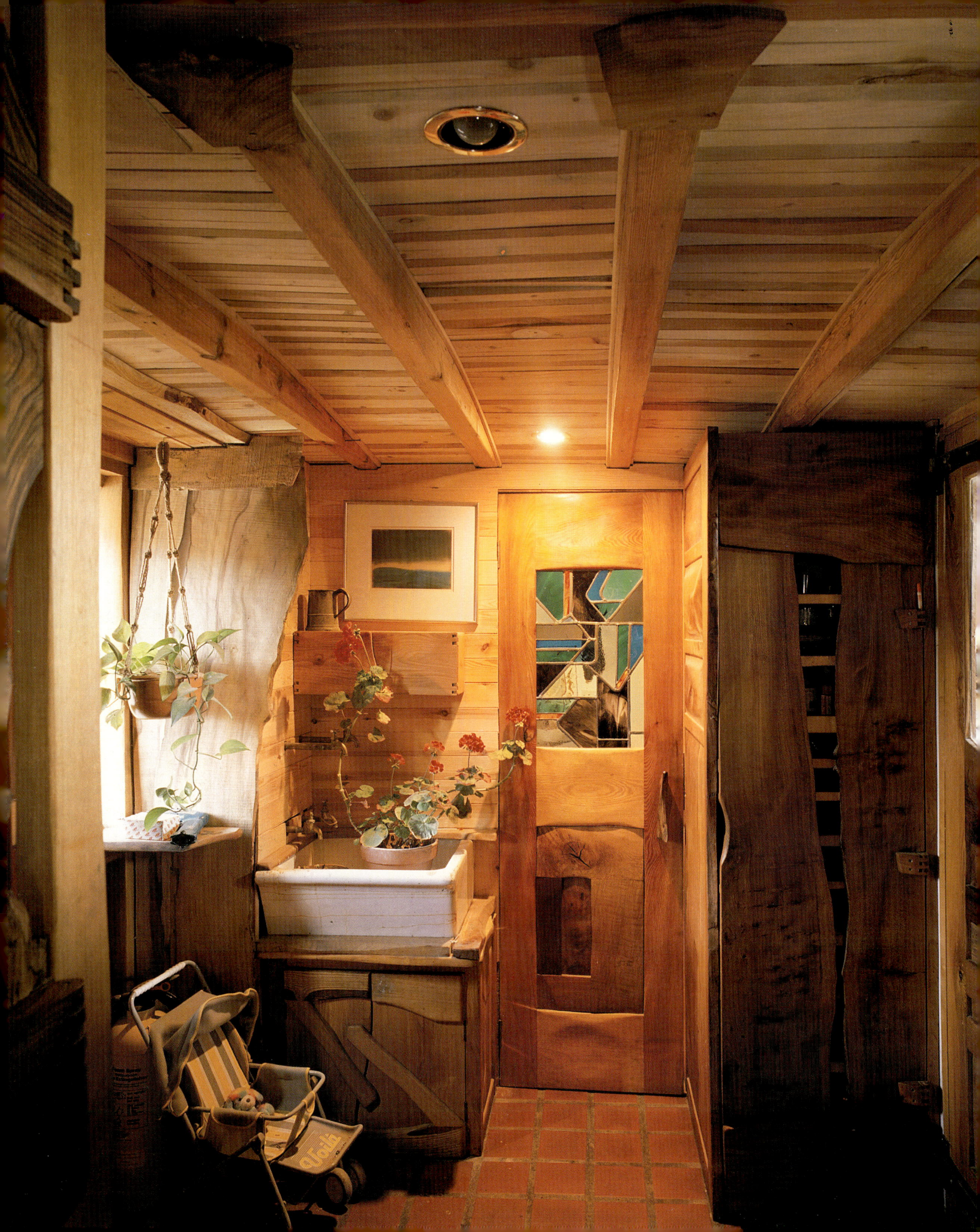

Opposite:
In a small space, the hallway, there are four doors leading to other rooms and five opening into cupboards. All the doors are different, as they are throughout the house. The perfect door may exist, but Stead prefers to enjoy a variety of imperfections. The stained glass in the facing door was made by Liz Rowley.
Photograph: Eric Thorburn

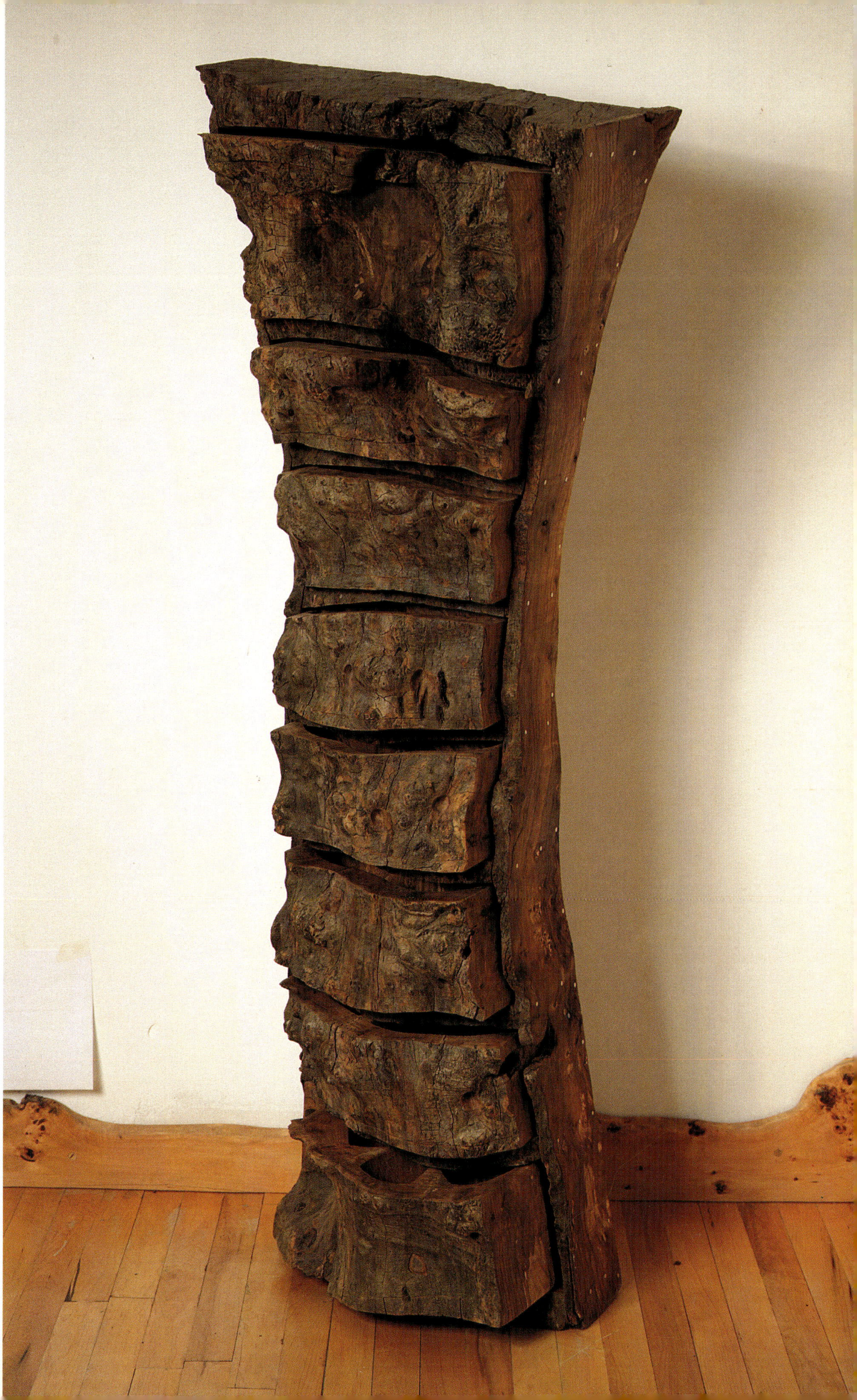

Chest of drawers from a solid six foot block of elm. The first plank cut from a tree – ' the slab'– is regarded as 'waste' and is usually sawn as thinly as possible. Stead now asks the sawyer to cut a generous slab so that he can use it. There is a strong interplay between the irregular tree features and the fine lines of the sawing. Although the drawers do not offer a great deal of storage, they offer a good excuse to bring this beautiful slab of elm indoors.
Photograph: Antonia Reeve

Overleaf right:
A modern interpretation of the grandfather clock. The workings were made by Jürgen Tübbecke in nearby Galashiels, while Stead made the ash casing. The numerals are arbitrary signs, which nevertheless echo characters from various ancient scripts.
Photograph: Roger Lee

Overleaf left:
Rear of elm corner shelves with 'Barrel' shelves between.
Photograph: Antonia Reeve

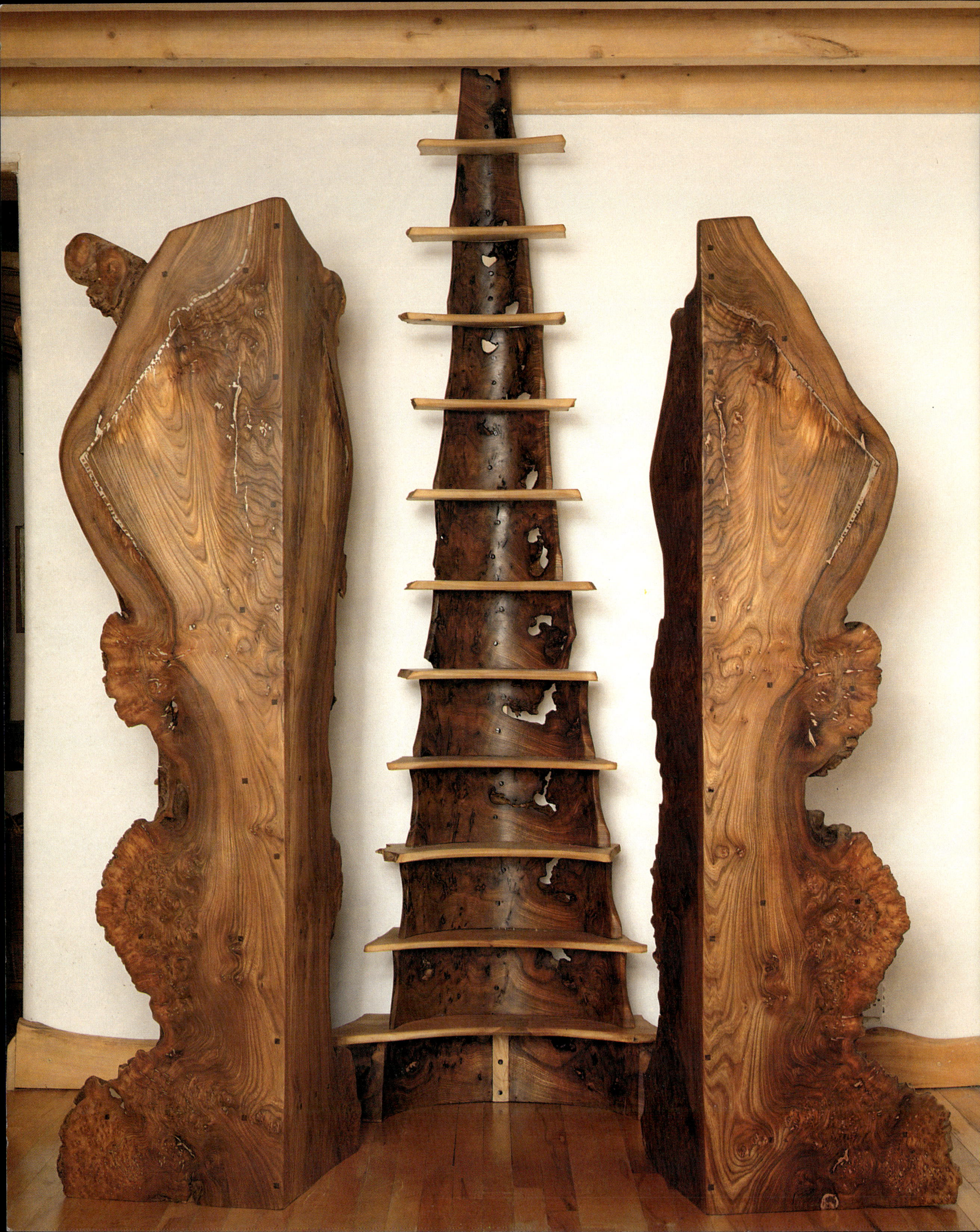

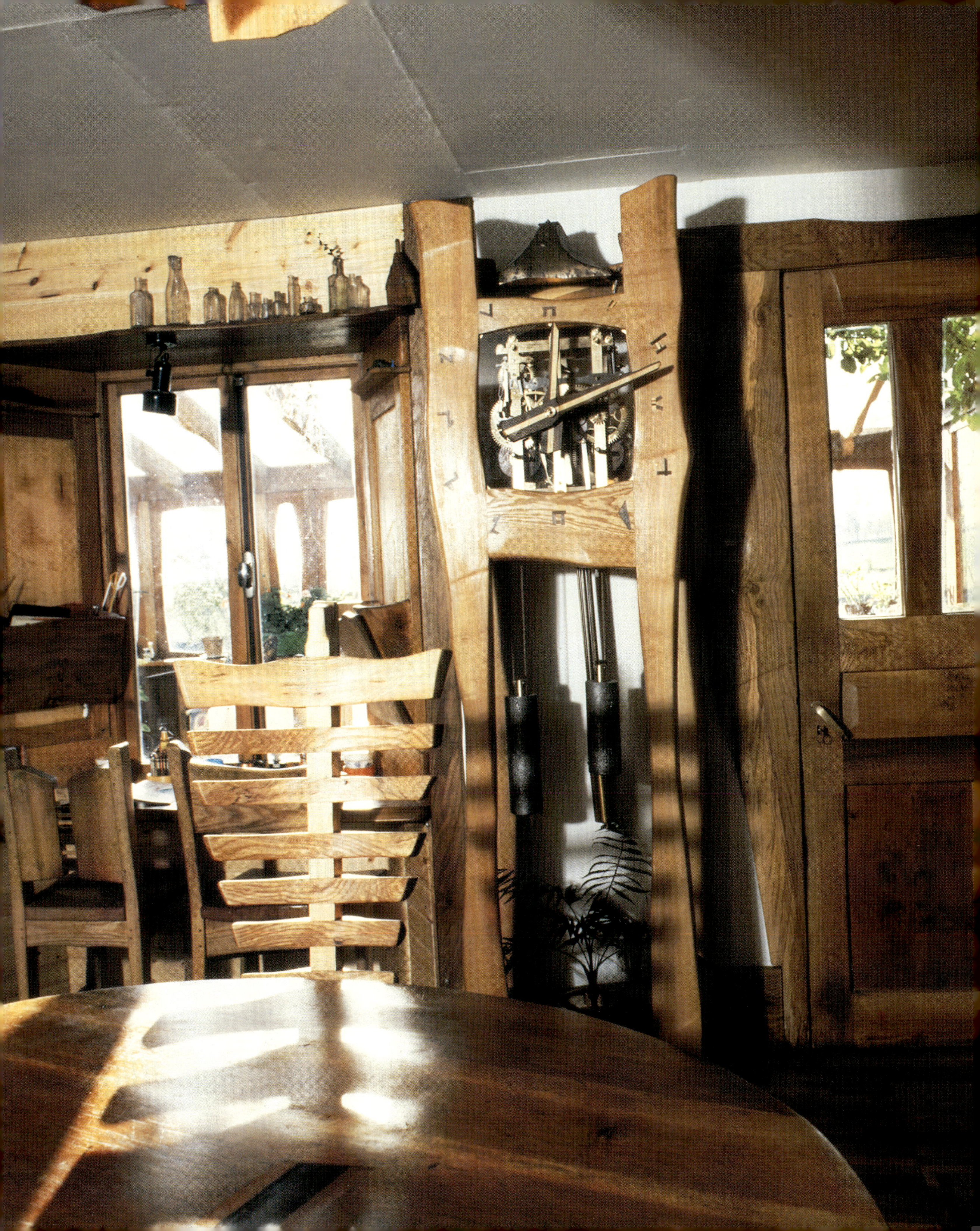

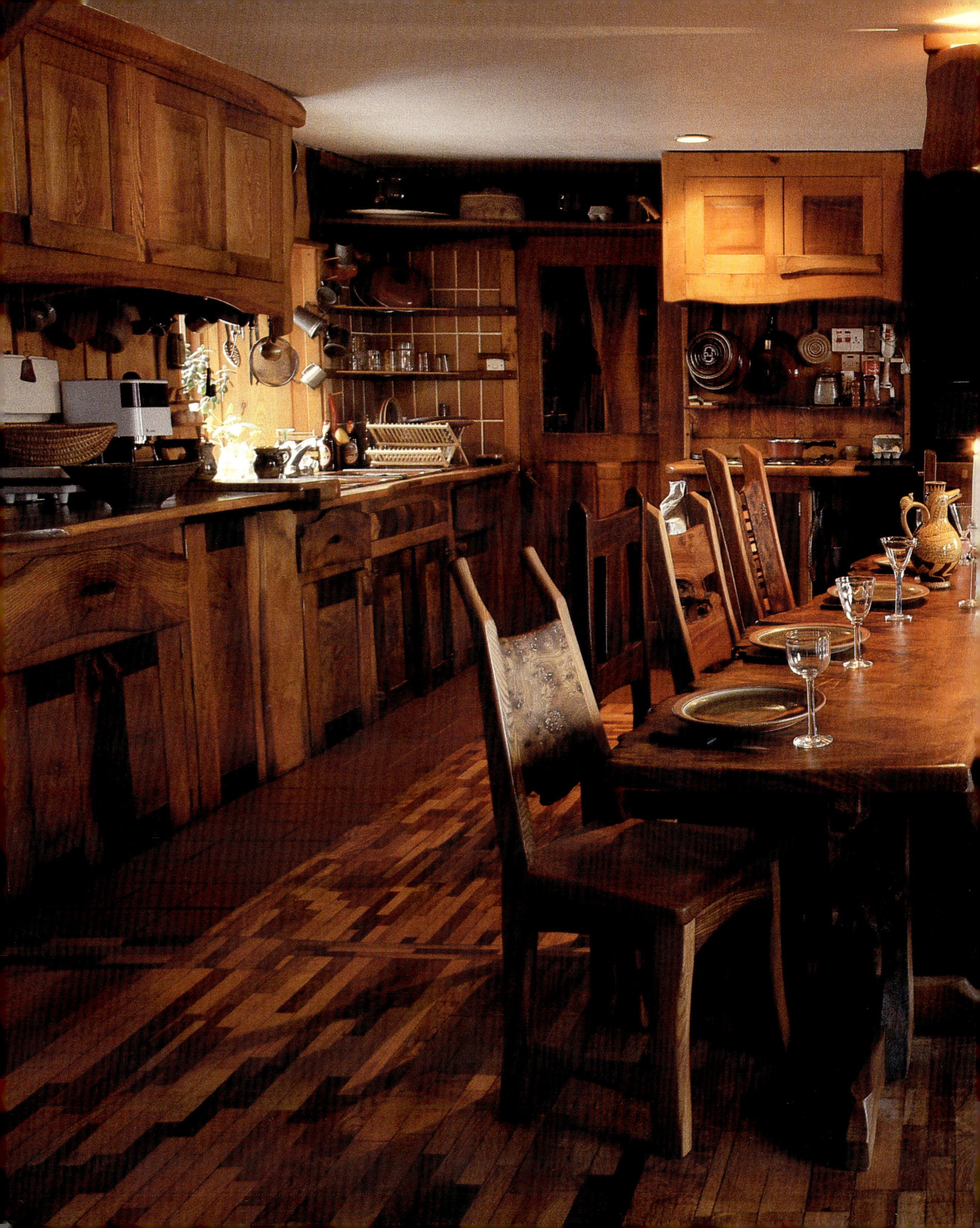

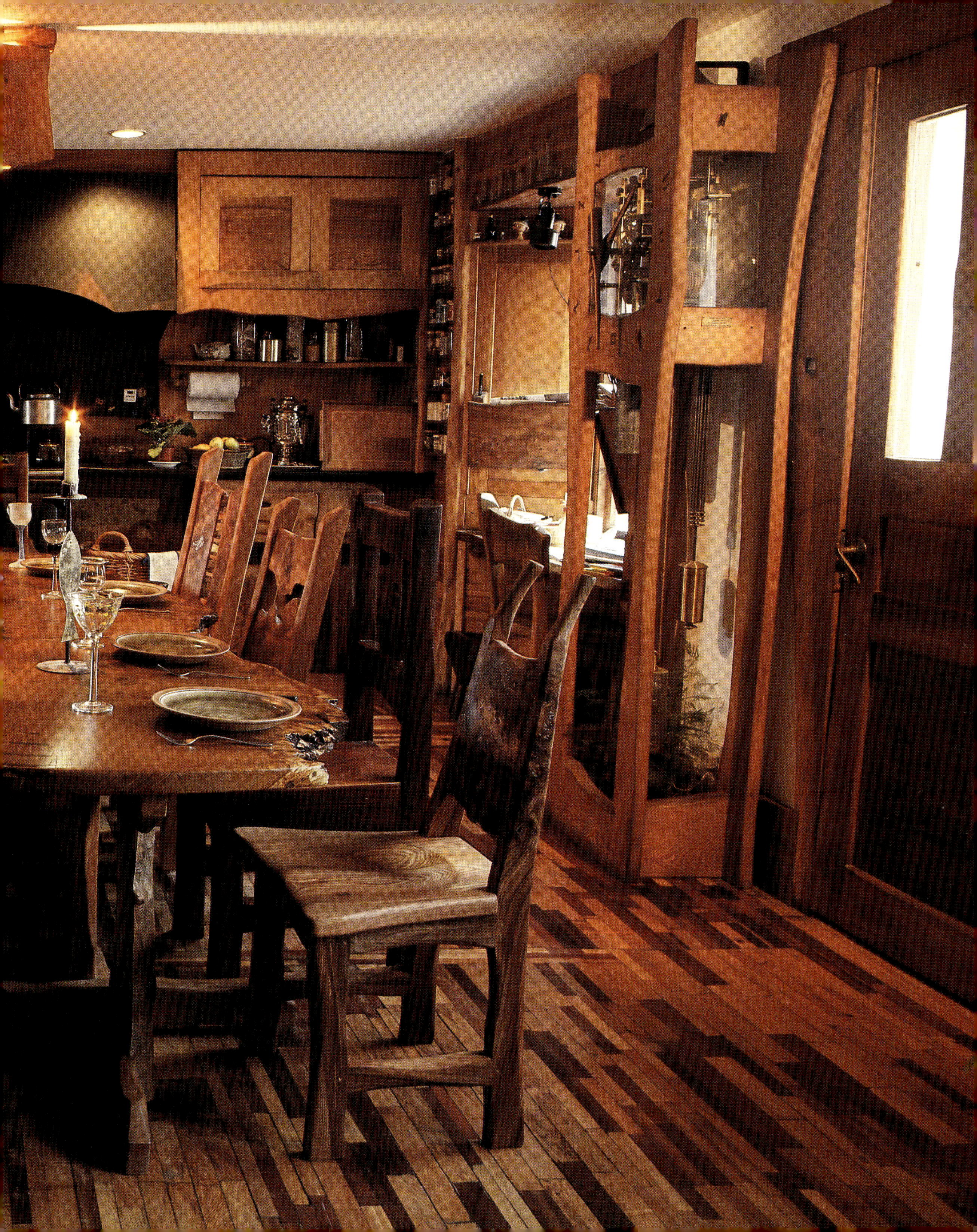

This pair of elm corner shelves was made in response to the very strong feature of a sawn off limb which has been sealed over by the natural processes of the tree. The four boards, all from the same tree, clearly show a large branch coming out from the main trunk. The straight edge means that it was sawn rather than broken. The bronze-filler closes a gap between the old wood and the seal. The filler also replaces the exposed wood which had rotted over the years. Ideally limbs should be sawn off when they are small – and as close to the main trunk as possible. Stead wanted to use these planks in a way where structural problems were unimportant, and where the fault could be seen to its best advantage.
Photograph: Antonia Reeve

Previous page:
Made from a single plank of book-matched burr elm, the table is more than a place to eat. It is a focal point for the room and somewhere to sit, talk and enjoy the company of friends.One main table and two additional pieces – all from a single plank.
Photograph: Antonia Reeve

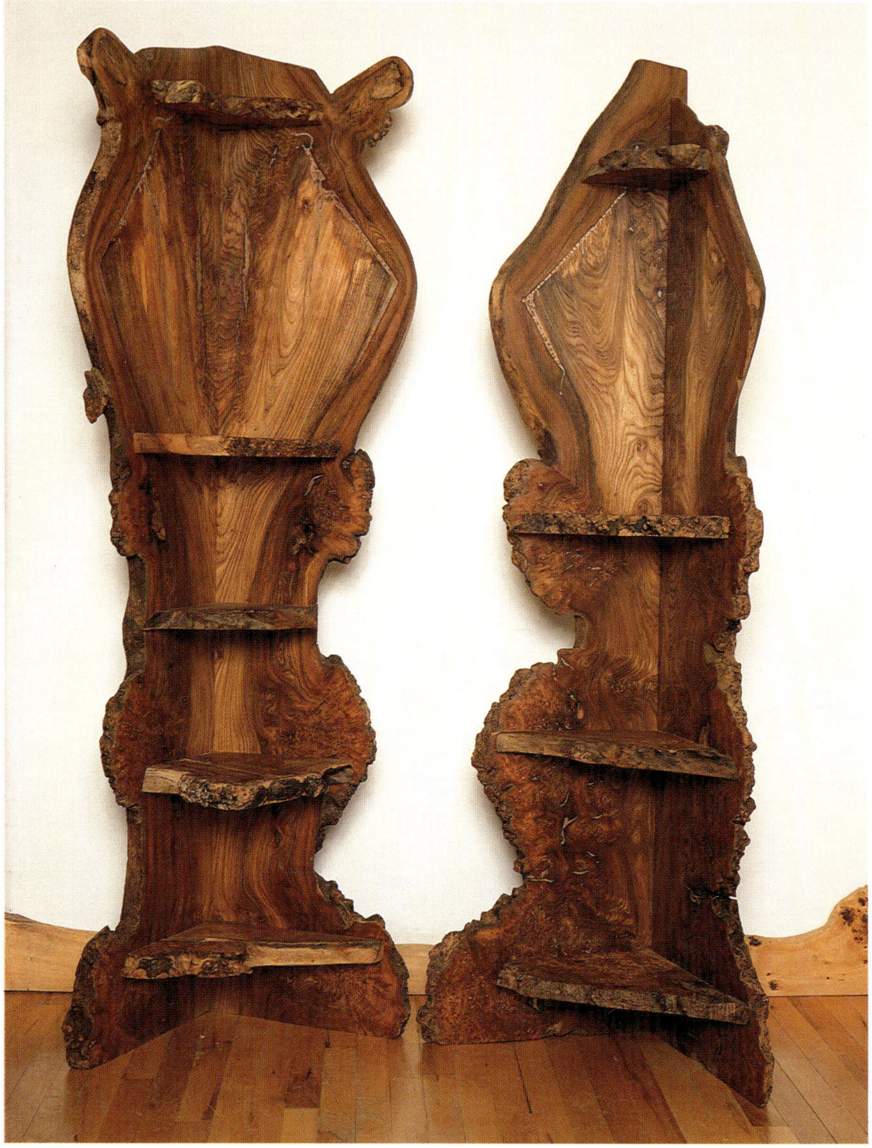

Opposite:
Made from elm, this desk houses a variety of objects including several notebooks which Stead made several years ago. The niches are cut from solid blocks in two of the uprights using a technique employed in the 'Layers' pieces.
Photograph: Antonia Reeve

Overleaf:
The main room of the house where everything happens. Central to the room is the table, made from one huge board of oak twelve feet long and four feet wide. This is too large for daily use. The near end is made up of two separate tables which are normally kept next door and are used as table and desk. The 'Dowling' stove, along with the dining table, acts as a focal point of the main room. The inspiration for the fireplace derives directly from the brochs and other structures, like Skara Brae, which Stead saw when he visited Orkney. The design is Stead's and the fireplace was built by a local stonemason, George Burns.
Photograph: Antonia Reeve

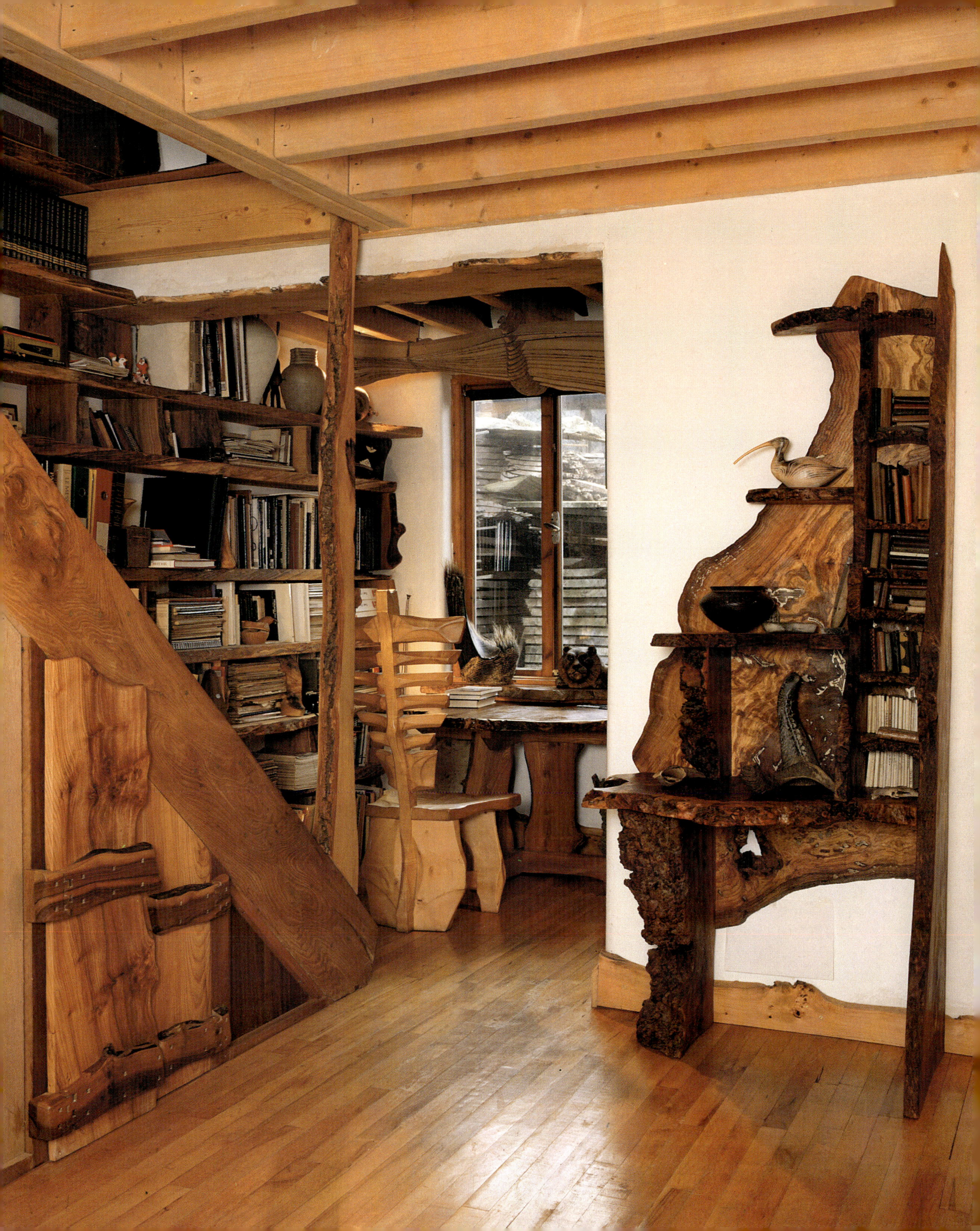

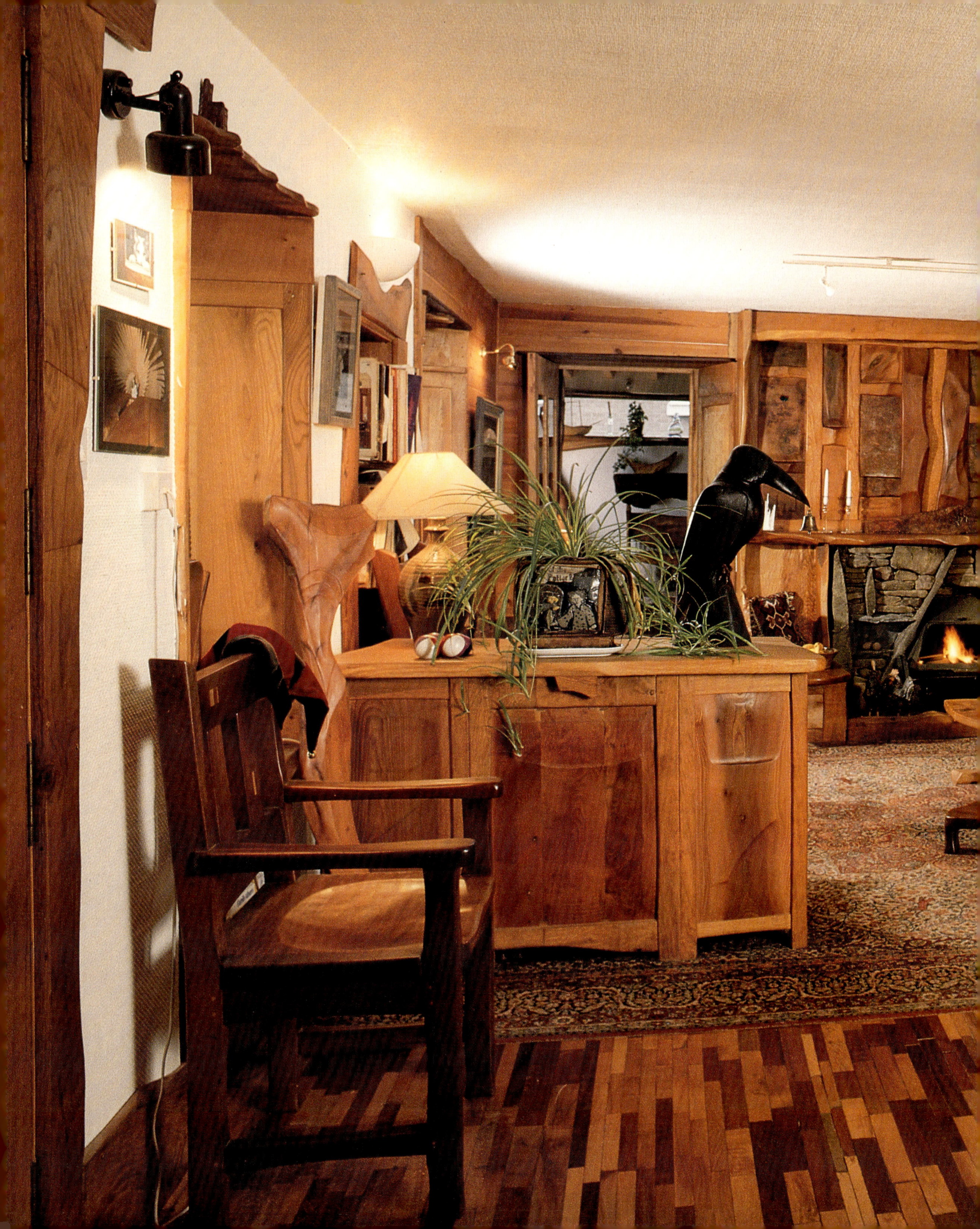

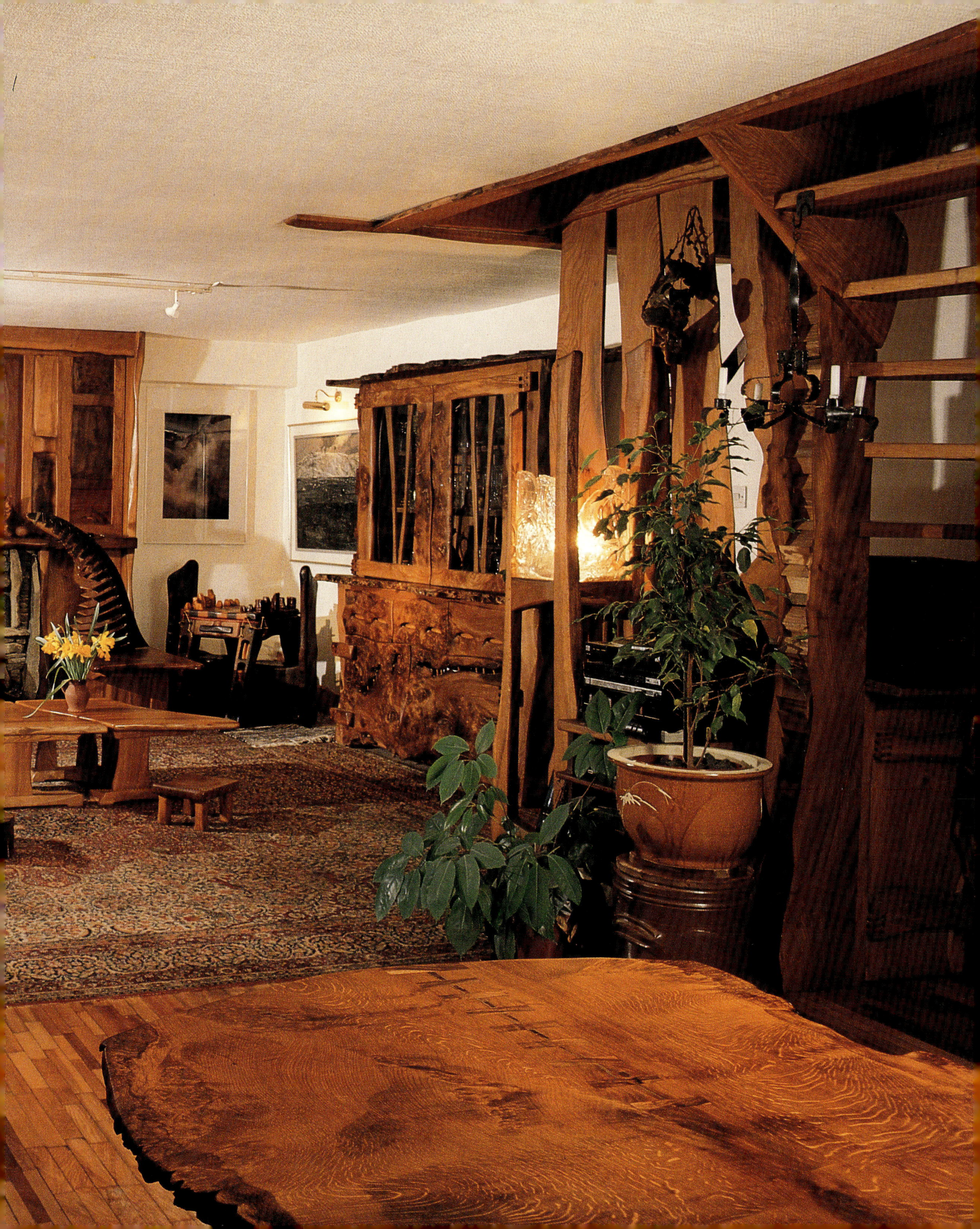

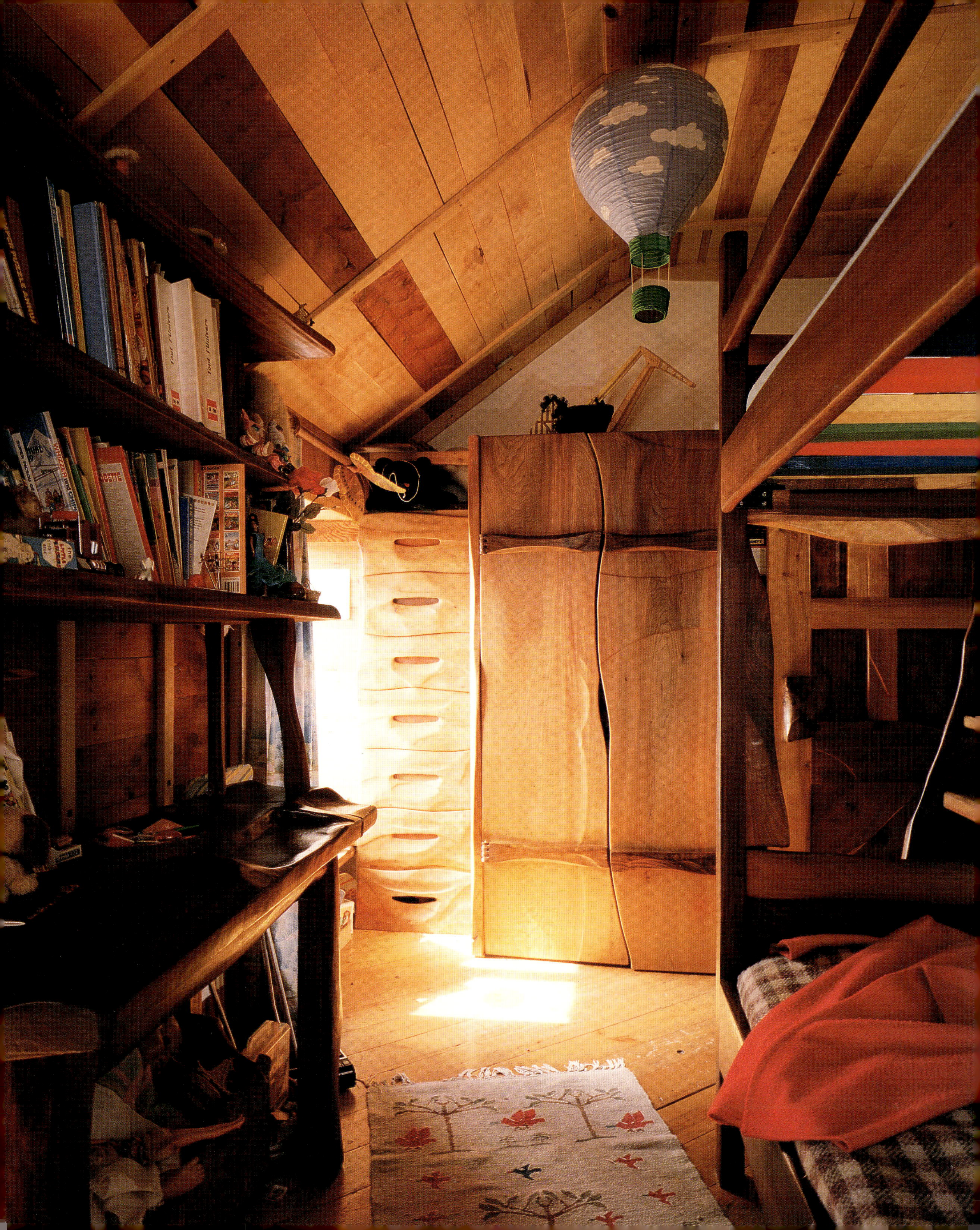

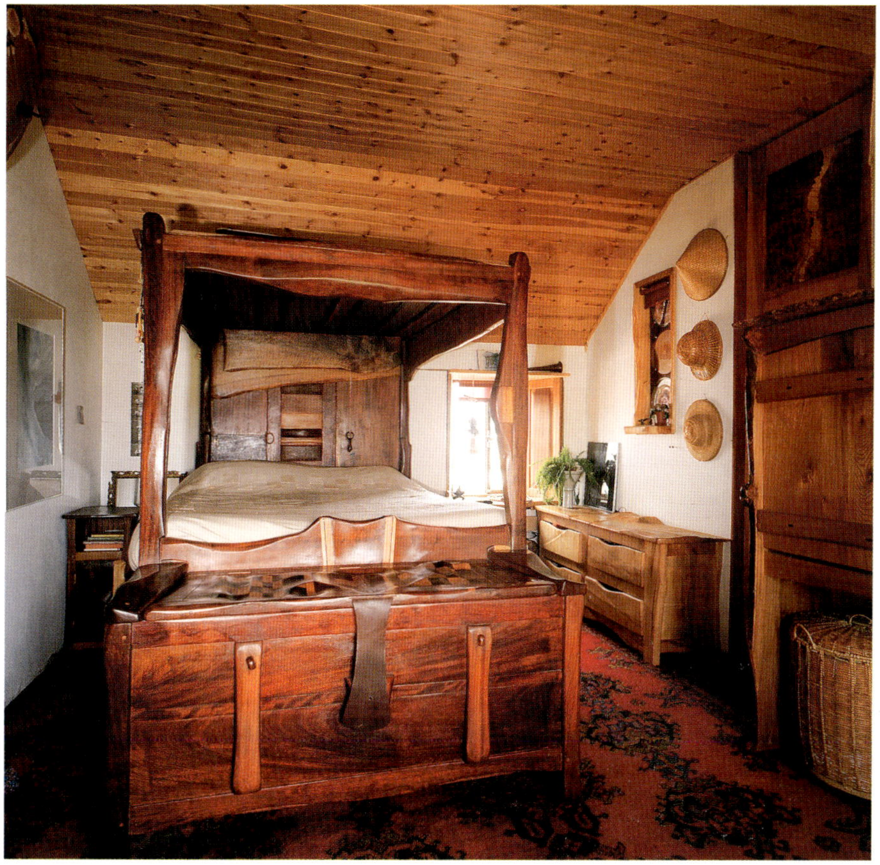

Sam and Emma Stead's beds. Stead made all the beds in his home. They range from bunks in his children's rooms, a low-lying bed in the guest room made from four planks of yew through to the four-poster beds in the main and second bedrooms.
Photographs: Eric Thorburn

The study seen from the top of the stair/bookshelf. This part of the house was once the end of the barn which adjoins the house. As with all the other rooms in The Steading, the study combines practicality with good design. The desk, which is fashioned from a single board of ash, houses a computer and printer. The drawer-fronts are again made from single planks of burr elm, as is the shelving. The chair completes the work area and testifies to the comfort of the space. Larger shelves, built on a walnut desk, on the opposite wall double up as steps leading to a mezzanine floor. This accommodates a bed and is used as a guest room.
Photograph: Eric Thorburn

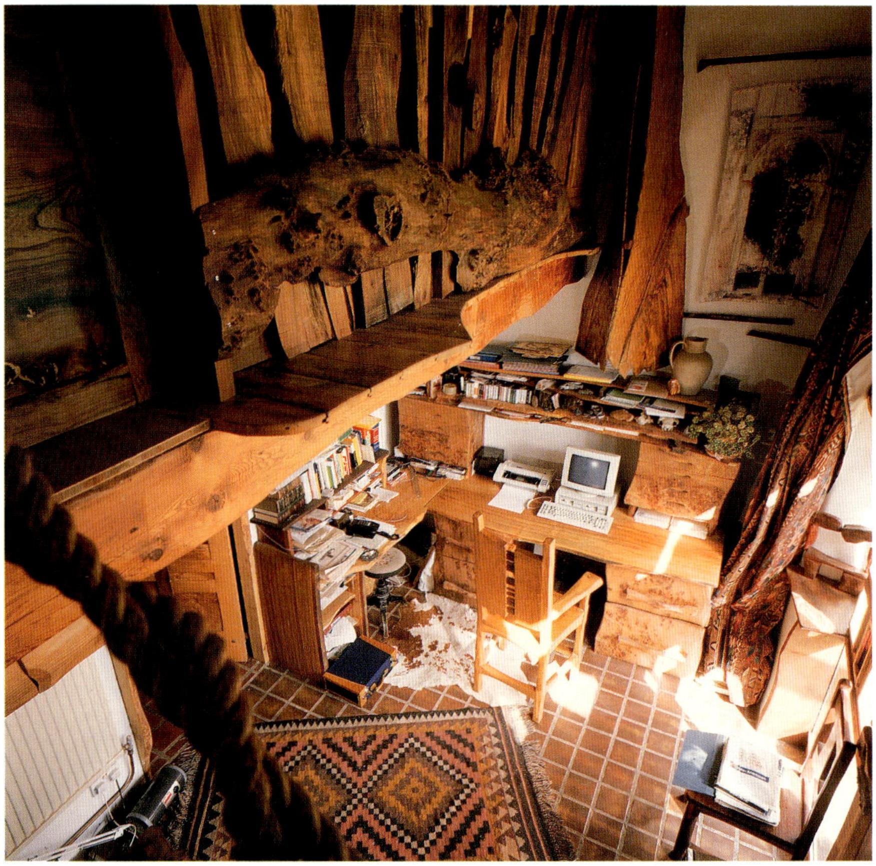

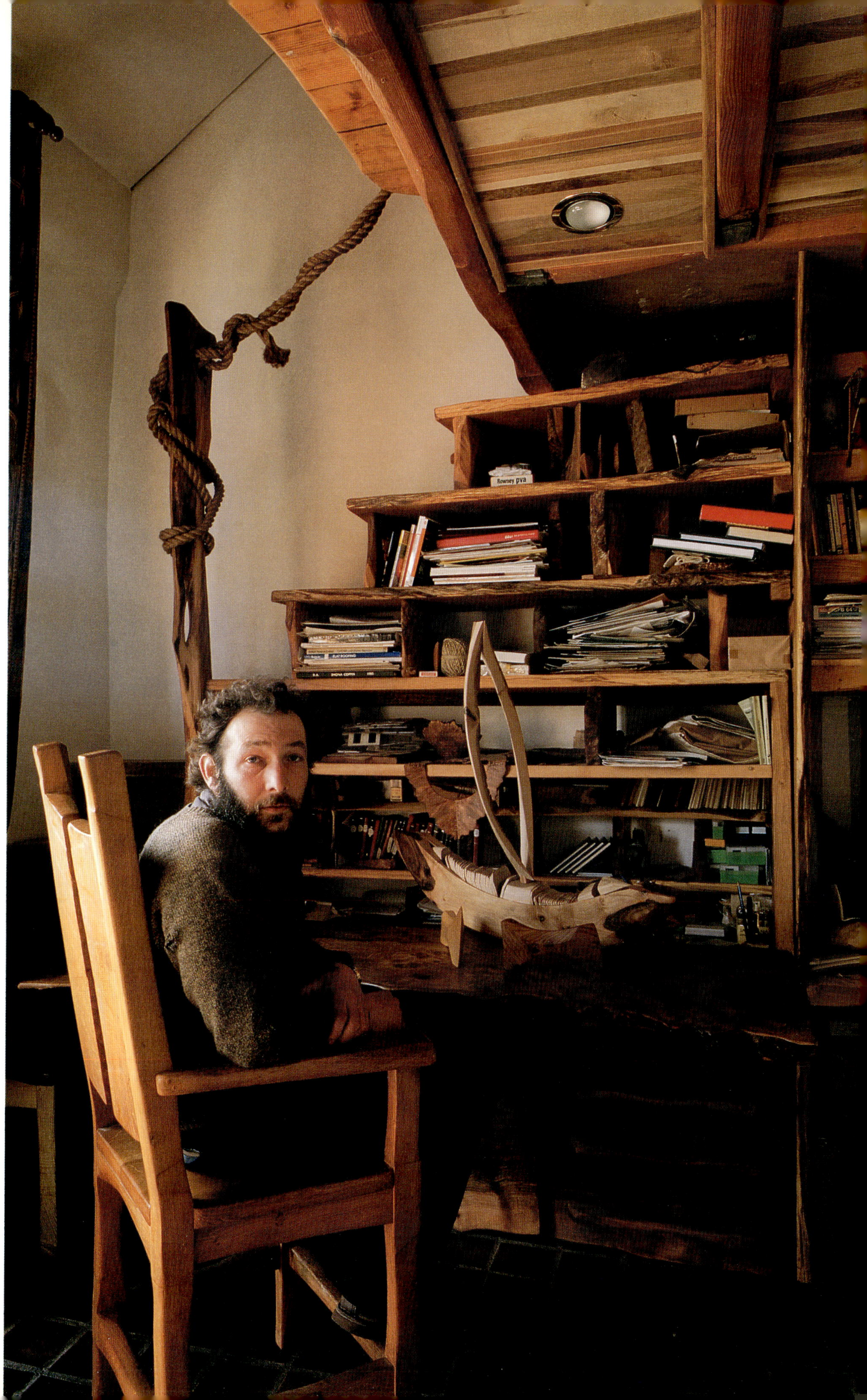

The desk is the focus of Stead's 'chaos'. The use of small notebooks is a discipline which he has maintained continuously for twenty years. The notebooks contain ideas, sketches and doodles.
Photograph: Eric Thorburn

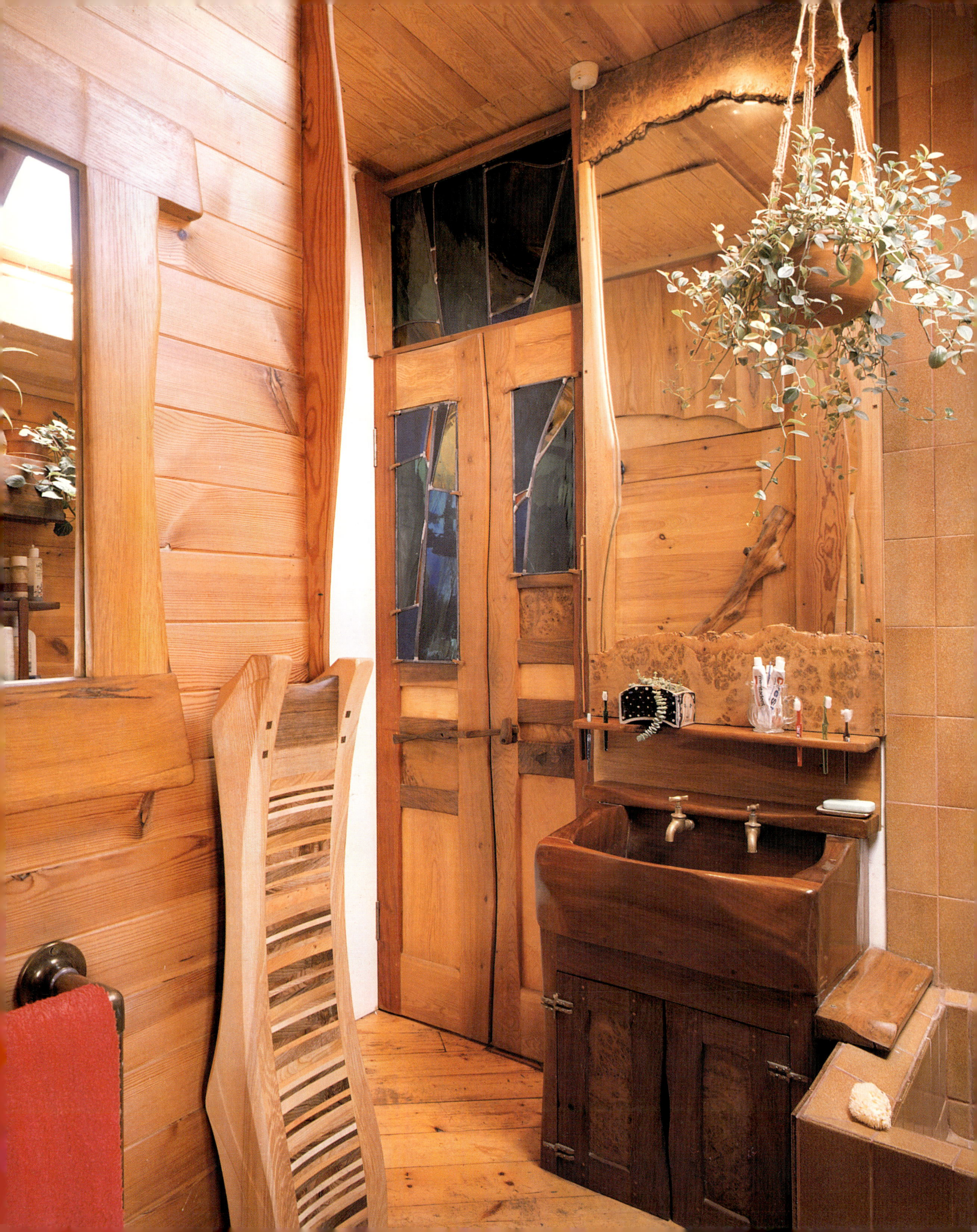

Opposite:
The glass in the bathroom doors was made with Liz Rowley. Wood and glass combine in harmony as sunlight brings the colours alive. The sink, made from iroko, at first seems more surprising than it should, until one remembers that wood was a commonly used material for this purpose before the widespread use of stoneware and vitreous china. The wood is protected from water-logging and rot by a heavy varnish. Water flowing over the surface of the wood creates intriguing patterns, shapes and sounds and it is possible to pretend that the water is fresh from the sky.
Photograph: Eric Thorburn

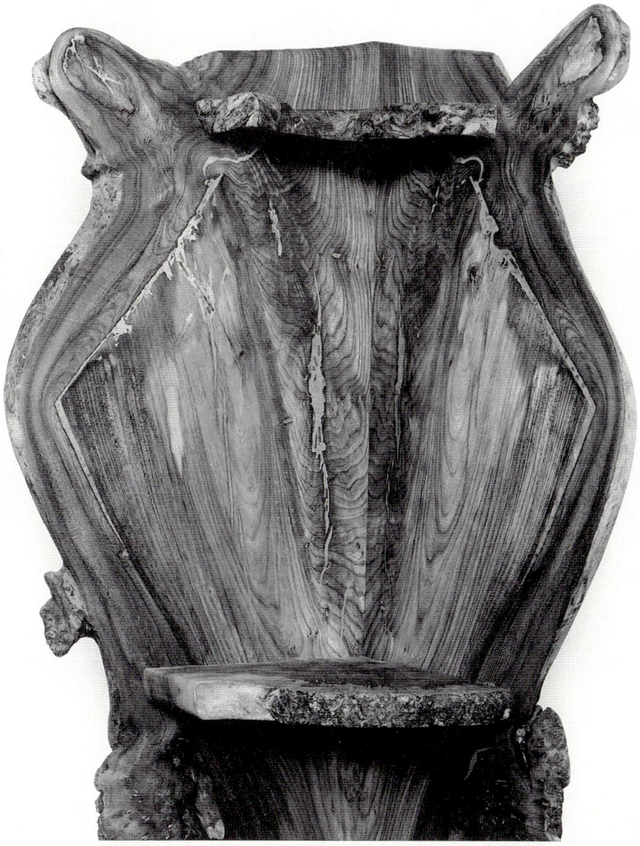

Detail of elm corner shelves
Photograph: Antonia Reeve

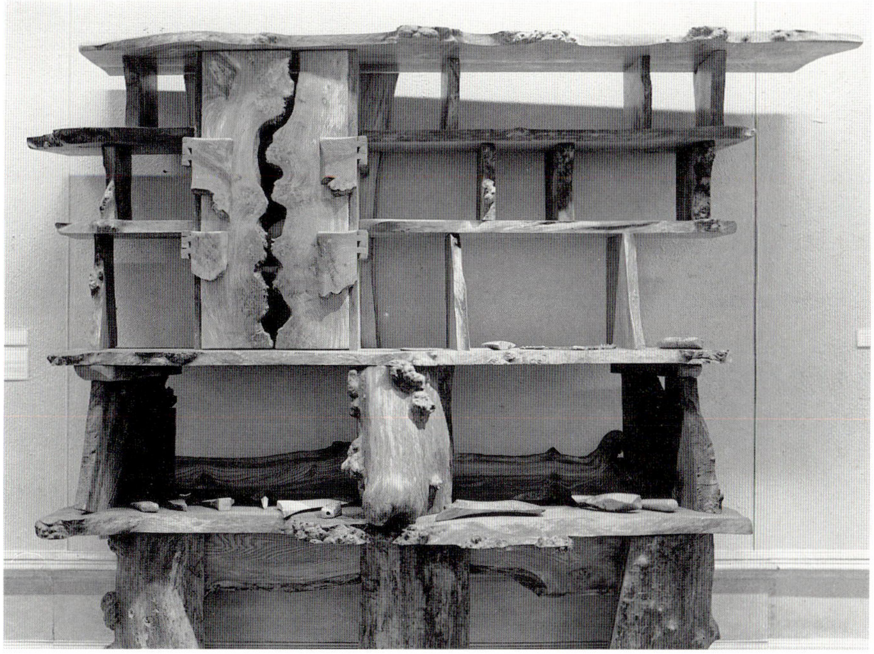

The 'Horse's-Nose Dresser' was a response to an invitation to show a piece of work alongside a wooden interpretation of Skara Brae. Stead was commissioned to make this for the exhibition 'Scotland Creates – 5,000 years of Art and Design in Scotland', which was held at the McLellan Galleries in Glasgow in 1990. Why 'Horse's Nose'? Because not only does the central support of the first shelf look like a horse's nose but it also has a leather-darkness and a hole inside.
Photograph: Sean Hudson

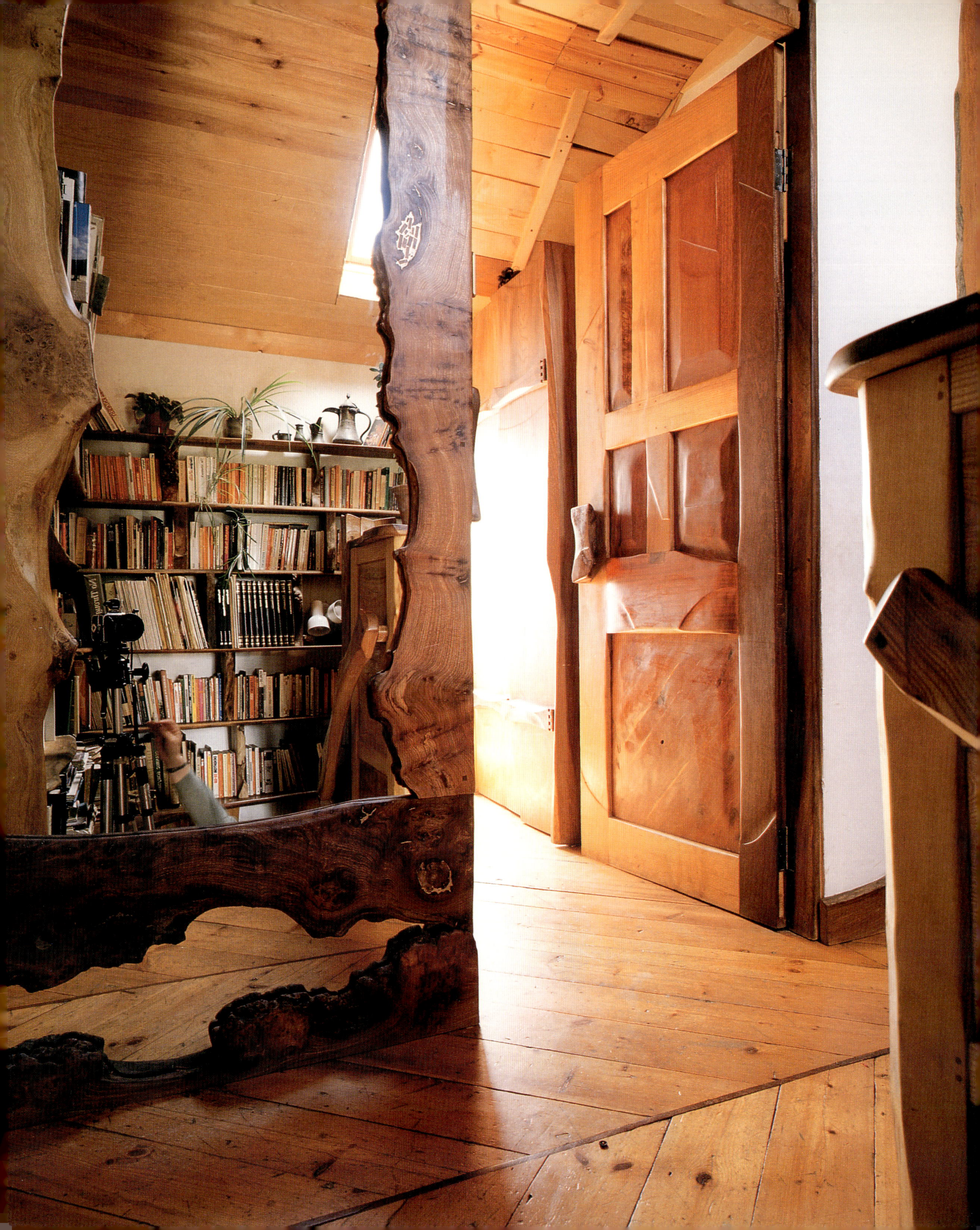

Opposite:
The landing is a very small area. When planning the building, Tim and Maggy wanted to minimise the space wasted on stairs and corridors: the stairs are lined with books and cupboards occupy any spare space. The large mirror is directly at the top of the stairs, which gives the space an open feeling. The reflection allows other elements to be seen at a greater distance.
Photograph: Eric Thorburn

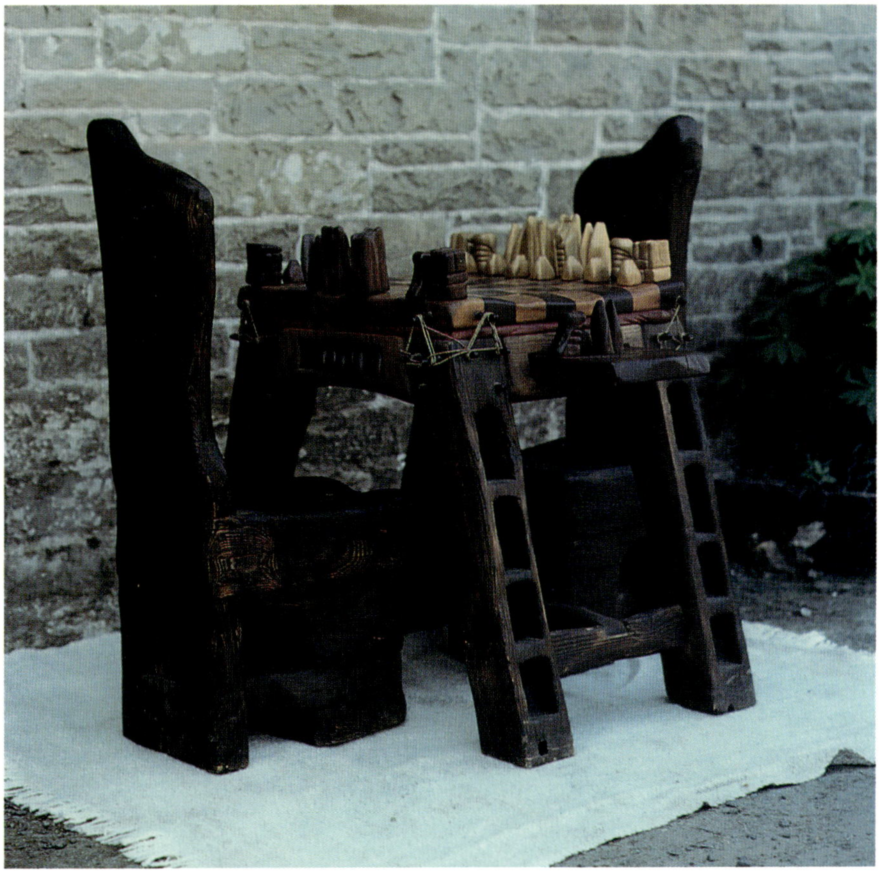

Over the years Stead has made a number of chess-sets. The first was Stead's first piece of real furniture and is very much a transitional work. It was made after most of Stead's sculpture at Trent Polytechnic. It leads backwards to the sculpture and forwards to the rest of the furniture which was made subsequently. Function was an area of interest in the piece, which was made from timber available at the time. The legs are from railway sleepers and the chairs from tenement joists.

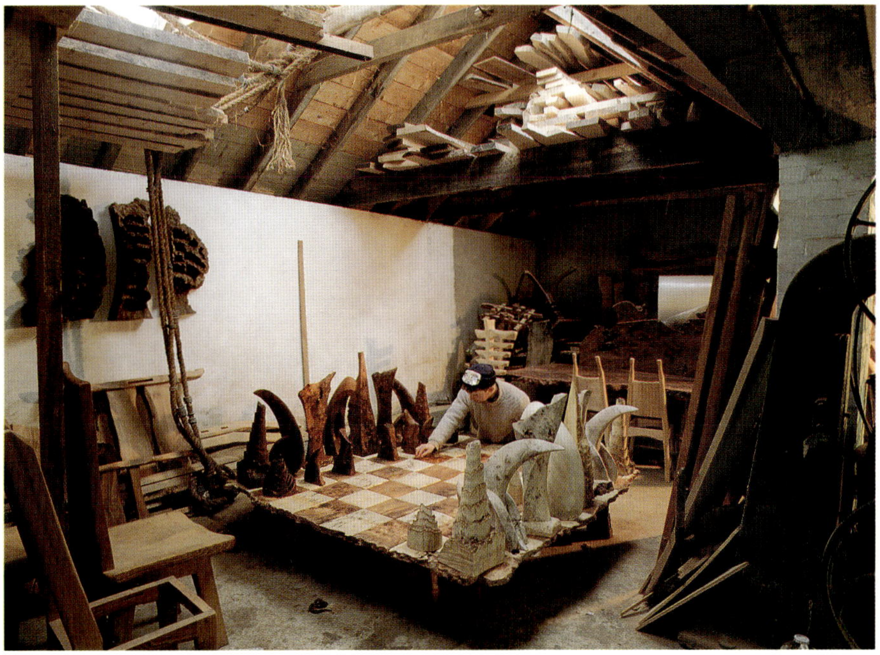

Stead's most recent chess-set is on a much larger scale. The board itself is made from a number of waney-edged planks with alternate bleached and oiled squares. The pieces consist of a number of dramatic sculptural forms from the smaller, simpler pawns to the larger tusk-shaped queens which stand about twenty-four inches high. The most inhibiting aspect of working on such a large scale is the problem of storage.

Commissions

Over the years Stead has undertaken a wide variety of commissions and other projects at the behest of others. Most famous of these is the Papal Chair he made for the visit of John Paul II to Scotland in 1982. The Pope celebrated mass at Murrayfield Stadium in July and Stead's chair was the centrepiece at the ceremony. It was commissioned privately by the Polish priest Ryszard Haluka. The commission required the representation on the chair of the four gospels of the New Testament – Matthew, Mark, Luke and John – by their respective symbols: the lion, the angel, the eagle and the bull. The chair, made from elm, was inlaid in a form of marquetry with various other woods.

In 1981 Ian Spence, former owner of The Round Table restaurant in Edinburgh, asked Stead to design and make a variety of furniture. The restaurant, which specialises in Scottish and Norwegian food, is a popular lunchtime and evening venue firmly established on the city's cultural map.

St. John's Chapel, The Kirk of St. Nicholas, Aberdeen

In 1989 Stead was commissioned by the North Sea Oil Industries to design and make the fittings for a new Memorial Chapel in the Kirk of St. Nicholas, Aberdeen. Stead was chosen from a group of seven individuals and companies originally proposed by the SDA. The organisation represents the major companies working in the British sector of the North Sea. This was a huge project in terms of Stead's previous experience and originally involved forty chairs, a lectern, communion table, and a minister's chair. Later, this extended to include a screen which would divide the chapel from the rest of the kirk. The requirements of the commission were simple – to provide seating which would be comfortable. In almost every other aspect Stead was given a free hand.

TS
A commission like this is a once-in-a-lifetime opportunity and I felt very privileged to have been given the job. I know now that it was close-run thing and that the Kirk elders were understandably hesitant about something original and new – they could have opted for a safer, more traditional choice. I also knew that there was uncertainty and tension about how it would finally look. However, I am overjoyed at the response which I have had and how pleased everyone else is with the overall effect.

As comfort was paramount, Stead's starting point was to take his most comfortable chair to date and modify it – this was the Skeletal Chair which had a single mast for supporting the back. Stead incorporated two masts into the new design while retaining the original chair's narrow back. The new design went through at least one prototype before a final design was decided.

TS
I liked the tall back and the way the legs come over the back. But if you imagine somebody sitting down – from the front it looks as if you've got Devil's horns and from the back it looks like rabbit's ears . . ! So unfortunately that had to be changed. The angle was slightly wrong – it was too far back so you tended to slip forward. This would have been impossible to see from a drawing.

The final design for the chairs involved setting different types of wood into two routed channels on the inside of the masts. The different textures and colours are reminiscent of a geological core sample. The initials of the different species spell out the simple message 'WE REMEMBER YOU':

Walnut.
Elm.

Rowan.
Elm.
Maple.
Elm.
Maple.
Beech.
Elm.
Rowan.

Yew

TS
I generally make pieces of furniture for individuals, and it is therefore easy to understand what they have in mind. On the very rare occasions when there have been misunderstandings they have not been difficult to rectify. With this project I was in many ways imposing my designs. I worked in close collaboration with Colin Fisher, the architect, who was a tremendous help. I also tried, as far as I could, to keep in touch with the people who used the kirk. But ultimately I was locked into certain ideas which had formed very quickly. The chair was the starting point and the design occurred to me within hours of the first phone-call and I had made it within a fortnight. Throughout, I worked with full-scale mock-ups, rather than drawings, because it is so easy to be deceived by the latter.

The screen separating the Chapel wing from the rest of the kirk was originally to have been of glass. However, this would have involved cutting into the stone pillars. The Rood Screen with its double-doors and vertically adjustable slats invoke the pillared trees of a forest, as well as the pipes of a church organ. The Memorial Chapel is now highly popular and is used by many denominations for all types of ceremony, from marriages to christenings. In 1991 the project received the Saltire Society Design Award for Art, Craft and Architecture. The architects for the project were the Jack Fisher Partnership, St Andrews.

Papal Throne made for the visit of Pope John Paul II to Scotland, July 1982

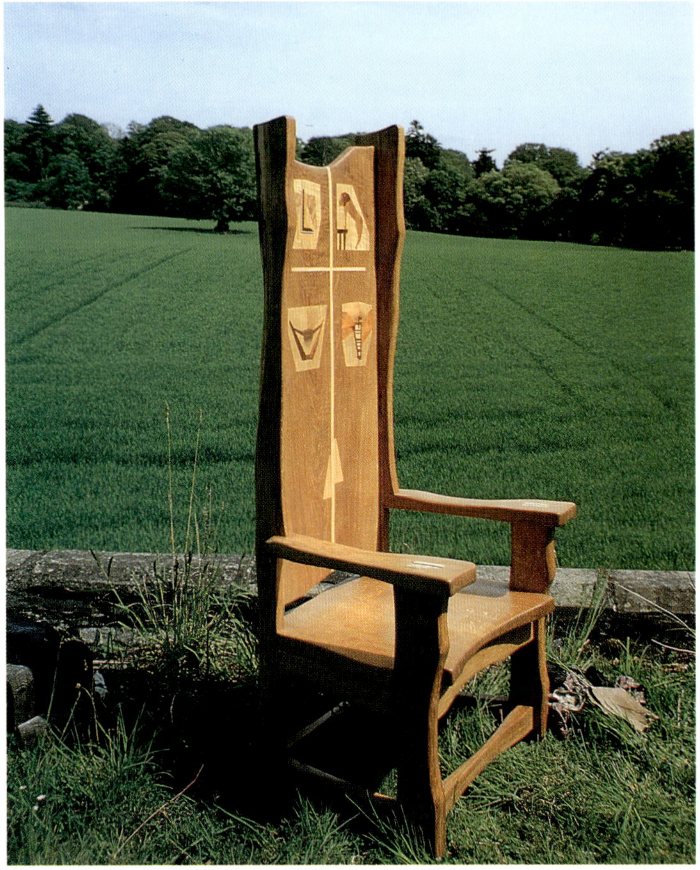

'Skeletal' chair
Photograph: Roger Lee

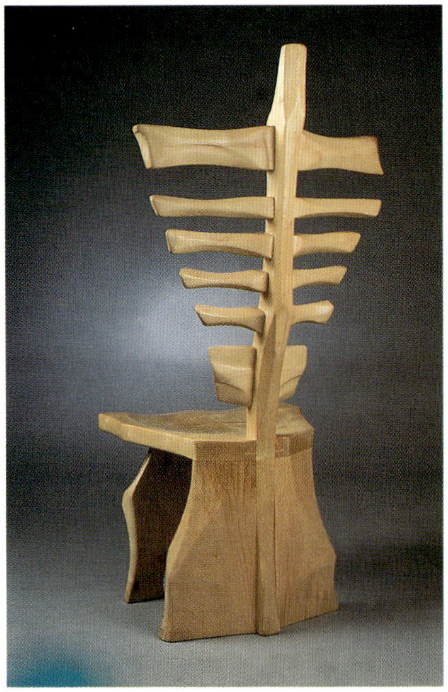

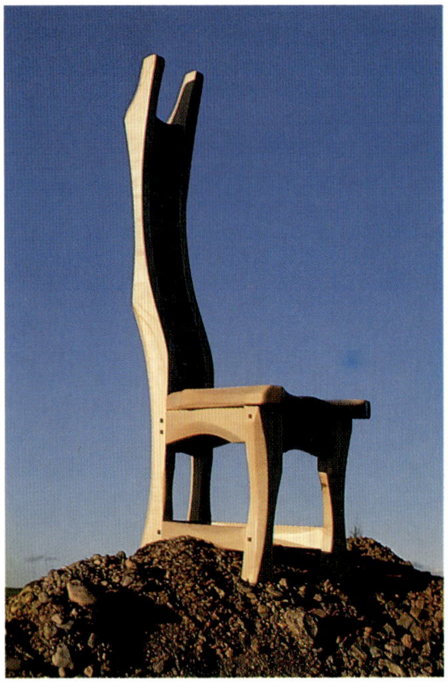

The first 'Strata Chair'

The slats of the Rood Screen in open and closed position.

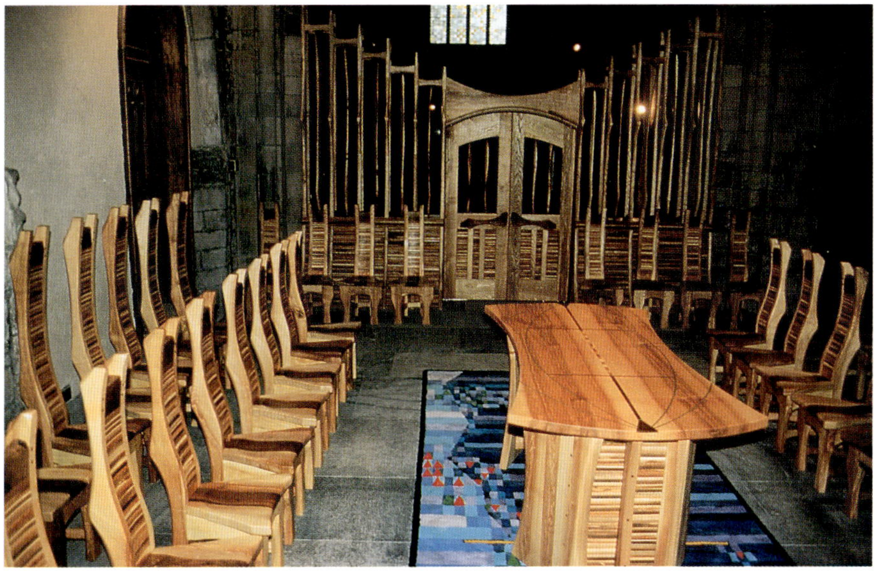

The stained glass window was designed by Shona McInnes, as was the rug which was made by the Edinburgh Tapestry Company.

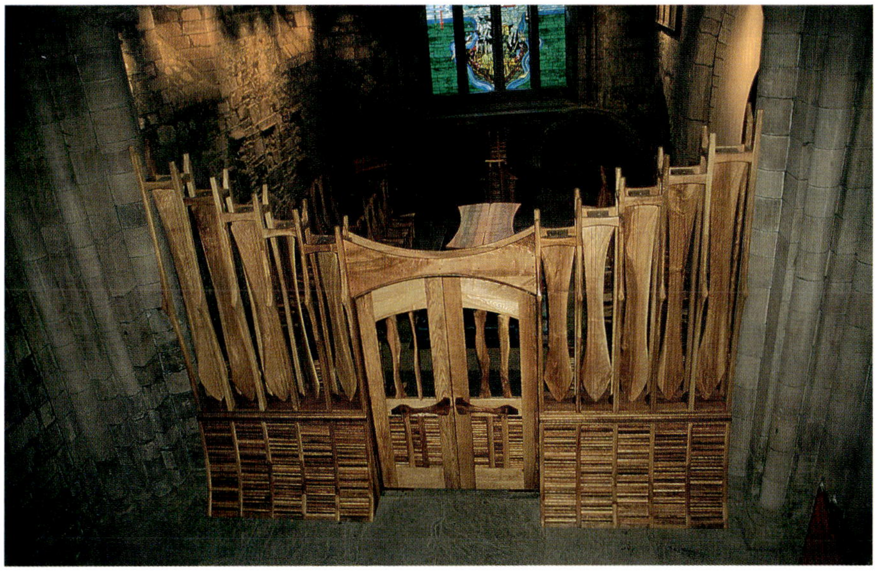

Axes for Trees

In 1986 Stead conceived the 'Axes for Trees' project. This came about through his own increasing awareness concerning the types of wood he was using for his work. For some time before this Stead had been making exclusive use of native British timbers. He considered woods like ash and elm to be more attractive than, say, mahogany. In addition, these trees were fairly readily available in his immediate locale.

By this time the plunder and destruction of the tropical rainforests was common knowledge. Although the motivation behind Stead's use of native timber had been almost exclusively aesthetic, the connection between an impoverished native resource and the damaging exploitation of foreign timber soon became clear. Having recklessly mismanaged our own timber reserves over the centuries, we are now hugely dependent on both hardwood and softwood from other countries.

As a wood-user who earned a living from this resource, Stead began to feel increasingly strongly about putting back some of what he had taken out.

TS
It was coming to a point where if I wasn't planting trees then it made the experience of working with wood incomplete. If you are not involved in putting back, it restricts your freedom to use what has been planted and come to the end of its life. I prefer to be a beneficial parasite, rather than a harmful parasite.

'Axes for Trees' involved making an axe-head for each day of 1986 and selling these to raise money to buy land on which to plant trees. Like each day, each of the three-hundred and sixty-five pieces was unique and made from various species of British hardwood. It is a lively irony that wood, always the material that had been cut by the metal axe, was now being used to make a sculptural interpretation of that tool.

TS
The axe-head is something which I've always liked. It's a most beautiful shape and something which links form and function perfectly. There are so many other things in nature which correspond to that – it's aerodynamic, water-dynamic, it's very much about natural laws. The axe has been used by man for millions of years – it's a very early tool, one which is used with rhythm, rather than the chain-saw which is much more destructive.

Stead took the decision to make the project as public as possible in order to attract the maximum interest and help. This included printing postcards depicting three of the axeheads and these were distributed widely. The tactic worked and Stead was approached by Alan Drever of the then Scottish Community Woods Campaign (now the Scottish Native Woods Campaign) and Donald McPhillimy, a forester and a director of the environmental charity Reforesting Scotland.

TS
At that time I knew nothing about planting trees. I had bought a few apple trees and stuck them in the garden. I met Alan Drever and Donald McPhillimy through selling the axes – people I wouldn't have met otherwise. They thought this was great. I was somebody from a different area who shared a common interest. I was fascinated to learn about what they knew and I was guided by their ideas.

Donald McPhillimy, who had initially trained as a doctor, gave a talk in the local village hall which set forward the idea of a 'Community Woodland'. He compared the concept to the human heart where he saw the woodland as an essential life-sustaining organ in the body of the community. Although the idea of a community woodland is widespread in other parts of Europe, it is a relatively new concept in Scotland. A Community Woodland involves much more than an area simply in which to plant trees; it should be able to accommodate a variety of functions and uses. There should be areas to plant, areas of existing woodland of different ages which can be managed and the trees themselves should be a mixture of hardwood and coniferous species. People from surrounding areas should be able to drive, walk or cycle to the wood and get involved in various activities including the planting of trees, thinning them out as they mature, weeding, building paths as well as picnicking, walking and simply enjoying their surroundings.

Although an 'ideal' existed in imagination, none of those involved in the project expected it to materialise in reality. Soon afterwards, however, a local farmer put an area of land up for sale. When Stead and others examined the land in question, the fifty-acre Wooplaw Wood, they recognised the ideal had almost miraculously appeared. The wood also included a small burn, which enhanced the proposition further. The bid to buy the wood received help in the form of donations and loans from the local community. Various environmental funding bodies including the World Wide Fund for Nature (WWF) and the Countryside Commission for Scotland also contributed. When this was added to the £3,500 Stead had by then raised from the sale of the axe-heads, the £30,000 needed for the purchase of Wooplaw Wood was raised within the seemingly impossible time limit of six weeks. Borders Community Woodland, of which Stead is Chairman, was formed to administer the wood.

An ambitious programme of work in now underway in partnership with the Scottish Wildlife Trust. Enhancement of wildlife habitats is considered important, as is the re-establishment of areas of native woodland. A further aim is to manage the area for timber extraction, creating revenue which can then be channelled back to enhance the woodland. But the project has not worked out in exactly the same way as was first envisaged.

The wood is not being used as much by the local community as we had thought initially, even though it's ideally situated several miles away from a number of villages and towns – Galashiels, Melrose, Tweedbank, Stow, Lauder, Blainslie and Earlston. There are a lot of people in the area but the

Axes for Trees. Stead made one wooden axe-head for each day of 1986. The proceeds from this signed, limited edition went towards planting a hardwood forest. To Stead, the axe is a symbol of slow individual progress and is in balance with nature. The rhythm of the axe has suddenly become the momentum of mechanised change.

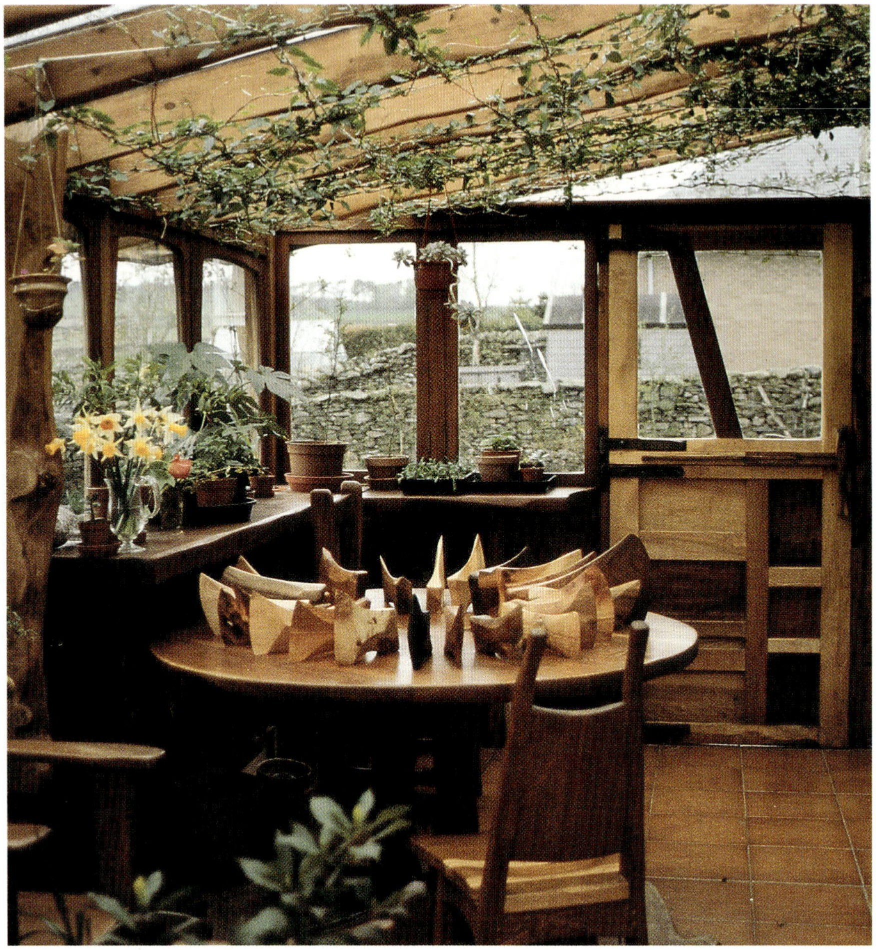

A ballet performance in the Borders Community Woodland.

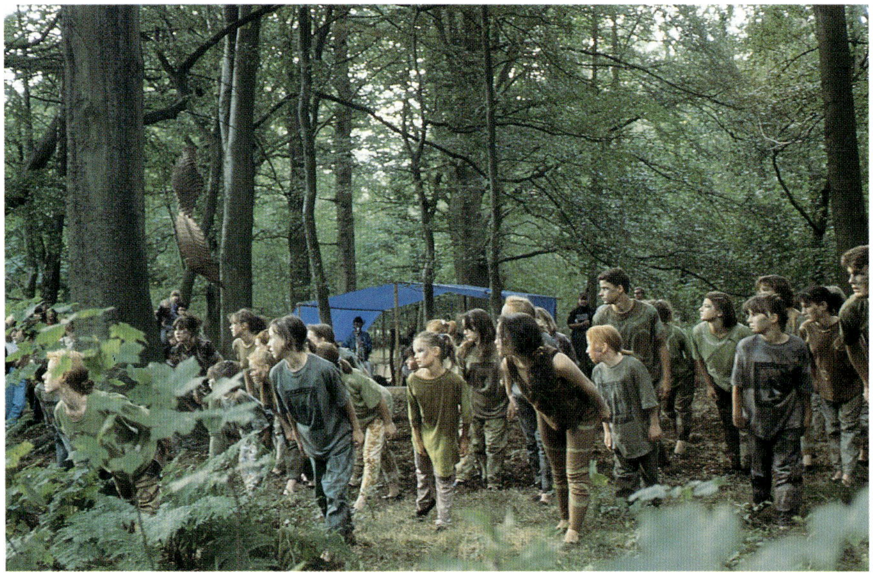

wood isn't on anyone's immediate doorstep. I think it's an idea that's ahead of its time. We thought we'd get more people coming out to work in the wood and to enjoy themselves. In fact, very few people are interested in that, although I'm sure that in ten years time it will be much more acceptable than jogging! There is a basic need for people to do physical work, to learn fairly simple skills and to achieve something which is useful. It is a leisure pursuit that will develop but these are very much the early stages.

Borders Community Woodland has allowed those involved to extend their awareness of trees and related issues. An important component of Stead's 'Layers' exhibition involved a minimum of ten percent of revenue from sales going towards the setting up of tree nurseries in Nepal. This was to help a project being co-ordinated by Chris Evans, a VSO worker, who was attempting to introduce the concept of permaculture to local farmers.

TS
Some of the money from 'Layers' went to promote tree plantations and tree nurseries in schools, so that the schools would be paid and the children could plant trees. It was really so good – a sort of community woodland approach. The project grows trees for fodder which involves cutting off a certain amount of branches. The leaves will feed cattle, and the wood is used for fuel. Those involved in the scheme weave cloth and are setting up looms linked to permacultural methods. Permaculture is a very nice approach to changing the land-use. A number of different farms have been set up and the farmers are telling other farmers that the methods work. It's not some European delegation that's getting a percentage for selling fertiliser; it's a very small exciting thing. The project has been running for five years.

There is a strong link, therefore, between Stead's position as a user of wood and his involvement as a provider, grower and sustainer of wood as a raw material. All of these aspects are strongly linked in a natural, organic and constantly evolving relationship. Another permaculture plan involves David Bellamy and David Norman. The latter is Managing Director of a Glasgow-based timber importer. In 1990, Norman launched the Scottish Hardwood Charter whose signatories (including Stead) have pledged only to import timber from sustainably-managed sources. Bellamy and Norman identified a tribe in Brazil who supply such timber. Despite the rich and complex ecosystem, the people are experiencing dietary and hygiene problems due to an influx of Western processed foods. Stead is supporting the project by providing sculpture to those who contribute more than £250-00; the ultimate aim is to help the people to start growing other crops on a small scale using permacultural methods.

In Scotland, in addition to replenishing supplies of timber for future generations, Stead also hopes to help provide a source of supply for the present, thereby creating a demand for home grown timber. He has proposed a scheme to the local authorities in the Borders where trees which are due to be felled are not burnt or used as mining chocks but are collected, milled and offered for sale to meet local needs.

TS
There's a lot of timber growing on farms, but often there are only a few trees on each and it's difficult to market and transport these individually. If the tree was at the roadside and accessible, it could be picked up and taken to a central point with a marketing area. Some of the butts could be sold as veneer logs or saw logs and the latter could be taken to other mills. The centre would also saw up the trees, air-drying them and kilning them as a material which could be used immediately by local people and schools. There are hundreds of places where you can buy imported timbers, whereas it's very difficult to buy ready-to-use British timbers. It's a catch-22 situation: nobody is using them because they're not available; and they're not available because nobody is asking for them.

A scheme of this nature already exists in Wales: Coed Cymru (Welsh Wood) – and operates remarkably successfully. Local authorities are obliged to use native woods and an infrastructure allows the use of available machinery and plant. Farmers, for example, are able to utilise timber growing on their own land which was previously inaccessible because of conversion costs.

As an essential component of this scheme, Stead envisages workshop facilities which will enable people to gain hands-on experience of working with wood. The costs of hiring workshop space and equipment, added to the difficulty of obtaining adequate instruction, effectively prohibit any real woodworking experience for the majority of people. We can look enviously in the direction of our continental neighbours like Denmark and Sweden who, as a matter of course, provide state-funded community workshops not only for woodworking but also for a wide range of other practical skills – glassmaking, metalwork and ceramics, to name a few.

TS
Ulrich Loening, for example, of the Centre for Human Ecology at Edinburgh University recognised the need for this kind of thing very early on and has tried to do something about it by setting up Lothian Tree Services. This involves using a portable band-mill which can convert trees to boards on-site, thereby immediately adding to the value of the timber. It's a business which needs a lot of capital and is a long-term project. In many ways it's too late for a lot of trees. For example, there should have been an intelligent policy of storing and planking the millions of trees which died because of Dutch elm disease.This is a major resource but most of it is burned. Similarly there was no infrastructure for dealing with the huge number of trees that fell in the gales a few years ago. A great deal of that was burned and a lot was exported, with only a small percentage being retained for home use.

Selected Exhibitions

Scotland Creates

In 1990 Stead exhibited at the McLellan Galleries' 'Scotland Creates' exhibition which celebrated 5,000 years of art and design in Scotland. The organisers, Barbara and Murray Grigor, invited Stead to re-create one of the houses in the Neolithic Orkney village of Skara Brae, in the main service-lift shaft in the gallery. The idea immediately appealed to Stead and he revisited Orkney to research the project and was soon consumed by an indeflectable enthusiasm.

TS

This was a very interesting and challenging job – it would have been more difficult to make happen had it been a museum contract to make an exact replica. Because the lift-shaft dropped below the level of the gallery floor, it conveyed a very good impression of the sub-terranean nature of Skara Brae. It was very much Murray Grigor's idea and inspiration. For me, it involved the discovery of aesthetic and cultural roots. I first heard about Skara Brae at Trent Polytechnic – a tutor referred to the stone dressers. It was a wonderful excuse to go back to Orkney and see Skara Brae.

Stead's Skara Brae was more of an interpretation of the original than a replica. It consisted of thousands of stone-shaped blocks of split wood – again mainly elm – which were fixed to sheets of particle-board using a combination of glue and screws. Out of necessity, Stead constructed the exhibit in separate sections so that it could be transported easily. 'The Scotsman' critic Emilio Coia wrote: 'Wood is to Tim Stead what paint was to Eardley or Van Gogh'. The installation was very well received and from 1995 will be on permanent display at The Hunterian Museum and Art Gallery in Glasgow.

TS

Skara Brae is one of the earliest landmarks of Scottish creativity. The project came down to how I interpreted that. Do you simply have photographs or slides . . .? Stone would have been far too heavy and there were only two days in which to install the piece. Wood is a good solution – much better, for example, than making a fibre-glass replica to make it look like real stone. It is a clear transposition from one material to another; the fact that it was made from wood gave it a very warm feeling. In Orkney there's usually a howling gale, it's wet and the stone is cold. You feel the Skara Brae houses would have been very uncomfortable places to live in. Whereas the wood is warm and makes it seem a civilised place to live – more like it would have been originally, bearing in mind that these would have been covered dwellings.

To accompany the Skara Brae exhibit, Stead made a variety of artefacts derived from actual Neolithic archaeological finds. While the purpose of many of these artefacts remains obscure, one important aspect was undoubtedly their tactile quality. The touching and handling of his work is always something Stead is keen to encourage.

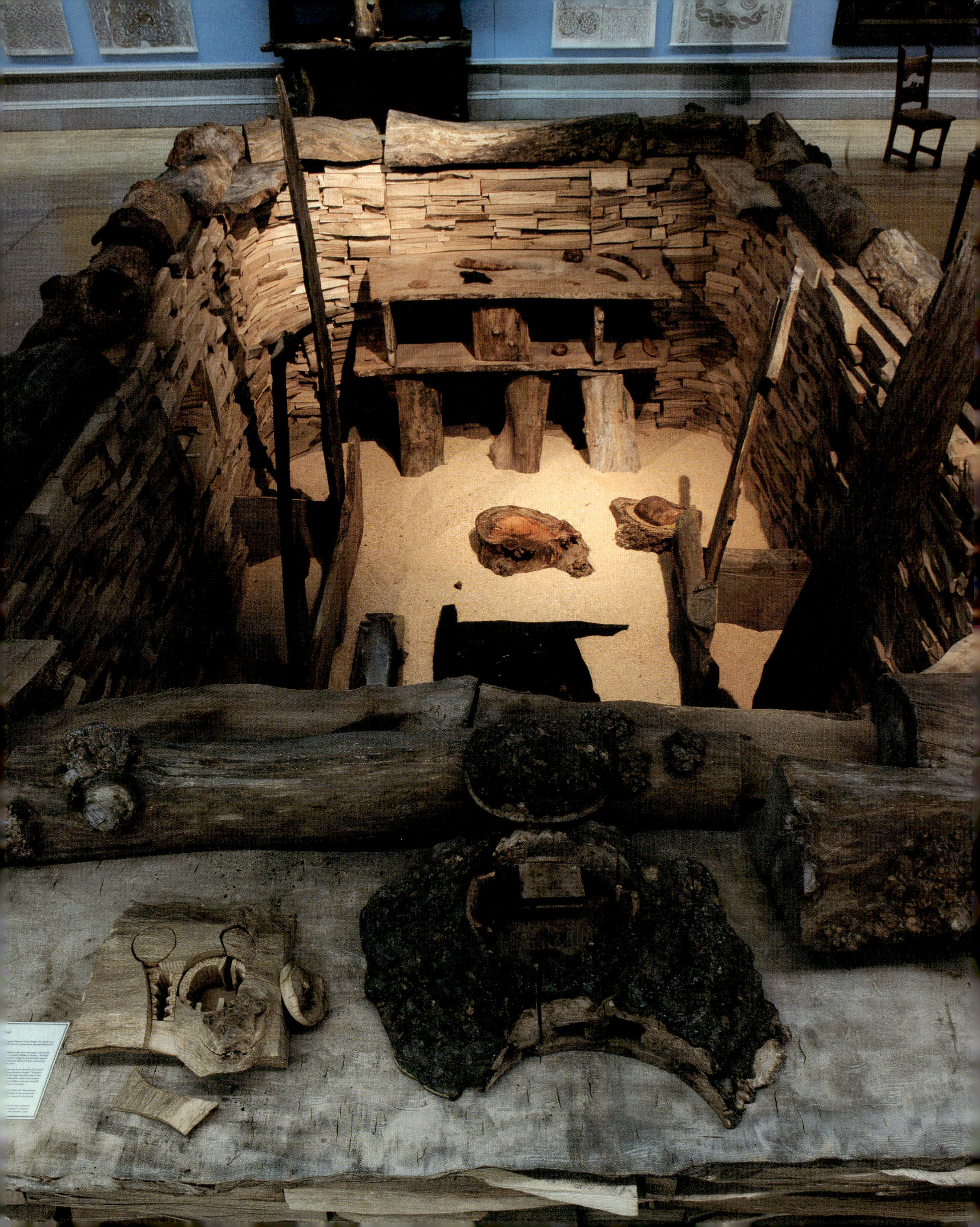

Opposite:
Skara Brae in a lift-shaft
Photograph: Sean Hudson

Right:
'Mountain Seed'

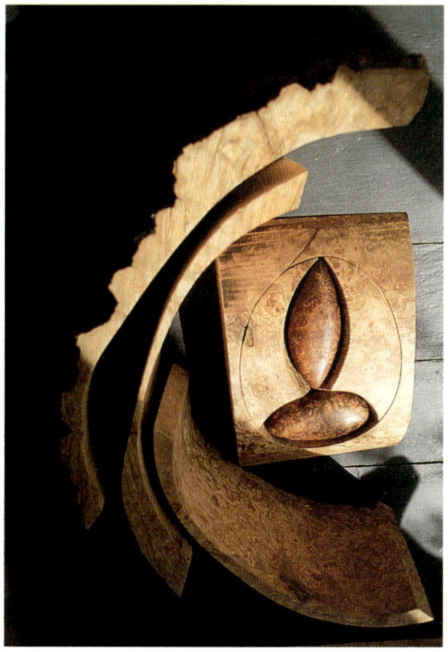

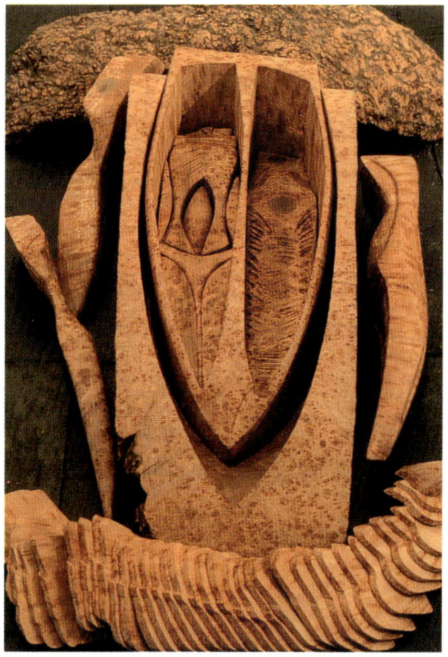

'Double Shuttle'
Photograph: Antonia Reeve

Left and Right:
'Whale Song'

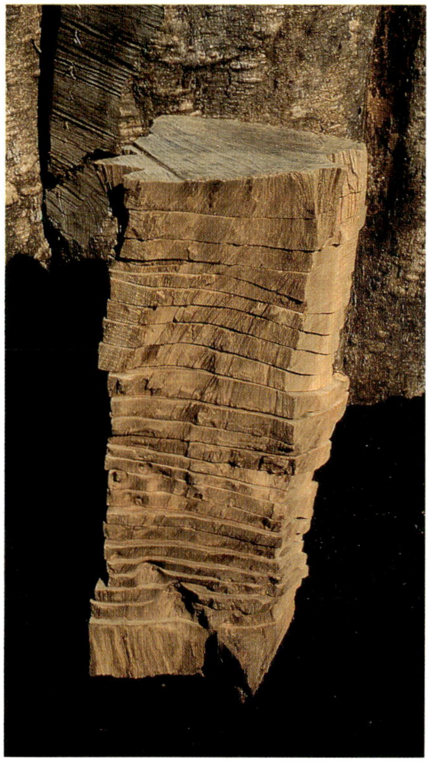

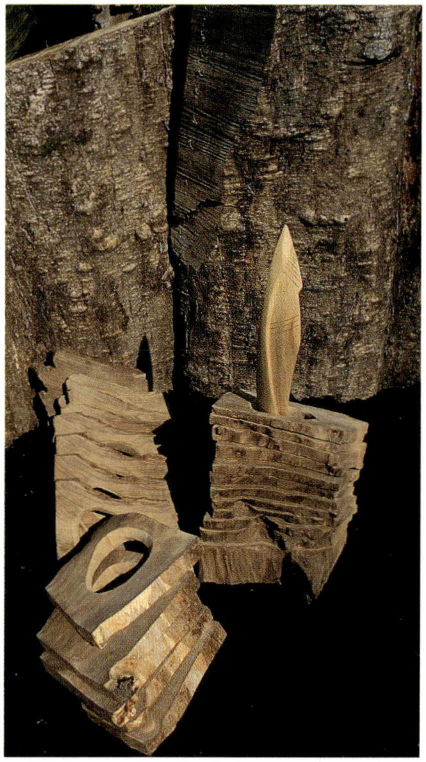

Layers

The work in the touring exhibition 'Layers' represented a fundamental departure for Stead in a number of respects. This was the first exhibition composed exclusively of non-functional, sculptural pieces – and in a gallery setting. Previously Stead had always combined sculpture and furniture, and this had predominantly been shown in contexts where the label 'art for art's sake' could not be applied. Initially, Stead was wary of showing his work in what could be perceived of as an élitist environment.

TS

I was very worried that people might ignore or dismiss the pieces, or not want to open them up and look inside them. I thought this might be asking too much – it could have been interpreted as an imposition and might have left people feeling self-conscious and unwilling to participate. But on the opening night there was such a good feeling – it sounded like a snooker hall! There were bits of wood being pushed in and pulled out. People were smiling, laughing and really enjoying themselves. Every weekend people were bringing children. Several groups of blind people came. It was really well received.

Integrating the functional with sculptural in previous work had always been a way of side-stepping the anxiety of being labelled 'élitist'.

TS

'Art' is very alienating to most members of the public and sculpture, particularly, is just not well-received at all. There's no real continuity within our culture of objects, outside of churches, having any special significance in people's lives. The big sculptures tend either to be of military figures on horses, or huge modern things which seem to be about saying so much – but nobody can quite understand what. It is very difficult to say something simple in a piece of sculpture and have it on big pedestal in a city centre. People will always assume that it is much more laden with meaning than it actually is. A lot of the work that I've done is about finding ways of making sculpture more available and accessible to people. They respond very well through a whole range of intellects and backgrounds.

In 'Layers', Stead's starting point was to take the most mundane of objects – 'a lump of firewood' – and reveal the mysteries that lay within. These mysteries take not only the form of the natural patterning within the wood but also, in combination, the shapes and structures created by the imagination of the artist. An essential element of the success of these pieces was to allow participation in the process. One of the pitfalls of most people's experience of art is that the relationship between artwork and audience is not fully participatory – best exemplified by the words 'DO NOT TOUCH'. All the 'Layers' pieces carried an invitation – 'Please Touch'. This extension of the normal experience of art allowed a full sensual involvement – not just looking, but also touching, smelling and hearing. If people are allowed to explore without inhibitions they will experience a greater feeling of reward and achievement.

TS
There is a fascination with the 'Layers' pieces of opening them up and having shapes and forms which you can touch and explore yourself, rather than having a piece of sculpture which is 'very important' because of its 'formal values'. The 'Layers' pieces don't have any of those pretentious values. Saying 'Please Touch' is like giving people a fiver– they respond so warmly! I think if I had said 'Do Not Touch' people would have taken offence and thought the whole thing was too distant; they would have disliked it. Touch is so important.

'Yew Bone', for example, is a log eighteen-inches in length, which has been sawn in half, lengthwise; from it Stead has created a layered puzzle of interconnecting shapes. Yew provides contrasting textures and colours for the bone-like forms which lie within. One is invited to take part in the unravelling like a ritualistic exhumation. 'Chambered Cairn' reveals Stead's fascination with the distant past, so that the puzzle becomes archaeology. Many of the 'Layers' pieces are a direct result of Stead's experience of Orkney. The Orkney landscape, littered with evidence of the ancient past – brochs, chambered cairns, burial mounds – provided rich inspiration.

TS
A number of 'boat' pieces like 'Double Shuttle' and 'Spawning Voyage' link the idea of seed, fertility and voyages. The piece entitled 'Vanished Gods & Banished Gods' gives an idea of what you find within hills and mountains: sacred areas. In a sense, when the belief stops the Gods die off or are put out. Almost what you would expect to find is a figure of a cowed God.

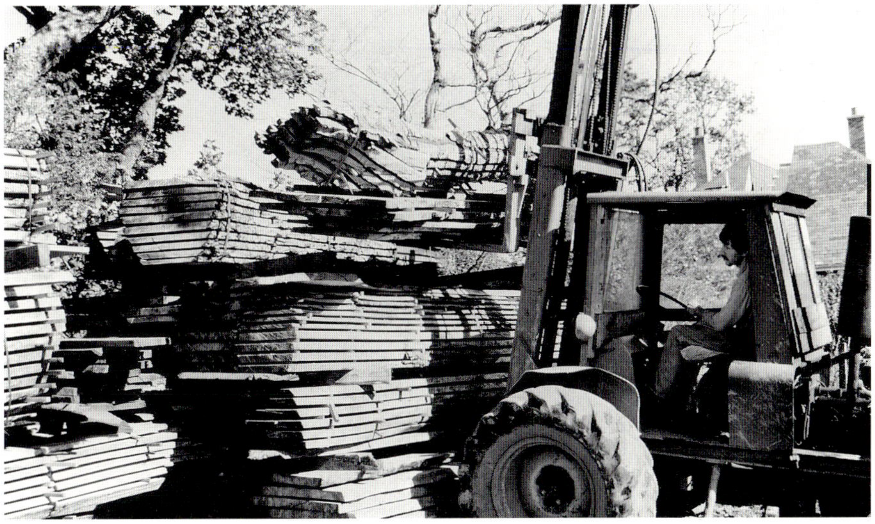

Lifting stacks of timber

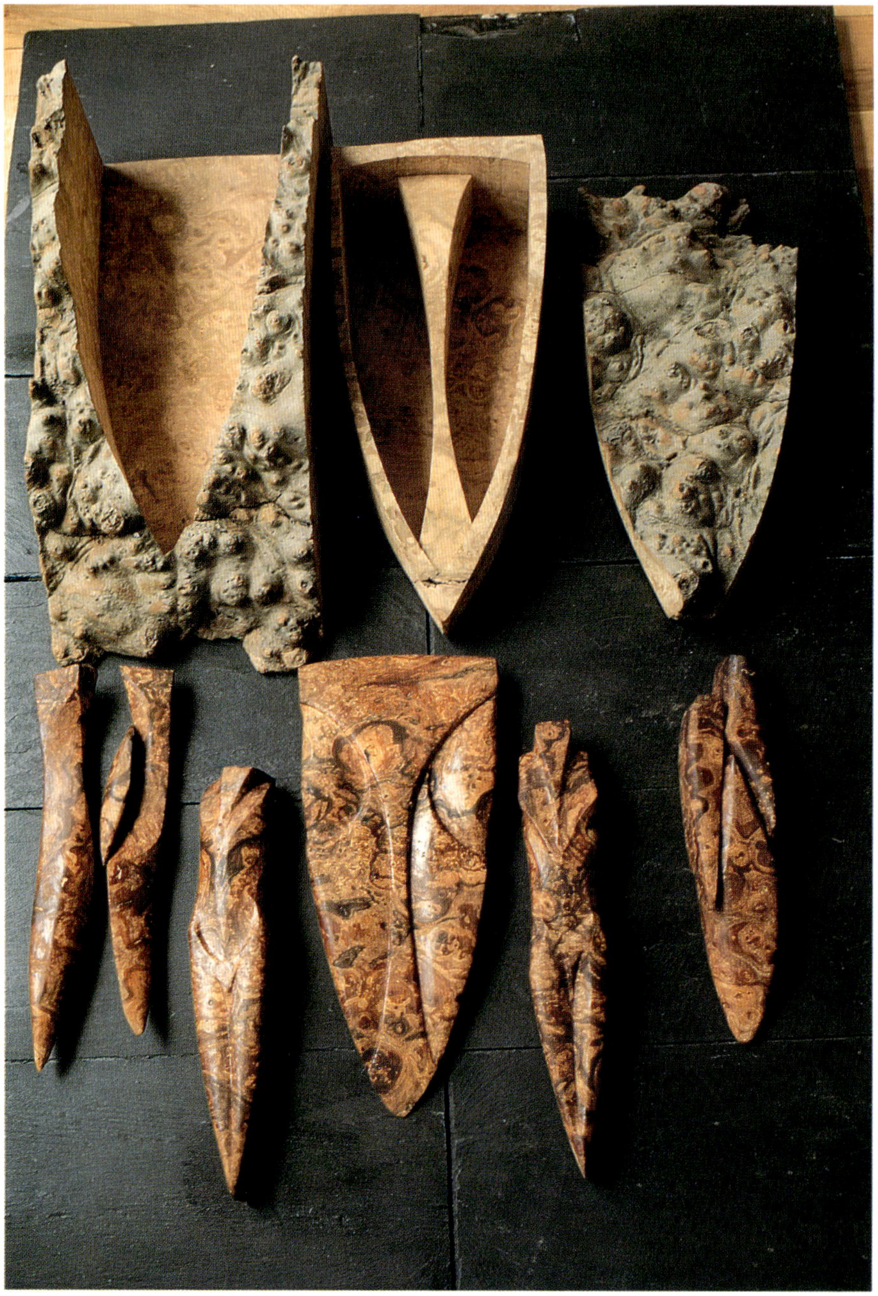

'Mask - Mime - Mumming'. A block of burr-elm is opened, revealing a boat-like form. Within this, a mask, elongated and pointed. Below this mumming surface, two figures – male and female. And beneath these, other shapes, strangely primitive: bone and seed, echoing the harmonious rhythms of nature. Layer upon layer of hidden meaning – an invitation to open and explore.

'*Yew Bone*'
Photograph: Antonia Reeve

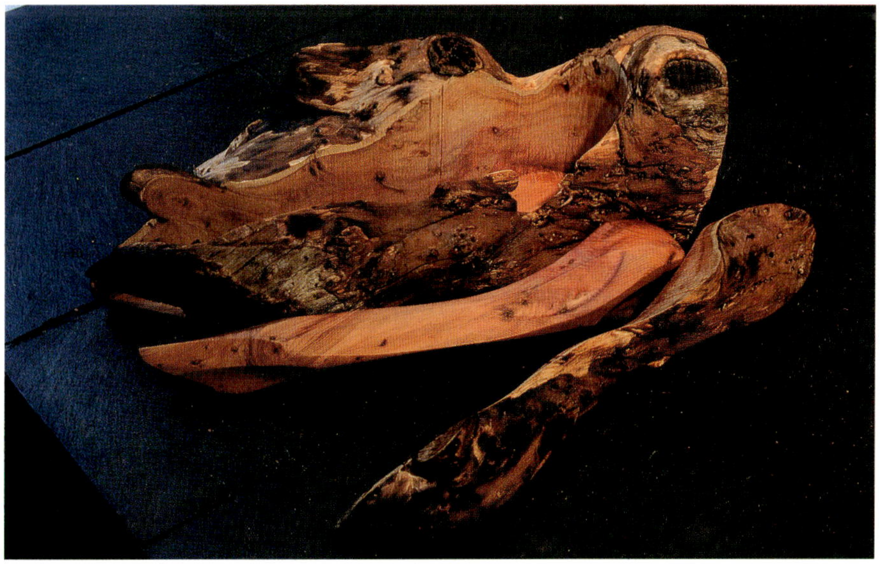

'*Chambered Cairn*'

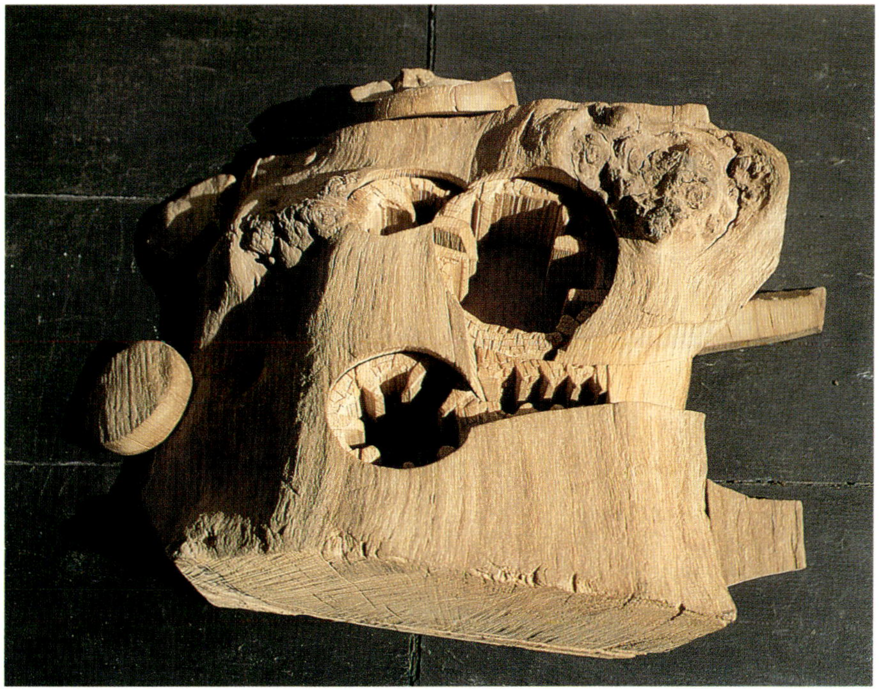

Spirits of the Forest

'Spirits of the Forest' was held at the Glasgow Arts Centre in October 1991. The season, which included sculpture, theatre, painting and demonstrations concentrated on wood and the many issues which surround it – papermaking, recycling, deforestation and conservation. Stead contributed both sculpture and furniture; the former category included hanging spiral 'bird' forms, two huge chairs with towering backs and an enormous 'trilobite' sculpture situated on the floor. These pieces were made from ash using a technique not previously used by Stead and involved band-sawing successive strips from a single block of wood. This revealed fascinating patterning echoed in other natural forms – wave ripples in sand, shells and cones. One obvious conclusion was that a similar 'chaotic' logic informs the geometry of a whole range of forms in nature.

TS

The exciting thing is to take simple lumps of wood and do something which is very easy and very obvious – it's taken me years to realise this and do it. Each piece, when cut away from the other, is bound to link and bound to have grain that matches. There's very little interference from me – apart from the cutting. But the imagery which comes from it is very strong. By slicing up logs you get references from one material to another material; it looks like bones or leaves or geological structures or insect bodies. Making sculpture gives that element of play – just do it and see what happens. Some of the images and some of the techniques and ways of working and looking at things start working back into the furniture.

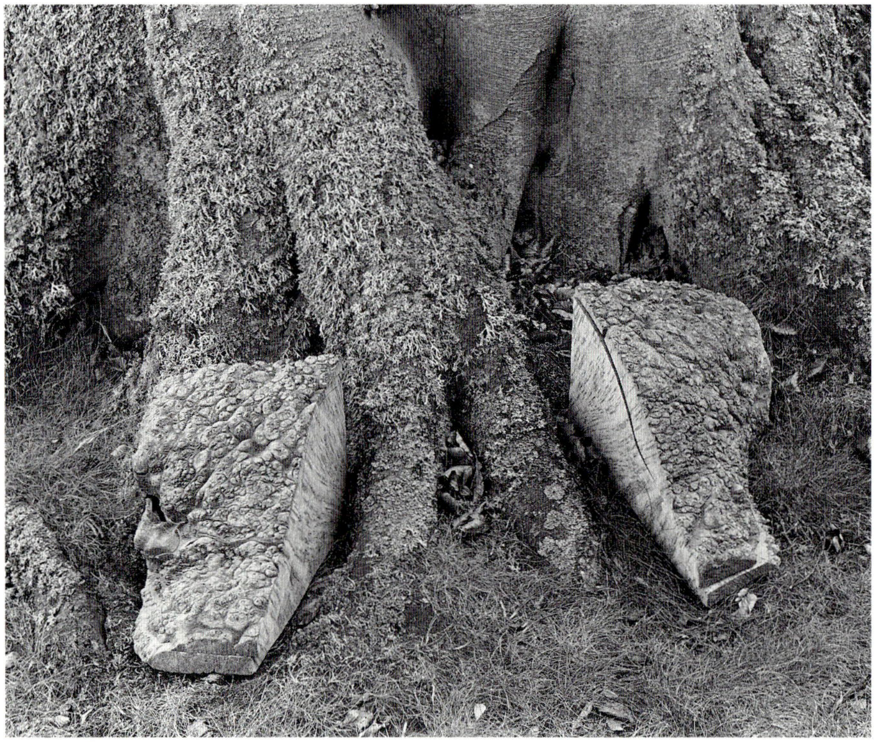

Opposite, right and below:
'Vanished Gods &
Banished Gods'
Photographs: Iain Mackenzie.

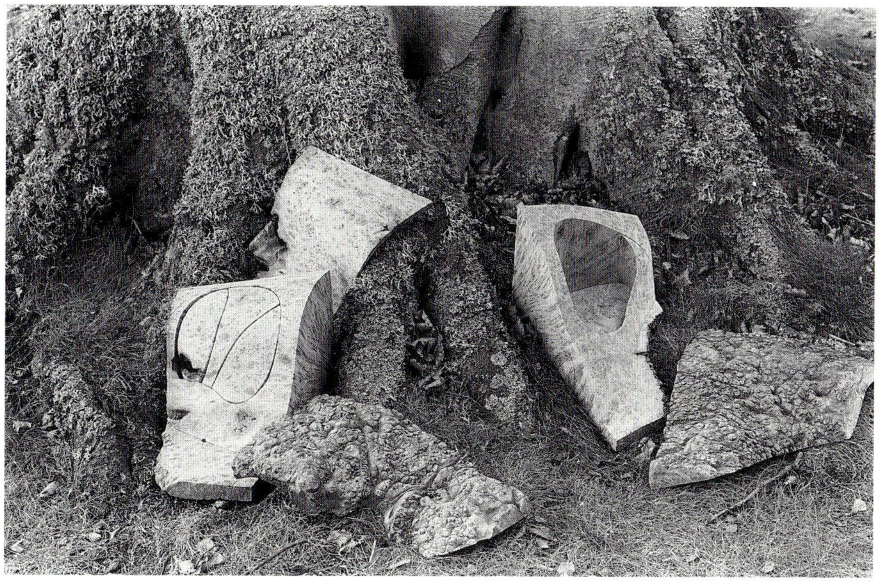

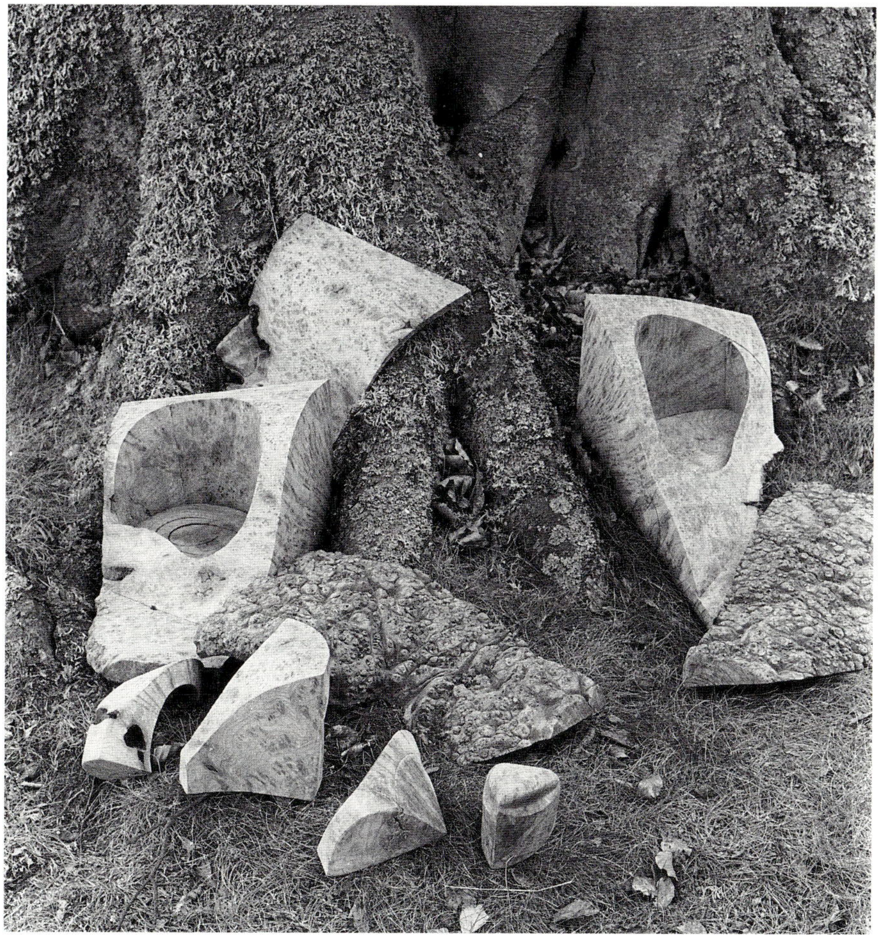

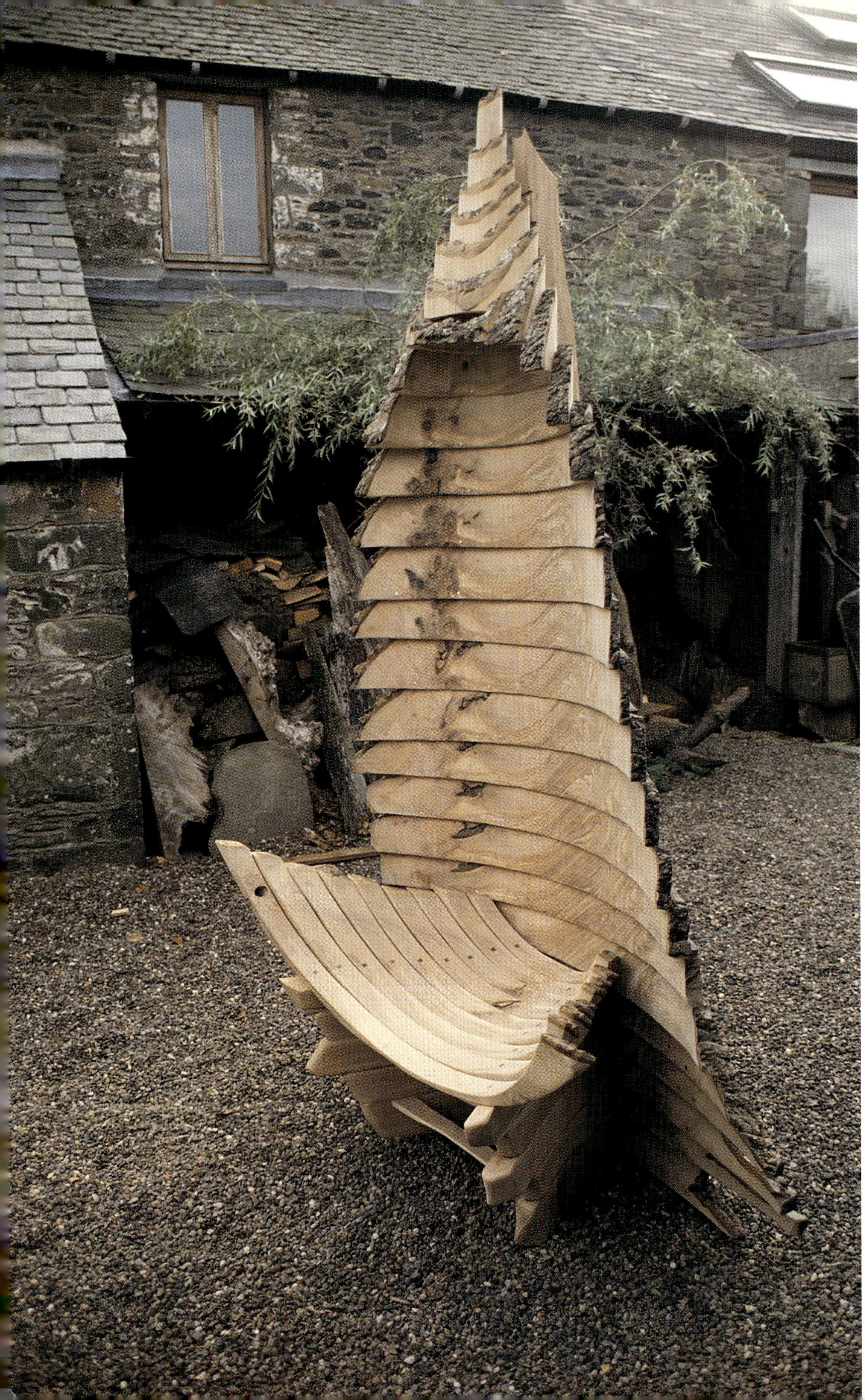

This chair is a direct result of Stead's experimentation with sculpture.

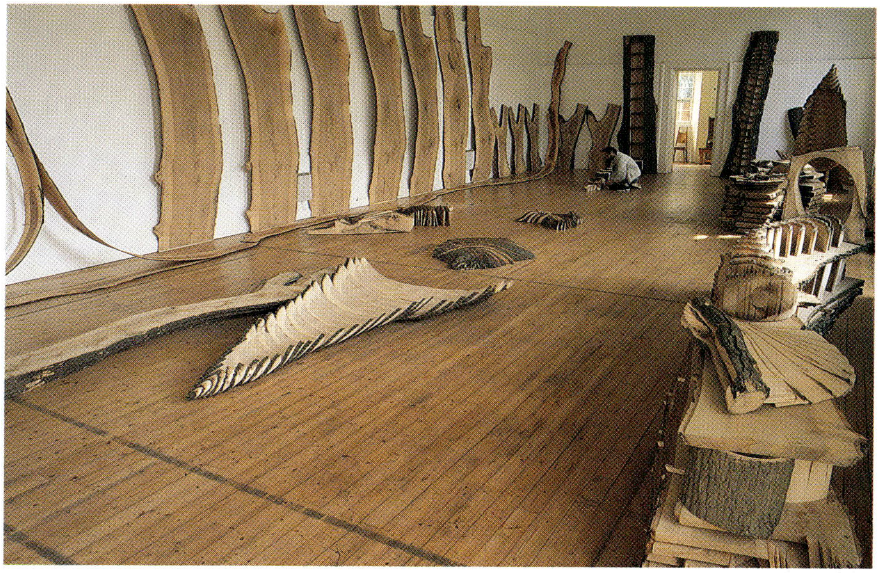

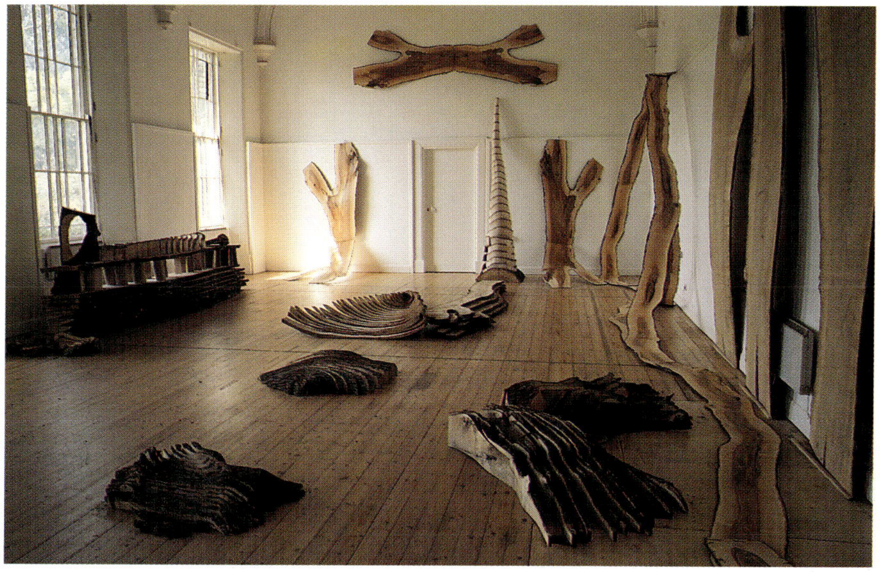

Above and below:
'The Botanic Ash'
displayed in The Royal
Botanic Garden's
Caledonian Hall.
Photograph: Debbie White

'Slip Knot'
Photograph: Iain Mackenzie

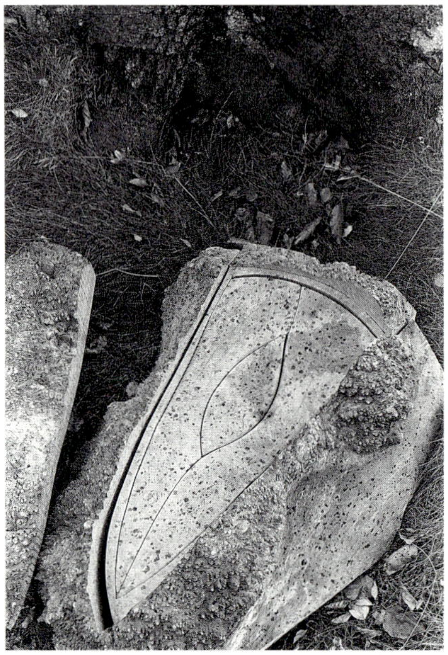

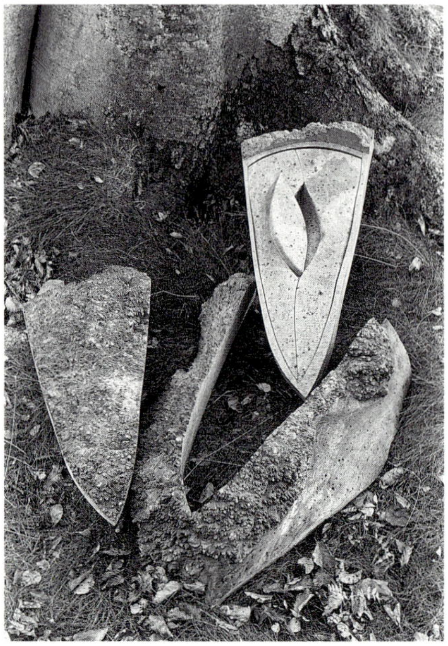

'Slip Knot'
Photograph: Iain Mackenzie

'Clutch'
Photograph: Iain Mackenzie

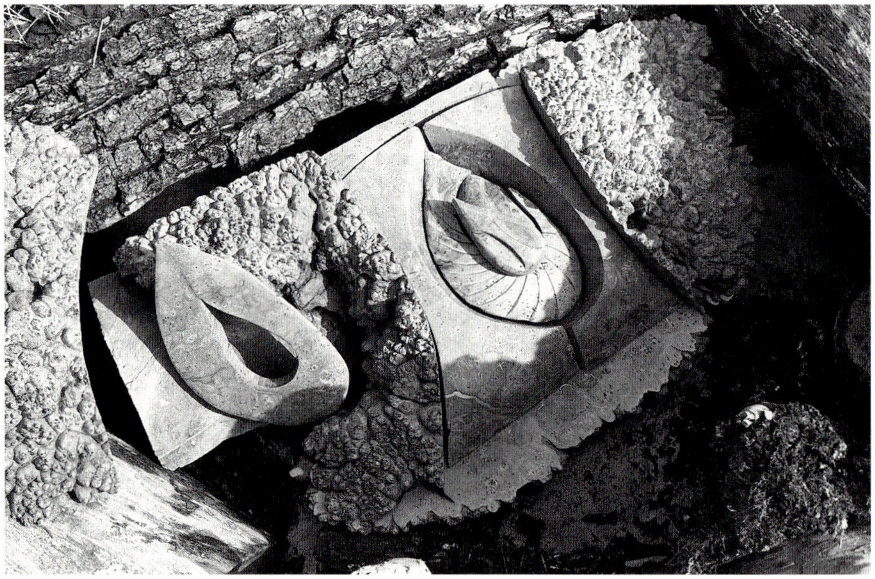

Opposite
'Mined Landscape'
Photographs: Iain Mackenzie

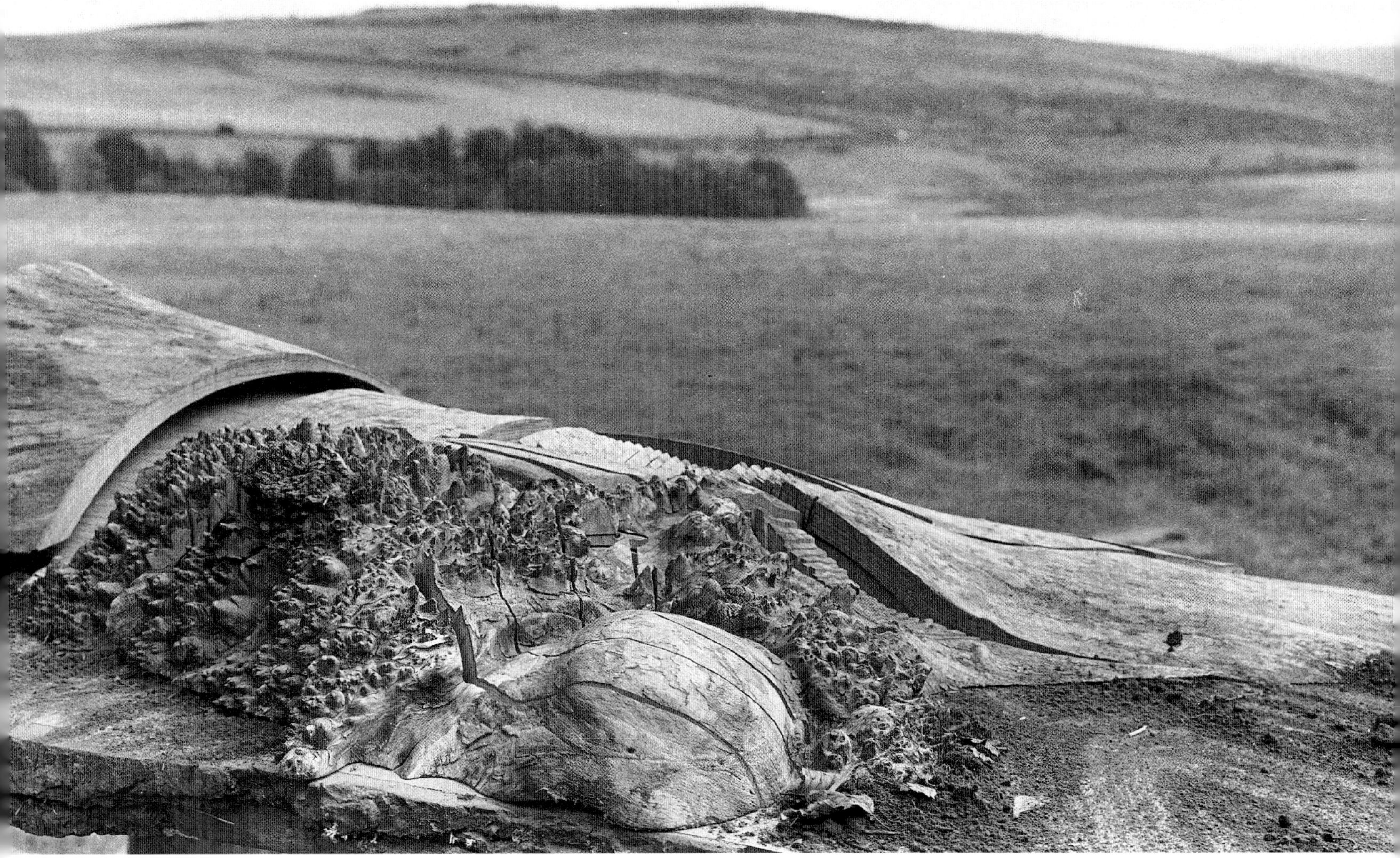

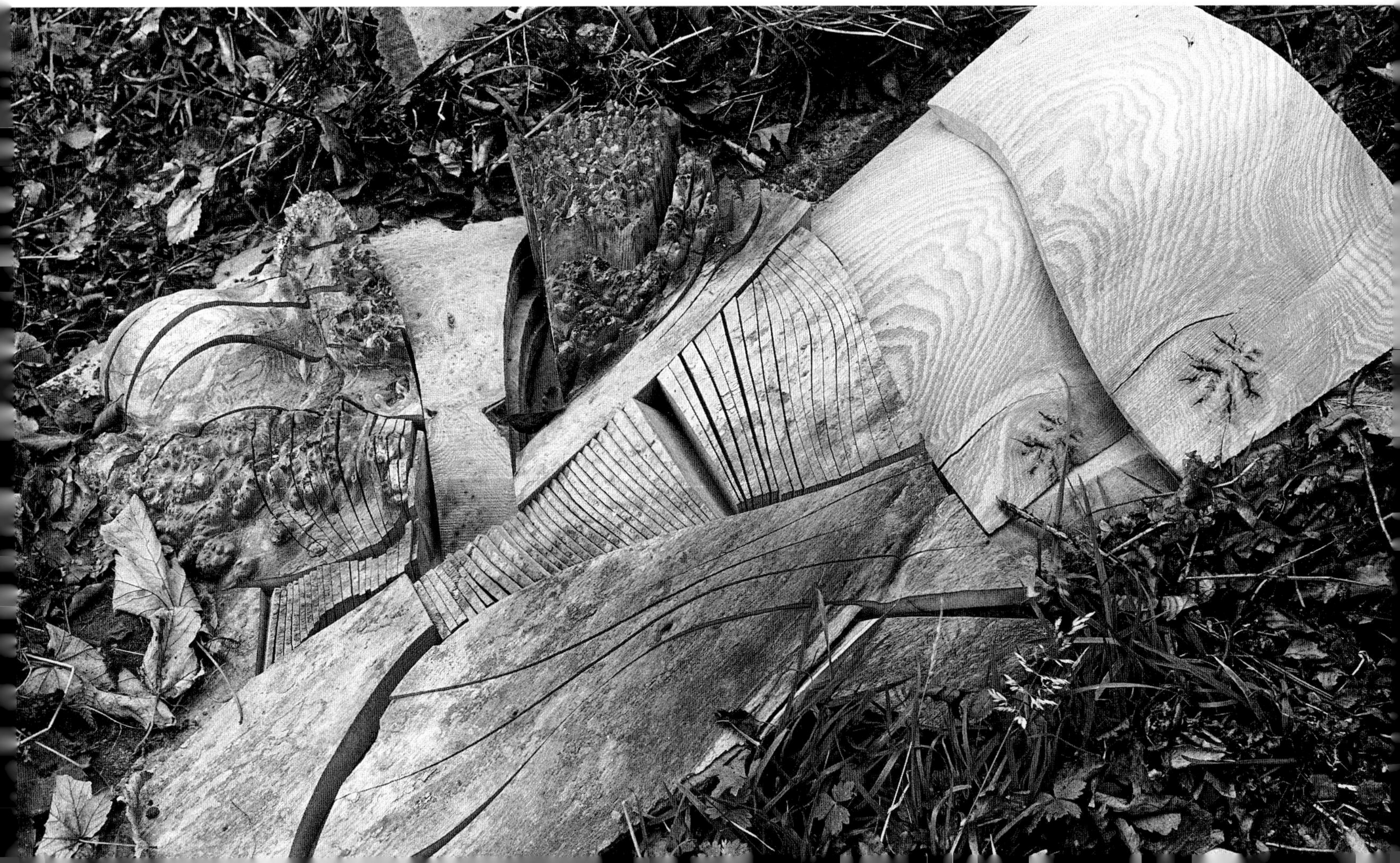

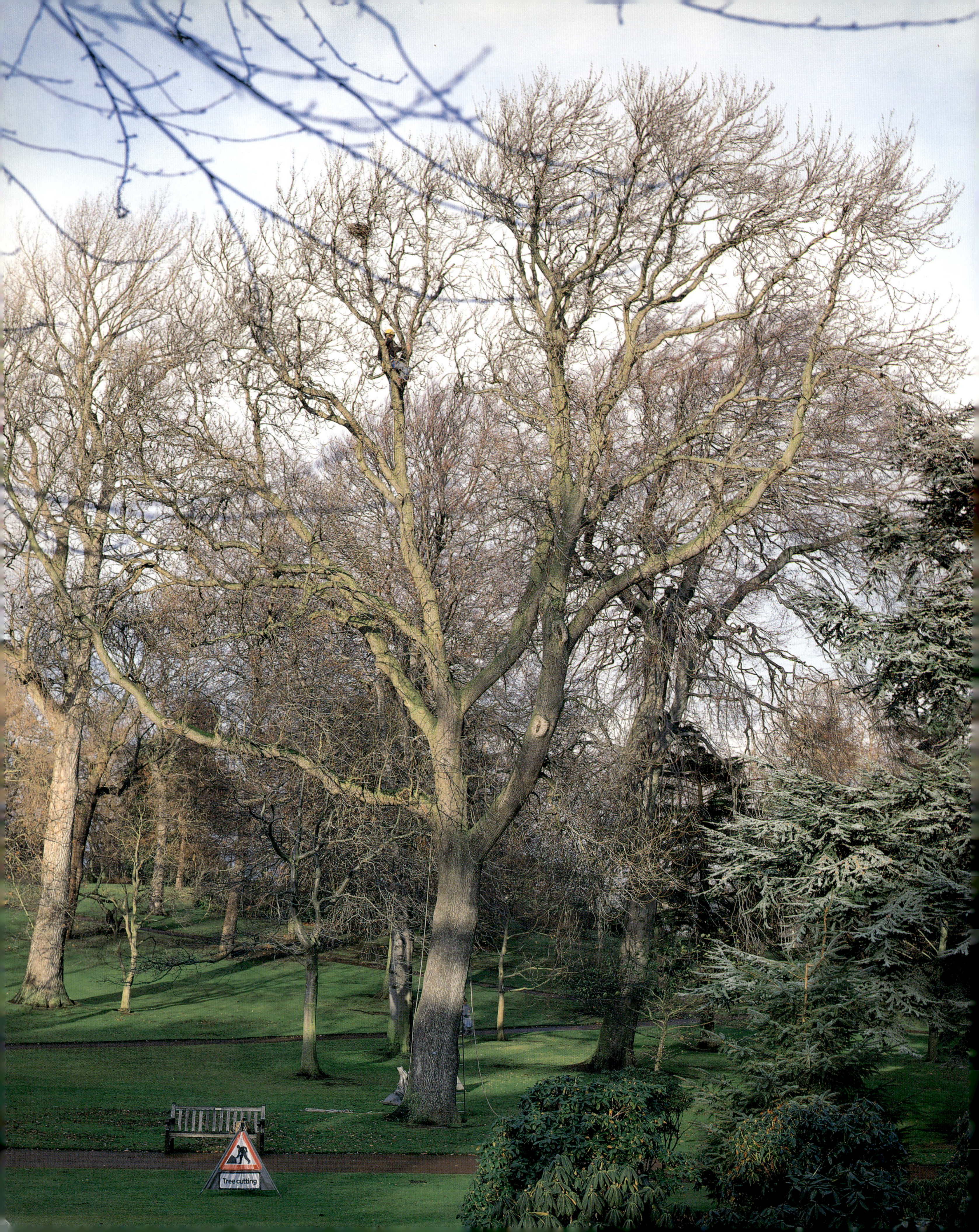
Tree cutting

The Botanic Ash

TS
I find it wonderfully difficult to grasp that the tiny seed which I hold in my hand contains all the necessary information to become a tree weighing many tons. This tiny pod carries a collection of messages which have been passed on over millions of years: when to germinate; how to make a bud; how to form a leaf; how to form a flower. As branches grow, this seed already has the information to construct grain which will support a ton of wood and leaves. The branches are able to bend in the wind and leaves can turn to seek out light. I often work with the wood of trees that are over a hundred and fifty years old: the grain has recorded a history which can be re-read. No matter how detailed the map of DNA becomes, it will always be theory; the fact that it happens will always be a miracle.

Edinburgh's Royal Botanic Garden is increasingly recognised as a major contributor to the world's understanding of botany and how this relates to wider ecological concerns. As well as specialising in plant taxonomy (the principles of botanical classification), the garden holds over two million seed samples of different plant species from around the world. It also undertakes an extensive educational programme which includes a series of exhibitions linking art and nature. Stead recognised this as a highly appropriate venue for his work and conceived an ambitious exhibition centred on a large 170-year-old ash tree which was due to be felled.

The exhibition set out to present the tree as a miraculous living organism. The majority of pieces in the exhibition were derived from this single tree. All the complicated stages of felling were recorded; and all limbs, branches and sections were numbered so that the finished work could be related back to the original structure. The main section of the tree's enormous root was extracted from the ground and washed to reveal a marvelously complex structure with many intricate forms, colours and textures.

TS
It is very sad when a tree is felled, but trees are not immortal and it is better that they are felled before they fall. If the timber is usable, then the tree has achieved its maximum potential. This was the case with the ash tree. There was very little rot or damage on its limbs, which had been well maintained by a succession of arboriculturalists. However, when it was cut down it was possible to see that the root section had been eaten away by fungus, which was slowly spreading up the butt. In a few years this tree would have been hollow and the hard usable timber would have been like sponge.

Opposite:
The 170-year-old ash tree in the Royal Botanic Garden, Edinburgh – fraxinus excelsior with homo sapiens in the correct scale.
Photograph: Debbie White

Working at the Inverleith saw-mill Stead oversaw the next stage of the project which involved cutting the main trunk into boards, some a thin as a quarter inch.

TS
When a tree is being milled, I am supposedly in control. I have to decide the

Opposite:
Setting up the bandsaw for the first cut.
Photograph: Debbie White

way the section should be positioned and at what thickness. However, the decisions I take are sometimes arbitrary. Decisions need to be made quickly and these are usually irreversible. If the relationship with the sawyer is bad then this spontaneous indecision is a potential nightmare.

The main root section of the ash was on display outside the garden's Caledonian Hall. The thinly sawn ash boards were placed around the walls inside the building. Boards were left 'in stick' to dry and a number of sculptural forms derived from the ash were also on exhibit. By revealing to a wider public the sights, smells and textures normally available to a much smaller number of people, Stead gave an immensely powerful yet simple demonstration of the miraculous nature of the tree. Another element of The Botanic Ash exhibition involved the making of an 'ash tunnel'.

TS
The ash tunnel was derived from a small section of a limb – I had never considered this before. When the limb was being milled, I initially wanted the thickness to be an inch-and-a-half, which is a very safe size. I suddenly had a thought about bending the wood and changed my mind. The whole log was cut at a quarter-inch thickness. When it was being sawn I did some sketches in a notebook and the idea evolved into a tunnel. Twenty-four boards which are a foot wide become a piece twenty-four feet long. I can't explain why this is so exciting, but I know that it was right . . . How can one explain a feeling of something being right? I spent over a year thinking about this project, yet when I am making these decisions I feel that I need to have every door of my brain open and to be almost blank.

Opposite:
The end of the first cut – removing the slab from the butt. When a tree is sawn through, each board is different and reads like a massive book revealing colours and lines which formed in the past. Suddenly they reflect light after a hundred years or more. The smell of wet sawn wood fills the air and the noise of the machines is drowned by the monumental clarity. Brushing away the sawdust, touching the wood which is cold, wet and solid never fails to release a cascade of thoughts and emotions.
Photograph: Debbie White.

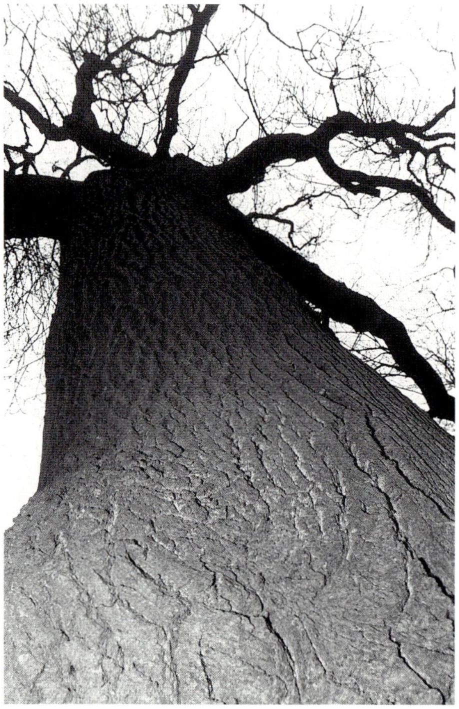

The Botanic Ash – child's-eye view. Stead was sent drawings from a group of primary school children who had visited Wooplaw Wood. The perspective of one of the drawings corresponded to that of the photograph. The child's point of view emphasises the correct scale between man and the enormous size of the mature ash.
Photograph: Debbie White

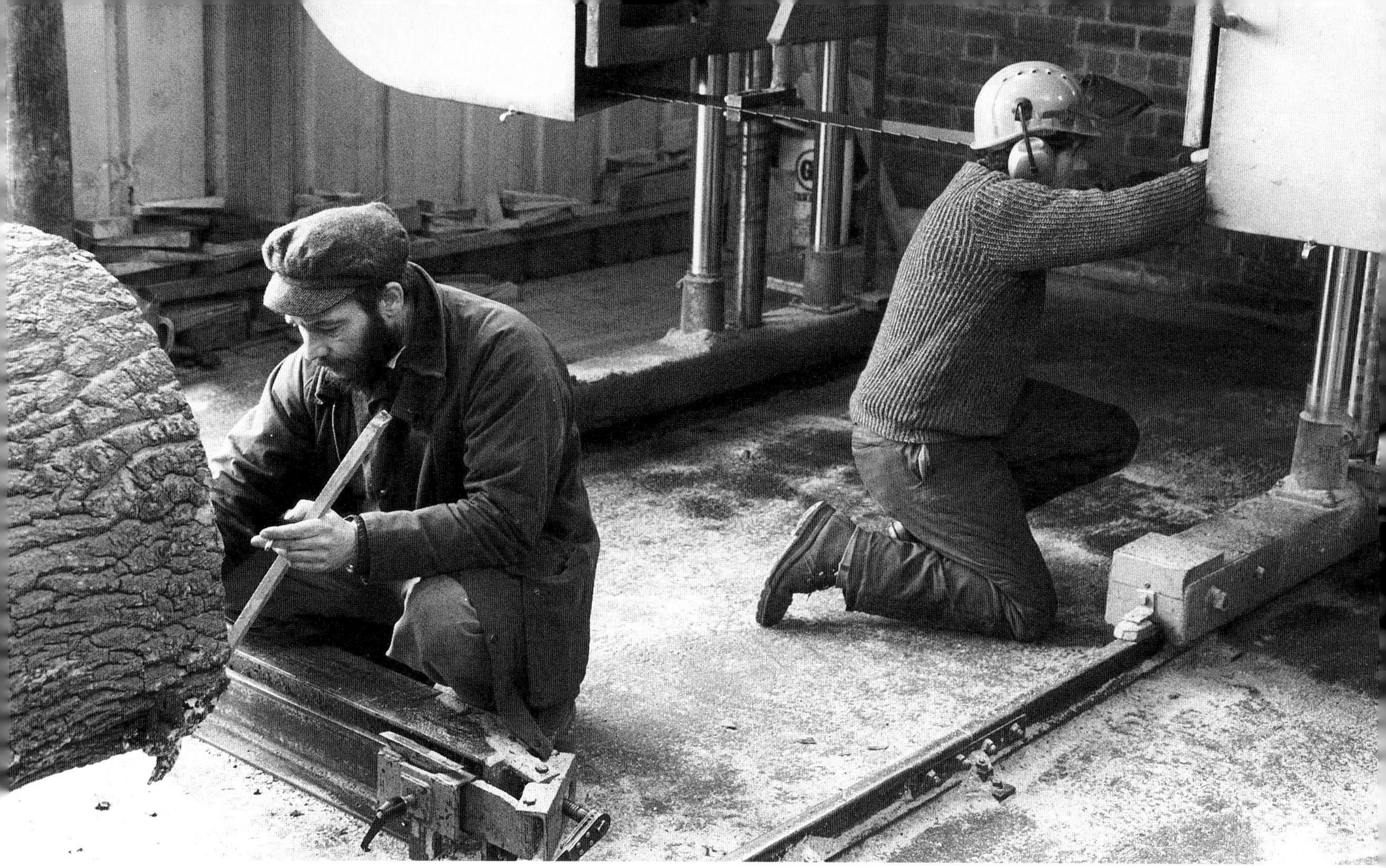

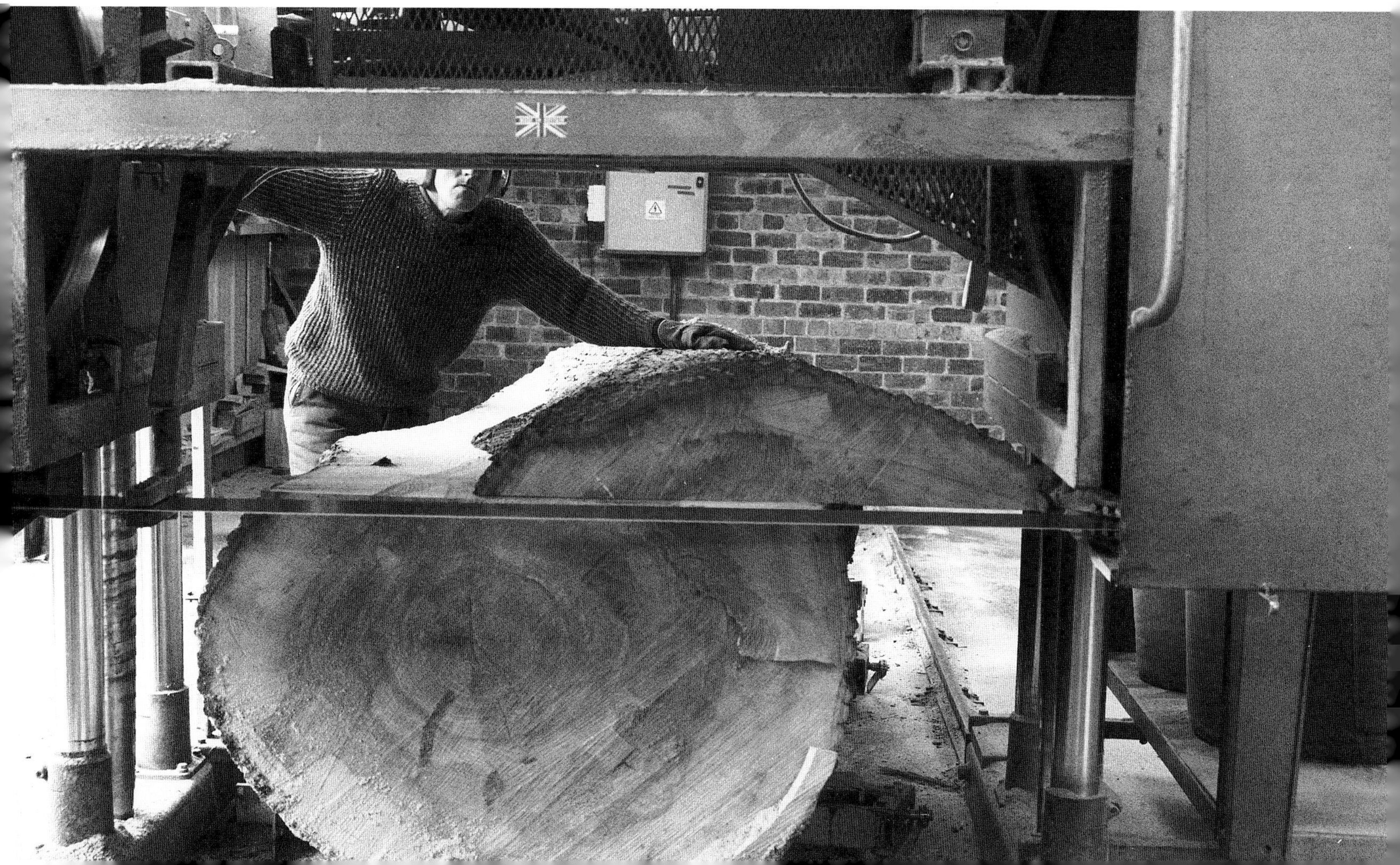

'Branch Limb'. A small limb with cut gaps which have been wedged open using sections of a smaller branch.
Photograph: Debbie White

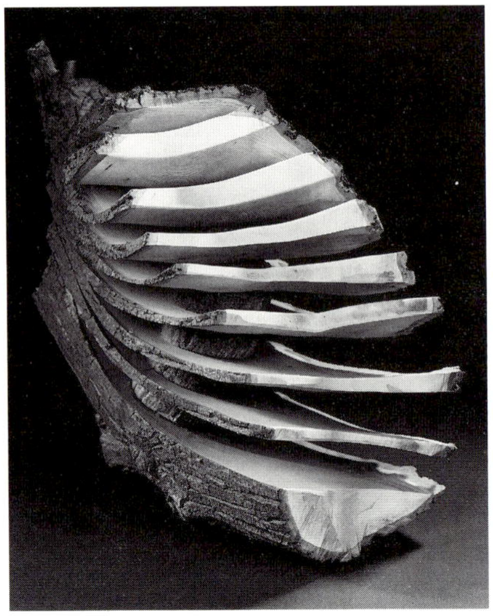

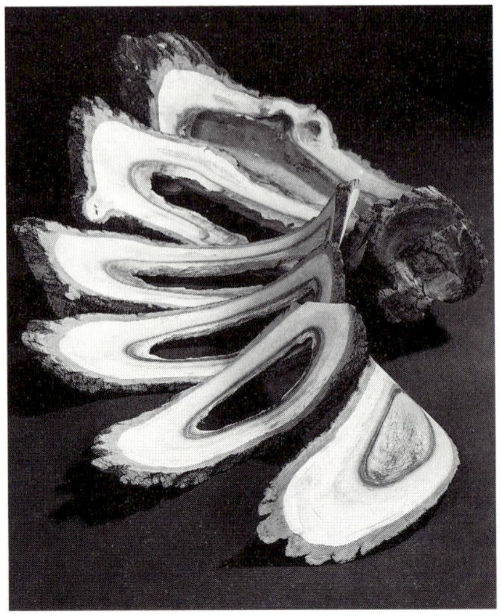

Section cut through a rotten limb.
Photograph: Debbie White

Setting up 'The Botanic Ash' exhibition.
Photograph: Debbie White

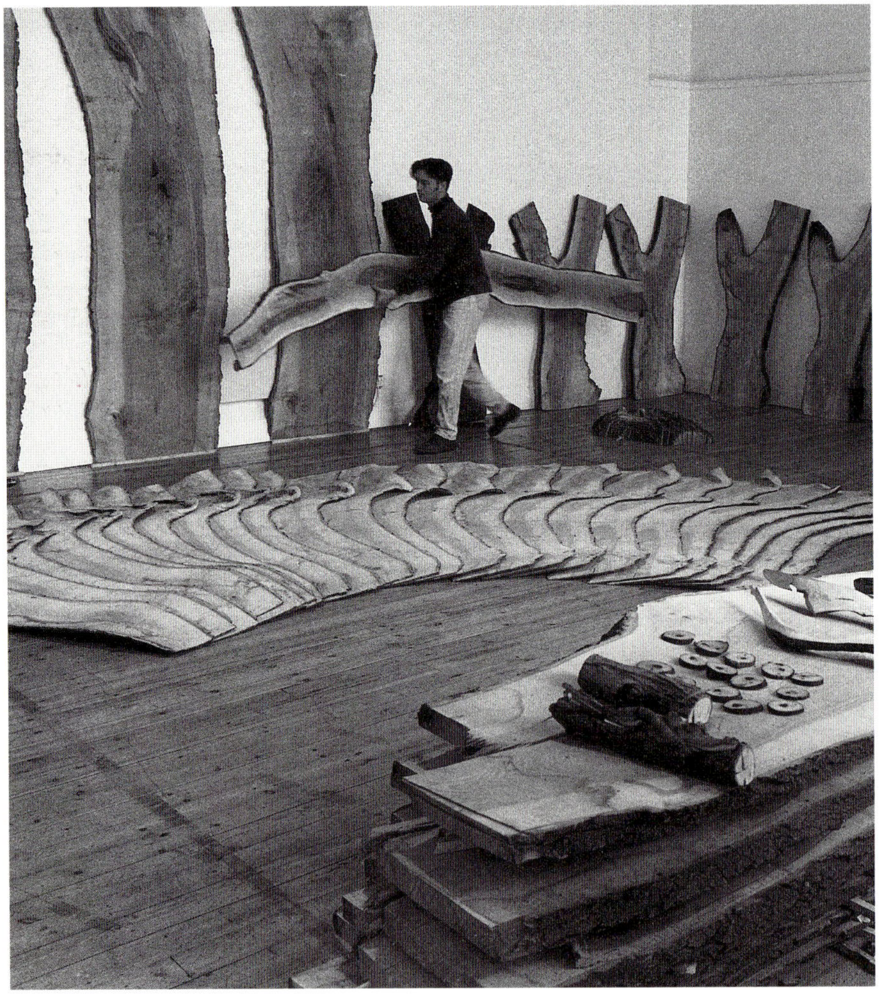

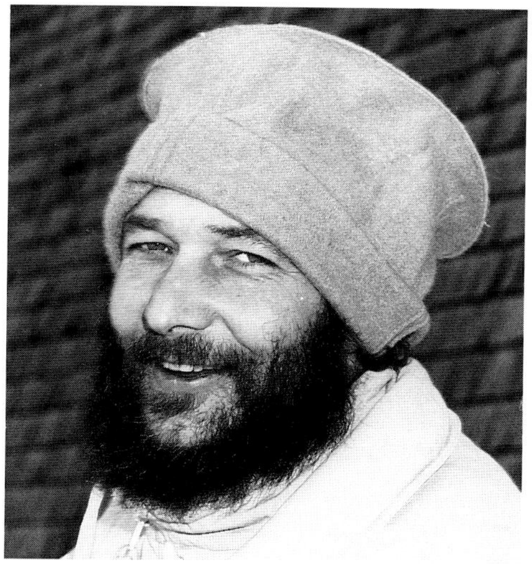

Tim Stead

Born	1952 Helsby, Cheshire, England
Trained	1974 Trent Polytechnic 1975 Glasgow School of Art
Awards	1975 Travelling Scholarship, Glasgow School of Art 1982 Crafts Fellowship, Scottish Development Agency 1989 Finalist in McGrigor-Donald sculpture competition 1989 Winner of 1989 Stella Artois Style awards 1990 Runner-up of the ABSA design competition
Member	Tent Co. Scottish Craft Centre Border Crafts Association Co-Labor Luxembourg Chairman, Borders Community Woodlands

Articles/Catalogues

'Cleavers', Craft , August 1975, Charlotte Mooney
'Fully Furnished', Craftwork, July/August 1981 (No. 42), Kitty Warnock
'Scottish Craft Furniture Antiques for the Future',Scottish Field, Feb 1981, Ken Wilson
'£3,500 Craft Award', Craftwork, May/June 1982
Tim Stead Catalogue, Collins Gallery, Helen Douglas, January 1983
'Tim Stead: Who Steers the Craft?', Craftwork, Spring 1984
'With the Grain', Woodworking Crafts, Nov. – Jan. 1985/86
'Doing What Comes Naturally', Homes & Gardens, August 1987, Judi Goodwin
'Timely Choice', House and Gardens, October, 1987
'Designers Crafts', Ideal Home, October, 1987
'Wood That Doesn't Go Against the Grain' Observer Scotland, January 1989, Kristina Woolnough
'Interiors', Scottish Field, July 1989, Sue Parrish
'His Style – Design & Anti-design', High Chic, Japan, 1989
'Kirk Commissions', Crafts, Richard Carr, 1989
'Layers – an exploration in wood by Tim Stead', Compass Gallery catalogue, January 1990
'Carved to Touch with Care and Confidence', The Glasgow Herald, January 1990, Clare Henry
'A Woodman Sparing Trees', Scotland on Sunday' January, 1990 Clare Flowers
'Carving a Reputation out of Wood', Southern Reporter, January 1990
'Glasgow 1990', Arts Review, January 1990, Clare Henry
'Chairs of Philosophy', The Observer Scotland, January 1990 W. Gordon Smith
'Endpiece', Artwork, January 1990
'Upland Trends', Crafts, March/April 1990 Kristina Woolnough
'The Corporate Solution', Crafts News, Autumn 1990
'Getting their act together for a fine exhibition', The Scotsman, November 1990, Allen Wright
'5,000 Years of Creativity', The Scotsman, November 1990, Emilio Coia,
'Liftshaft genius adds a wow factor', The Glasgow Herald, November 1990, Clare Henry
'Relishing the Rugged and Rustic', The Christian Science Monitor, April 1991, Christopher Andrea
'The Caddis and the Carpenter', Reforesting Scotland, Autumn 1991, Bernard Planterose
'Taking Wood to a Higher Plane', The Scotsman, January, 1993, Giles Sutherland
'Tim Stead' Prospect (RIAS magazine), January, 1993, Jamie MacFarlane

Solo Exhibitions

1976 Scottish Craft Centre, Edinburgh
1978 Collins Gallery, University of Strathclyde, Glasgow
1983 Collins Gallery, University of Strathclyde, Glasgow
1985 Galerie Arcoma, Paris
1986 Galerie Co-Labor, Luxembourg
1986 Wetheriggs Country Pottery, Cumbria
1987 Gossipgate Gallery, Cumbria
1990 Compass Gallery, Glasgow
1990 Museum of Natural History, Dundee
1990 Indesign, Chester
1990 Friends Meetings House, Edinburgh
1990 Iona Gallery, Kingussie
1990 Swanson Gallery, Thurso

Group Exhibitions

1973 Northern Young Contemporaries
1974 Southern Young Contemporaries
1975 Edinburgh Festival (with Peter Reeve)
1977 Glasgow Group, McLellan Galleries, Glasgow
1978 Four Young Sculptors, New 57 Gallery, Edinburgh
1978 Craft Exhibition, Norfolk, Virginia, USA
1978 Art and Craft in Scotland, Cercle Municipal, Luxembourg
1978 Inter-celtic Festival, Lorient, France
1979 Glasgow Group, McLellan Galleries, Glasgow
1979 Wood and Glass with Lindean Mill Glass
1979 Scottish Crafts, Heidelberg, West Germany
1980 Broughton Gallery, Lanarkshire
1980 Scottish Crafts, Goteburg, Sweden
1980 Glassmarket Gallery, Edinburgh
1981 Furniture in Wood, South Shields
1981 New Faces, British Crafts Centre, London
1981–89 The Tent, Edinburgh Festival
1982 MacRobert Arts Centre, Stirling
1985 Le Salon de l'Artisanat d'Art, Paris
1986 The Direct Design Show, London
1986 The Fourth Stirling Bienniale Exhibition
1986 Prescote Gallery, Beauly, Inverness-shire
1986 Glasgow Group, McLellan Galleries, Glasgow
1988 Wrought Wood, Turton Tower, Bolton
1988 The Scottish Gallery, Edinburgh
1988 Carlisle Museum & Art Gallery
1989 McGrigor-Donald Sculpture Exhibition, Edinburgh, Glasgow and London.
1990 Borders Art Bienniale
1990 'Spirits of the Forest', Glasgow Art Centre
1990 'Scotland Creates', McLellan Galleries, Glasgow
1992 Simpson's of Piccadilly, London
1992 Ancrum Gallery, Borders

Commissions

1975 Sculpture, Rufford Country Park
1978 Furniture, Houndwood Lodge Restaurant, Berwickshire
1979 Furniture, Café Gandolfi, Glasgow
1980 Three doors for Central Govan Housing Association Ltd, Glasgow
1980 Furniture for the European Language Lab, Lauder, Berwickshire
1981 Outdoor seat for Lyndock House Old People's Home, Edinburgh
1981 Chair, visit of Pope John Paul II, Edinburgh
1981 Furniture, The Round Table Restaurant, Edinburgh
1985 Furniture, The Wallace Cave, Lanark
1985 Doors, Loreburn Housing Association Ltd, Dumfries
1987 Door, Polskeoth Bothy, Dumfries-shire
1988 Quaich Stand, Keepers of the Quaich
1988 Library table, St. Mary's Cathedral, Edinburgh
1988 Three Bedrooms, The Castle, Castletownlaroche, County Cork, Eire
1989 North Sea Oil Industries Memorial Chapel, Kirk of St. Nicholas, Aberdeen

Collections

The National Museum, Goteburg, Sweden
The Kelvingrove Art Gallery & Museum, Glasgow
The Scottish Craft Collection, Edinburgh
The Contemporary Art Society, Tate Gallery, London

Television

'After Image', Channel 4, May 1987
'Bookcase Scotland', BBC 2, February 1988
'The Furniture Maker', BBC Scotland, January 1989
'NB', Scottish Television, January 1990
'Excess', BBC Scotland, November 1991
'The Insider', BBC Scotland, September 1992